Simple Thai Food

Simple Thai Food

Classic Recipes from the Thai Home Kitchen

Leela Punyaratabandhu

Photography by ERIN KUNKEL

TEN SPEED PRESS

Berkeley

To Isaac, in whose shade
my heart finds rest.

CONTENTS

อาหารจานเดียว
ONE-PLATE MEALS
· 119 ·
ahan jan diao

ของหวาน
SWEETS
· 149 ·
khong wan

สูตรพื้นฐาน
BASIC RECIPES and PREPARATIONS
· 167 ·
sut phuenthan

Introduction

When I started my website, shesimmers.com, in 2008, I had no idea where it would lead. At the time, my only goal was to document the best, most tried-and-true Thai recipes from my mother's cookbook collection. She had passed away a few weeks earlier, and cooking, photographing, and sharing the recipes was my way of honoring her memory.

My mother started sending her cookbooks to me in the early 2000s, when I moved to Chicago for school. Although I continued to return frequently to my hometown of Bangkok, Mom was concerned that I would forget how to cook the dishes that I grew up with—or, worse yet, that I would forget how Thai food in Thailand tastes.

She need not have worried. Cooking from Mom's collection helped me stay connected to my roots, and blogging about Thai food on my website inspired me to share my love of Thai history, culture, and language—as well as different food spots in the country—with others.

Today, I write about Thai food and culture not only for my website but also for other online and print publications, and I love interacting with my readers, most of whom are non-Thais living in the West. What I have learned is that many of them—too many—are filled with dread at the thought of trying to make their favorite Thai dishes at home.

I sympathize with them. Acquiring the fresh ingredients necessary to make a classic Thai dish entirely from scratch is often either impossible or too costly to be worth the effort. At the same time, many American cooks feel that cracking open a can of Thai curry paste is cheating. They worry that if they take shortcuts, an angry Thai grandmother will jump out from behind the nearest potted plant with a stun gun.

Although it is true that several Thai dishes absolutely require that you invest time and money in sourcing hard-to-find ingredients, such as kaffir lime and galangal, to replicate their flavors faithfully, many dishes that are just as traditional are made with everyday ingredients that are stocked in most markets.

My goal with *Simple Thai Food* is to show readers how easy it is to re-create traditional flavors—and the classic Thai dishes I grew up eating—at home. Once you have built a pantry of essential Thai ingredients (see page 3), whipping up delicious *tom yam kung* (page 86), drunkard's noodles (page 133), or cashew chicken (page 61) takes less time and is more affordable than calling up your local takeout joint.

In choosing which recipes and methods to include in this book, I have unwaveringly adhered to three guiding principles: foundation, feasibility, and fun. The alliteration, trust me, is accidental.

Foundation. This book is rooted in the food that I grew up eating and cooking in Bangkok, where I was born and raised. The recipes represent Thai food as I have experienced it in my life. These are dishes that I am proud to serve to my family and friends, dishes that I know will not make them back slowly away from the table with their hands up, demanding to know what on earth this unknown, made-up fare is. This is *my* foundation. This is the food I cook when I am longing for the taste of home.

None of the recipes is unique to this book. In other words, my goal is not to invent new Thai-inspired recipes but rather to guide you through the process of re-creating dishes that are well known in Thailand as well as in Thai restaurants in the United States. Because I was raised in Bangkok, my tastes naturally skew more toward the dishes I grew up eating. But today, with the gap between how Thai food is made in Thailand and how it is made elsewhere in the world narrowing with each passing year, the recipes in this book will not be foreign to anyone.

Feasibility. My goal is not only to faithfully re-create the food I love but also to ensure that Thai food fans everywhere can cook the dishes at home. That means that I have had to choose and adapt recipes for home cooks whose kitchens are not equipped with every tool necessary to make Thai dishes the traditional way, and I have had to offer substitutions for harder-to-find fresh Thai ingredients.

The unavailability of fresh ingredients is one problem that affects everyone from veteran chefs to novice cooks. But the good news is that as Thai food becomes more popular, more and more Thai pantry staples, such as tamarind pulp, coconut cream, and curry pastes, are available at well-stocked grocery stores. Better yet, if you live in an area with an Asian market, you can often find affordable, Thai-imported versions of these and other essentials, such as thin soy sauce, dark sweet soy sauce, and dried shrimp. If you do not have access to an Asian grocer, your best shot for finding some ingredients will be to order them online, and I have listed some reliable online sources on page 217. But because some of you may be hesitant to take the plunge into online grocery shopping, I have provided many ingredient substitutions, particularly for fresh produce items (Chinese broccoli, Chinese water morning glory, long beans) that are hard to locate in many areas of the United States.

Fun. Cuisine exists to serve us, not the other way around, and cooking should be enjoyable. Some of the recipes in this book are ridiculously easy; some take a bit of effort. I have attempted to lay out the steps for every recipe in a way that makes them doable for even the novice cook. Complicated steps have been streamlined, and substitutions are suggested. None of the recipes requires any gadget or gizmo that you do not already have or cannot easily find.

How the Book Is Organized

At first glance, the structure of this book may seem unusual to anyone unfamiliar with the Thai way of cooking and eating. There are four main chapters, each of which corresponds to a different Thai meal category. The first chapter, Noshes and Nibbles, covers a few simple dishes that Thai people like to eat as between-meal snacks. These dishes often fall in the appetizer section of Thai restaurant menus outside Thailand. But Thai people do not think of these dishes as "starters" to a meal. Rather, they are just small bites to be enjoyed throughout the day and into the evening.

The second chapter, Rice Accompaniments, covers dishes that are eaten with rice as part of a family meal, or *samrap*. Traditionally, a *samrap* is composed of a handful of different dishes, all of which are meant to accompany the main player of the meal: rice. If you want to create a traditional Thai-style meal, choose several complementary dishes from the Rice Accompaniments chapter and serve them together.

The third chapter covers one-plate meals, that is, dishes that are a complete meal on their own. These recipes contain noodles or rice. Then comes a chapter on sweets, which can be consumed after a meal, like a Western-style dessert, or between meals as a snack, the most common way they are eaten in Thailand. Finally, I have included a short section of basic recipes for homemade stocks, curry pastes, coconut milk, chile jam, and more.

The Thai Starter's Kit: Pantry Ingredients and Equipment

What follows is a list of the most frequently used pantry ingredients and basic cooking tools that I recommend for making the recipes in this book. It is far from a comprehensive list of every item in the traditional Thai kitchen. Of course, if you want to invest in all of the tools that make Thai cooking easier, such as a large clay mortar for making papaya salads, a separate granite mortar for making curry pastes, and a bamboo basket for steaming glutinous rice, you can. But if you are anything like me, you will find that it is hard to store any more tools in an already-crowded kitchen. So, I have narrowed down the list to the essentials: the starter's kit.

Similarly, the ingredients listed below in no way encompass all of the ingredients used in Thai cooking. For a more detailed explanation of the vegetables, fruits, herbs, spices, sauces, and condiments used in this book, turn to the Ingredients Glossary on page 197. For now, here are what I consider the essential ingredients and equipment you will need to cook from this book.

PANTRY INGREDIENTS

Long-grain white rice. I cannot imagine Thai cuisine without rice. In fact, if I were asked to eliminate everything from my pantry except for one item, that one item would be rice. As long as I have some rice in the pantry, I know I will be okay. Plain rice is my canvas, and there are many things around me with which I can paint on it.

If you eat rice as often as I do (almost every day), always buy a 25-pound bag, which is considerably less expensive than a smaller one. Kept in a tightly lidded container in a cool, dry, bug-free place, long-grain white rice will keep indefinitely (unlike brown rice, which becomes rancid quite quickly and should be kept in the freezer for longer storage). See page 213 for more information on selecting long-grain white rice, and page 168 for cooking directions.

Thai glutinous white rice. Although I do not eat glutinous rice as often as I eat long-grain rice, I always have a bag of it on hand in case I get a craving for sweet coconut sticky rice and mango (page 161). Like long-grain white rice, glutinous rice, also known as Thai sticky rice, will keep in a cool, dry, bug-free place indefinitely. See page 213 for tips on singling out *real* Thai sticky rice from the myriad types of Asian "sticky" rice, and page 169 for cooking directions.

Coconut milk. Curries, soups, noodle dishes, rice dishes, sweets, snacks—you will find coconut milk used in nearly every category of Thai food. So, unless you are willing to make coconut milk from scratch (see page 172) every time you want to prepare a dish that calls for it, you will want to have canned or boxed coconut milk on your kitchen shelf. It is best to use full-fat coconut milk for the recipes in this book, as many of them call for the fatty cream that rises to the top of the can or box. (For more information on coconut milk and coconut cream, see page 198.)

Ready-made curry paste. Ready-made curry pastes are a great help for those who cannot find or afford the ingredients for making fresh pastes. I have included recipes for red, green, yellow, and *matsaman* curry pastes on pages 175 to 177, most of which call for kaffir lime rind, galangal, and dried red chiles, ingredients that can be hard to find in the United States. Believe me; I have tried! I have lived in the Chicago area for many years and still have to mail-order kaffir limes whenever I make a curry paste.

All of the ingredients I call for in my curry paste recipes are essential to producing the traditional flavors of Thai curry. If you want to go the mail-order route, I have listed some good online sources on page 217. If you do not have the time or the budget, it is better to buy a commercial curry paste than to attempt a homemade version in which key ingredients are either left out or poorly substituted (ginger for galangal, for example). Do not feel badly about using a store-bought paste. Even in Thailand, good cooks often buy ready-made pastes from the market.

When buying commercial curry paste, stick to imported Thai brands if possible, as they offer the flavors most consistent with what you find at Thai restaurants run by competent cooks. Mae Ploy, Mae-sri, Pantai, Nittaya, and Lobo are the easiest brands to find, but any Thai brand will work fine. If you cannot find curry pastes imported from Thailand, any curry paste made specifically for Thai food can be used. See "Curries" on page 36 for tips on using store-bought pastes in my recipes.

Fish sauce, soy sauce, and oyster sauce. When it comes to Thai food, especially food from Bangkok and the central plains region, the number one source of salinity is fish sauce (*nam pla*). I use it often as both a condiment and a cooking ingredient. (For more information on fish sauce, see page 209.)

In the past, in the areas where fish sauce ruled, soy sauce and oyster sauce did not play a significant role in the traditional Thai kitchen. But they have become essential in modern Thai food, which has been heavily influenced by Chinese cuisine. Cooks regularly turn to them for easy and flavorful stir-fries and marinades. In this book, I use two types of soy sauce, thin soy sauce and dark sweet soy sauce. (For more information on these soy sauces and on oyster sauce, see page 209.)

Chile jam (nam phrik phao). One of the most versatile ingredients in modern Thai cooking, *nam phrik phao*, variously labeled "chile jam," "roasted red chile paste," "chile paste in oil," and "roasted chile jam," is made of dried red chiles, garlic, shallots, and seafood in the form of dried shrimp and shrimp paste and is flavored with fish sauce, palm sugar, and tamarind. It is regularly used as a condiment, stir-fry ingredient, and accent ingredient (notably in some versions of *tom yam* soup) and can even be used as a spread on bread.

I hope that you get to know this multipurpose ingredient. You can use it, along with nearly anything in the refrigerator, to improvise a simple stir-fry with big, complex flavor. I use this powerhouse ingredient so extensively that I cannot imagine not having it in my pantry. You can make your own chile jam (page 184), buy a Thai brand at an Asian grocery or online, or try one of the widely available American brands, such as Thai Kitchen.

Sweet chile sauce (nam jim kai). Originally created to accompany grilled chicken, this sweet-and-sour sauce goes by "dipping sauce (for) chicken," the literal translation of its Thai name. But, oh, talk about a sidekick whose fame far surpasses that of the show's star. That does not come as a surprise considering its versatility: it is good with everything from sweet potato fritters (page 11) and spring rolls (page 22) to fish cakes (page 41).

Like chile jam, you can either make your own sweet chile sauce (page 187), buy a Thai brand at an Asian grocery or online, or try one of the American brands, sold at many well-stocked grocery stores.

USEFUL EQUIPMENT

None of the equipment listed below is *essential* for cooking the recipes in this book. In fact, I have provided alternative tools in every recipe should you decide not to invest in a wok, mortar, or steamer. But if you find yourself preparing Thai food fairly often, certain tools—a mortar and a wok, for example—will make cooking and cleanup easier.

Mortar and pestle. Pastes of all kinds—curry pastes, chile pastes, aromatic pastes—are at the heart of Thai cuisine, and a traditional Thai kitchen relies heavily on a mortar (*khrok*) and pestle (*sak*) set to make them. Before you decide to toss this book aside and exclaim, "I don't have room for one more kitchen gadget!" let me assure you that you can get by without a mortar and pestle. Indeed, I recommend alternatives in the curry paste discussion on page 175. That said, a mortar and pestle set is a serious Thai cook's most important tool for a reason: pounding the herbs and spices bruises them and extracts their flavor better than grinding them with a metal blade, which can only chop them finely. It also allows you to make a small amount of paste more efficiently, without having to dilute it with water to get the blade going. That is why I believe that a good-size mortar and pestle is a worthwhile investment. I use my set for many things, from making a few tablespoons of an aromatic paste, an amount that is too small to puree fully in a food processor, to making a large batch of curry paste.

When choosing a mortar for Thai cooking, steer clear of a marble mortar, which is too fragile and prone to breaking and chipping when you attempt to make a Thai curry paste in it. Also pass up a shallow Mexican-style mortar, which is useful for muddling spices and herbs but is not deep enough for pounding a Thai curry paste. Select a smooth-surfaced granite mortar that measures at least 6 inches across and 6 inches from the rim to the middle point of the bottom. With a mortar of this size, making a cup of curry paste, which is enough to cook up a huge pot of curry that will yield 10 to 12 servings, is a breeze. The depth of the bowl ensures that the paste ingredients—notorious escapee-wannabes—stay inside the mortar as you pound them. In fact, the depth of the bowl should be the main deciding factor when you buy a mortar, rather than the overall size and weight of it.

A clay mortar and wooden pestle set is also useful, but less versatile than a granite mortar and pestle. A clay mortar is good for grinding spices and making a simple aromatic paste. Most notably, it is used to mix and bruise the classic green papaya salad (page 79). However, a clay mortar is not ideal for making most curry pastes, since a wooden pestle does not break down fibrous herbs as well as a granite pestle does. Most Thai cooks have both a clay mortar and a granite mortar, but if you can only invest in one, I recommend the more versatile granite mortar. Just be gentle when you make a green papaya salad in it.

Wok. For the recipes in this book that require deep-frying, you can use whatever vessel you already have, such as a Dutch oven, a deep skillet or sauté pan, or a deep fryer. I recommend a wok, however, because the sloped sides form a well to hold the oil. That means that the same amount of oil in a wok is much deeper than in a flat-bottomed Dutch oven or skillet, so that you do not need to use as much oil to create a sufficient depth for frying.

If you do not have a wok, you will need one small skillet, 6 to 8 inches in diameter, and one large skillet, 14 inches in diameter, to make the recipes in this book properly. The former is appropriate for deep-frying small amounts, such as when making fried garlic (page 185) or fried shallots (page 183), without having to use much oil. The latter is suitable for stir-frying and other shallow frying.

I prefer cast-iron and carbon-steel cookware, which develops a nonstick patina when it is seasoned properly and used repeatedly. However, for the purpose of making the recipes in this book, you can use nonstick cookware if it is all you have.

Regardless of what type of wok or skillet you use, you will also need either a steel wok spatula or a wooden spatula to go with it.

Rice cooker. Because I eat rice often, I have found that my rice cooker was a good investment and more than justifies the space that it takes up in my kitchen. With a rice cooker, you push a button and that is it. There is no need to babysit the rice or constantly monitor the temperature. All things weighed, I find making rice in a rice cooker to be the most practical and efficient method.

You do not need an expensive model. If you can afford a fancy one with many functions, go for it. But a low-end rice cooker that costs under twenty dollars will work just fine and last a long time. If you decide that you do not have the space or the budget for a rice cooker, I have included a stove-top cooking method on page 168.

Steamer. If you want to make sweet coconut sticky rice to pair with mangoes (page 161) or prepare plain sticky rice to eat with a salad (see page 74) or grilled chicken, you will need to steam glutinous rice. The rice is steamed *above* boiling water, rather than *in* water. Thai cooks traditionally use a cone-shaped bamboo basket that rests inside the rim of a tall, narrow aluminum pot (it looks like a spittoon), so

that base of the basket is above the boiling water in the pot.

But like all of the equipment here, you do not need a bamboo-basket steamer to cook glutinous rice. I do not even use one because I do not have the space to store this single-purpose tool. Instead, I use a splatter guard or a metal colander to steam my sticky rice. A tiered steamer will work, too. See page 169 for details on how to use these equipment alternatives.

Hand grater. I use this little gadget a lot in my kitchen because I make *som tam* (page 79) every few days. Traditionally, Thai cooks shred a green papaya by hacking the surface of a peeled papaya with a chef's knife. But I prefer to use a hand grater, which is easier and safer. It also gives you a lot of control over the thickness and length of the strands.

Look for a gadget called Kiwi Pro Slice, a well-known brand that is inexpensive and widely used in Thailand. It is available at larger Asian grocery stores or online. Kuhn Rikon makes a julienne peeler that works almost as well as the Kiwi Pro Slice, though it costs four times as much. You can definitely use a mandoline, which works similarly to a hand grater but is less safe and convenient.

Handheld citrus juicer. If you juice as many limes as I do each week, a handheld, clamp-style citrus squeezer is a gadget in which you will want to invest.

Leaf-Wrapped Salad Bites, page 25

ของว่าง
NOSHES and NIBBLES
khong wang

In Thailand, the word *khong wang* or *khong kin len* is used to describe snacks that the Thais eat between meals. Here in the United States—and elsewhere in the world where Western menu standards are traditional or have been adopted—these same Thai foods are generally served as appetizers at the beginning of a meal.

Thais eat three good-size meals a day in much the same way that many cultures do, but they also like to graze on various noshes and nibbles throughout the day and often late into the night. These casual snacks can be anything from savory crullers to meat-filled dumplings to rich and starchy desserts that are too heavy to eat immediately after a meal. Even a small portion of the many salads or grilled meats that are usually considered rice accompaniments and part of a family-style meal (see the next chapter) are nibbled on as a snack.

มันทอด

SWEET POTATO FRITTERS with PEANUT–SWEET CHILE SAUCE

man thot

I cannot think about sweet potato fritters without also thinking about my grandfather and all of the lazy Saturday afternoons we spent together working on crossword puzzles and snacking. When I have friends over, I make this easy appetizer to tide them over until dinner is served. Crunchy on the outside, soft and creamy on the inside, these fritters, which may remind some readers of thick-cut French fries, go brilliantly with the sweet dipping sauce and are always a hit even among self-professed picky eaters. **SERVES 4**

Fritters

1½ pounds sweet potatoes or yams

¾ cup rice flour (preferred) or all-purpose flour

¼ cup cornstarch

1 teaspoon baking soda

½ teaspoon salt

¼ cup unsweetened dried coconut flakes

1 tablespoon white sesame seeds

½ cup plus 1 tablespoon water (¾ cup if using all-purpose flour)

1 tablespoon basic aromatic paste (page 179)

Vegetable oil, for deep-frying

Dipping Sauce

1 cup sweet chile sauce, homemade (page 187) or store-bought

½ cup roasted peanuts, finely chopped

¼ cup loosely packed fresh cilantro leaves, coarsely chopped

1 fresh bird's chile, chopped (optional)

To make the fritters, peel the sweet potatoes, then cut them lengthwise into French-fry-like sticks about ½ inch thick and of any length. In a large bowl, stir together the flour, cornstarch, baking soda, salt, coconut, and sesame seeds. Whisk in the water and aromatic paste until thoroughly combined. The batter will be thick and pasty, which may send your Spidey sense tingling. But do not worry, as that is the way the batter is supposed to be. Add the sweet potato sticks and use your hands to turn them in the batter, coating them as evenly as possible. Your hands will work better than a spoon or spatula here because the batter is thick. You will see coconut and sesame seeds adhering to the sticks in random spots, much like coarse salt on hard pretzels. That is great—that is what you want. Leave the sweet potatoes in the bowl and set the bowl aside.

To make the dipping sauce, put the sweet chile sauce in a small serving bowl. Sprinkle the peanuts, cilantro, and chile on top. Do not mix them together until serving time.

continued

To fry the fritters, pour the oil to a depth of 3 inches into a wok, Dutch oven, or other suitable vessel and heat to 325°F to 350°F. To test if the oil is ready without a thermometer, stick an unvarnished wooden chopstick into the oil; when the oil is hot enough, a steady stream of tiny bubbles will rise from the tip of the chopstick. Line a baking sheet with paper towels and place it next to the stove.

One at a time, drop the sweet potato sticks into the hot oil. Fry them in batches, being careful not to crowd the pan. Because sweet potatoes have orange flesh, it is difficult to know when the sticks are golden brown. But after about 2 minutes, the crust should start to darken and form a solid shell, and that is when the fritters are ready. Using a wire-mesh skimmer or slotted spoon, transfer the fritters to the towel-lined baking sheet. Repeat until all of the sweet potato sticks are cooked.

To finish the dipping sauce, stir the peanuts, cilantro, and chile into the chile sauce. Arrange the fritters on a platter and serve with the dipping sauce alongside. Any left-over fritters can be reheated in a 375°F oven until they are crispy again.

ม้าห้อ

PINEAPPLE with SWEET PEANUT-CHICKEN TOPPING (Galloping Horses)

ma ho

It is likely that this dish was introduced to the culinary scene in Thailand sometime in the early twentieth century, thanks to foreign-educated royals and aristocrats. Early adopters of Western customs, these elite groups often served visitors tea with dainty canapés and petits fours. And so a new category of dishes entered the Thai cooking repertoire: elaborate bite-size nibbles—the Thai equivalent of hors d'œuvres—that were served at court or in households of the gentry.

Although many of these appetizers require a lot of time, labor, and dexterity, galloping horses, or *ma ho*, do not. Each bite is made up of a piece of fruit—most commonly pineapple—topped with a spoonful of a sweet and sticky yet savory meat-and-peanut mixture. The topping can be made ahead, shaped into balls, frozen in an airtight container for up to 1 month, and then thawed just before using. The only catch is that you must assemble the bites just before serving, as the topping tends to draw out the juice from the fruit if left in contact too long. **MAKES 20 PIECES**

1 tablespoon vegetable oil

1 tablespoon basic aromatic paste (page 179)

¼ cup minced shallots

3 ounces ground chicken or pork

2 ounces shrimp meat, finely chopped

1½ tablespoons fish sauce

⅓ cup packed grated palm sugar, or ¼ cup packed light or dark brown sugar

3 tablespoons finely chopped roasted peanuts

20 pineapple rectangles, each 1½ by 2 inches by ½ inch thick (from ½ of a 4-pound pineapple)

20 fresh cilantro leaves, for garnish

20 thin slivers fresh red Thai long chile or red bell pepper, for garnish

Heat the vegetable oil in a 14-inch skillet over medium heat. When the oil is hot, add the aromatic paste and shallots and fry until fragrant, about 1 minute. Add the chicken, shrimp, fish sauce, and palm sugar, increase the heat to medium-high, and cook, stirring constantly and breaking up the ground meat as finely as you can with the blunt end of a wooden spatula. After 5 minutes, add the peanuts and continue to cook, stirring constantly, for about 5 minutes longer, until no moisture remains and the mixture has become sticky, glistening, and medium brown. Remove the pan from heat, transfer the topping to a flat plate, and spread it out in a round, even layer. Let cool completely.

When the chicken mixture is completely cool, divide the round into pie-wedge-shaped quarters. Then divide each wedge into 5 roughly equal portions. Form each portion into a loose ball, keeping the remaining mixture and the balls covered with plastic wrap or a kitchen towel as you work.

To serve, arrange the pineapple pieces on a large platter, top each piece with a ball, and press down lightly to secure the topping. Place 1 cilantro leaf and 1 red pepper sliver on top of each bite. Serve immediately.

ถุงทอง

CRISPY DUMPLINGS (Gold Purses)

thung thong

These little dumplings look more complicated to shape than they really are. In fact, after you make just one, you will realize that they are easier to form than spring rolls. You simply plop the filling in the center of a spring roll skin, gather the corners and press them together, and then secure the corners in place with a "string" made from blanched green onion blades, creating what looks like a small bag. Frozen spring roll skins can be difficult to find, but you can also use fresh or frozen wonton skins, which are widely available. If the dumplings are made with wonton skins, their exterior develops a bubbly appearance when fried (see photo at left); if they are made with spring roll skins, the surface is smooth. Both versions are delicious.

You can assemble the dumplings up to 24 hours in advance, cover and refrigerate them, and then deep-fry them just before serving. **MAKES 18 DUMPLINGS**

7 green onions

1 tablespoon vegetable oil, plus more for deep-frying

1 tablespoon basic aromatic paste (page 179)

4 ounces white mushrooms, cut into ½-inch dice

8 ounces ground chicken or pork

1 tablespoon thin soy sauce

1 tablespoon oyster sauce

1 teaspoon fish sauce

½ teaspoon granulated sugar

1 (8-ounce) can whole water chestnuts, drained, rinsed, patted dry, and cut into ¼-inch dice

18 (4-inch) square or round frozen spring roll skins or fresh or frozen wonton skins, thawed if frozen and kept covered with a kitchen towel

¾ cup sweet chile sauce, homemade (page 187) or store-bought, for serving

Trim off and discard the roots of the green onions. Cut each onion into 2 pieces, separating the white bulb end from the green blades. Slice the white parts crosswise ¼ inch thick and reserve for the filling. Set the green blades aside.

Heat 1 tablespoon of the oil in a wok or a 14-inch skillet over high heat. When the oil is hot, add the sliced onions, aromatic paste, and mushrooms and stir-fry for about 2 minutes, until the onions and mushrooms have softened. Add the chicken, soy sauce, oyster sauce, fish sauce, sugar, and water chestnuts and stir with a spatula, breaking up the chicken as finely as you can with the blunt end of the spatula. Continue to stir-fry for 5 to 8 minutes, until all of the chicken is cooked through and all of the liquid has evaporated. Remove the pan from the heat and let the filling cool to room temperature.

To blanch the "strings" for tying the bags, fill a 1-quart saucepan half full with water and bring the water to a boil. Place a bowl of iced water next to the stove. When the water is boiling, add the green onion blades, pushing them down gently with a spoon

continued

to submerge them in the water. After 30 seconds, transfer the onion blades to the iced water. Within 1 minute, the onions should be cool enough to handle. Remove them from the water and, with your fingers or the tip of a paring knife, split each blade in half lengthwise; set aside.

To assemble the dumplings, lay a spring roll skin flat on a work surface and put 1½ tablespoons of the cooled filling in the center. Gather together the corners of the skin and adjust the dumpling so it takes on a round, rather than flat, profile. Using 1 piece of onion blade, tie it around the gathered corners twice to secure them. With a pair of kitchen shears, trim off the dangling blade ends. Repeat with the remaining spring roll skins and filling.

To fry the dumplings, pour the oil to a depth of 3 inches into a wok, Dutch oven, or deep fryer and heat to 325°F. To test if the oil is ready without a thermometer, stick an unvarnished wooden chopstick into the oil; when the oil is hot enough, a steady stream of tiny bubbles will rise from the tip of the chopstick. Line a baking sheet with paper towels and place it next to the stove.

Using a slotted spoon, carefully lower 3 or 4 filled pouches into the hot oil and deep-fry for 2 to 3 minutes, until golden brown all over. Using the slotted spoon, transfer the dumplings to the towel-lined baking sheet. Repeat until all of the dumplings are cooked.

Do not serve the dumplings right out of the oil, as the filling will be much too hot to eat. Let them cool down to slightly warmer than room temperature, then arrange them on a platter and serve with the sweet chile sauce.

หมูสะเต๊ะ

PORK SATAY

mu sate

Thai-style satay is served with a flavorful yet mild and slightly sweet peanut sauce based on curry and coconut milk. A light, refreshing side of cucumber and shallot relish cleanses the palate between bites and counterbalances the richness of the pork and the sauce. In most places in Bangkok, thick slices of white bread, toasted on the grill and cut into bite-size pieces, are served as part of a satay set.

If you actively look for a way to make satay complicated, you will find it. I like this quick and easy version, however. It comes from one of my grandparents' former employees, who left her job to run a pork satay shop. One of the tricks that she shared with me is the addition of pineapple juice to the marinade to tenderize the pork and keep it moist. The marinade is heavy on dried spices and does not contain pulpy fresh herbs, which is more in line with the way Chinese vendors—the people who have popularized the pork version of this dish in the central part of Thailand—do it. (It is also the way I like it!) If you prefer to make chicken satay, you can substitute the same weight of skinless, boneless chicken breasts or thighs for the pork.

Thais do not use any silverware when eating satay. Instead, they use the bamboo skewer left behind after finishing a piece of meat to pick up the cucumber, shallot, and pepper in the relish and to dip the toast in the peanut sauce. **SERVES 4 TO 6**

1 pound boneless pork shoulder	½ cup fresh pineapple juice or freshly squeezed orange juice
2 teaspoons ground turmeric	½ cup water
1 teaspoon ground coriander	2 (1-inch-thick) slices soft white sandwich bread (optional)
1 teaspoon ground cumin	
1 tablespoon grated packed palm sugar or light brown sugar	Cucumber relish, for serving (page 191)
1 cup coconut milk	1½ cups satay sauce, for serving (page 188)

Slice the pork into strips about 3 inches long, ¾ to 1 inch wide, and ¼ inch thick. In a bowl, combine the pork, turmeric, coriander, cumin, sugar, ½ cup of the coconut milk, and the pineapple juice and mix well. Cover and refrigerate for at least 2 hours or up to 8 hours.

While the pork is marinating, soak 24 bamboo skewers in water to cover for at least 30 minutes or up to 12 hours.

To grill the satay, prepare a medium fire in a charcoal or gas grill. If using charcoal, allow the charcoal to develop a gray ash before you start grilling. Oil the grate with vegetable oil. (Alternatively, heat a well-oiled stove-top grill pan over medium heat until hot or preheat the broiler and oil a broiler pan.)

continued

While the grill is heating, remove the pork from the marinade and the skewers from the water. Thread 2 strips of pork onto each skewer, filling each skewer about three-fourths full and leaving the bottom one-fourth empty to use as a handle. In a small bowl, stir together the remaining ½ cup coconut milk and the water to use for basting. Place the bowl and a small basting brush near the grill.

Working in batches if necessary to accommodate all of the skewers, arrange the skewers on the grill grate directly over the fire and grill, brushing the skewers lightly with the coconut milk mixture and turning them once until the pork is cooked through, about 5 to 8 minutes. (If using a stove-top grill pan or the broiler, cook the skewers the same way using roughly the same timing.) Grill the bread slices, turning once, just until toasted on the outside but still soft on the inside.

Cut the toasted bread into bite-size pieces. Arrange the skewers on a platter with the bread alongside. Accompany with the cucumber relish and the satay sauce. (The cucumber relish should be enjoyed as a palate cleanser, similar to the pickled ginger served on the side of your sushi.)

เม็ดมะม่วงหิมพานต์อบสมุนไพร
HERB-BAKED CASHEWS

met mamuang himma-phan op samunphrai

I drink so little alcohol that the amount that I consume each year is barely enough to fill a soup bowl. And much of that is in the form of a wine cooler or a light beer. I just do not have a taste for alcohol. But all my friends and cousins love me because I am the perfect designated driver, the person who is willing to go sit with them at a bar in Bangkok and drink overpriced soda and nosh all night on the quintessential Thai bar snack, seasoned fried cashews.

This is the baked version of those sweet-and-sour fried nuts, with a touch of herbal fragrance and a little bit of heat. **MAKES 2⅓ CUPS**

1 pound raw whole cashews

2 tablespoons vegetable oil

¼ cup freshly squeezed lime juice

Grated zest of 1 lime

1 tablespoon minced fresh cilantro leaves

1 tablespoon minced fresh mint leaves

1 tablespoon minced green onion, green part only

2 tablespoons honey

1 teaspoon salt

1 teaspoon red chile powder

Preheat the oven to 300°F. Line a large baking sheet with parchment paper or a silicone mat.

In a large bowl, combine all of the ingredients and mix well, making sure that the cashews are evenly coated with the seasonings. Spread the cashews in a single layer on the prepared baking sheet, leaving as much space as possible between them.

Bake the nuts, stirring them every 5 minutes, until golden brown, about 20 minutes. Remove from the oven and let cool completely on the baking sheet before serving or storing. The cashews can be stored in an airtight container at room temperature for up to 1 week. But trust me: they will be gone long before that.

ปอเปี๊ยะทอด
FRIED SPRING ROLLS
popia thot

Gather ten Thai cooks in a room and ask them what goes into the filling of these Chinese-influenced spring rolls and you will get ten different lists of ingredients. If there are any over-laps among those lists, they will most likely include glass noodles and bean sprouts and maybe wood ear mushrooms. That said, it is not uncommon to come across street hawkers selling cheaply made spring rolls that contain little more than sliced cabbage and grated carrots.

Good spring rolls must taste great on their own, even without a dipping sauce. In other words, the filling needs to be more than just cheap roughage to keep the tubes from collapsing. The recipe I use is based on how one of my aunts makes her *popia thot*. You can play around with which meat or combination of different meats to use in the filling. When I have extra cash or I am under the illusion that I am rich, I use lump crabmeat. When neither is the case, I stick with whatever is on sale. You can even skip the meat altogether and replace it with chopped firm tofu.

Once rolled and sealed, the spring rolls can be deep-fried right away. They can also be arranged in a single layer in a freezer bag and frozen for up to 2 months. That way, whenever you have a hankering for a spring roll or two, you can fry them without having to whip up a big batch. Never thaw them before frying them. If you do, the wrapper will become soggy and burst open in the hot oil. **MAKES ABOUT 20 (4-INCH-LONG) SPRING ROLLS**

1 ounce glass noodles

6 dried wood ear mushrooms, or 4 ounces fresh white mushrooms

1 tablespoon vegetable oil, plus more for deep-frying

1 tablespoon basic aromatic paste (page 179)

4 ounces ground chicken or pork

1 tablespoon fish sauce

1 tablespoon oyster sauce

½ cup water

8 ounces mung bean sprouts

20 (6-inch square) frozen spring roll skins, thawed and kept covered with a kitchen towel

5 or 6 leaves green, red, or red oak lettuce, for serving

¾ to 1 cup sweet chile sauce, homemade (page 187) or store-bought

Immerse the glass noodles in a bowl of room-temperature water and soak for 20 min-utes, until pliable. Drain and cut into 4-inch lengths with kitchen shears. Set aside.

If using dried mushrooms, immerse them in a bowl of hot water and soak for about 20 minutes, until soft. Drain, rinse off any sandy sediment, and squeeze dry. If the mushrooms have hard, knobby ends, trim them off. Then slice the mushrooms into ¼-inch-wide strips. If using fresh mushrooms, cut them into ¼-inch cubes. Set aside.

Heat 1 tablespoon of the oil in a wok or a 14-inch skillet over medium heat. When the oil is hot, add the aromatic paste and fry until fragrant, about 1 minute. Turn up the heat to medium-high, add the chicken, mushrooms, fish sauce, and oyster sauce, and sauté, breaking up the chicken with a spatula along the way, for about 3 minutes, until the chicken is cooked through. Add the glass noodles and water and cook, stirring, for about 1 minute, until the noodles are soft and most of the liquid has evaporated. If there is too much moisture in the pan, increase the heat to high and continue to cook until all of the liquid has evaporated.

Remove the pan from the heat. Add the bean sprouts and stir to combine them with the chicken mixture, letting the residual heat in the pan wilt them. Transfer the filling to a large plate and allow it to cool completely. It must be completely cooled before you begin to assemble the spring rolls.

If you have just a single wok like I do, you may want to clean and dry it now so that it is ready for frying the spring rolls later on. You will have time as this point, as it is going to take a while for the filling to cool down.

To assemble the rolls, place a small bowl of water and a brush to one side of your work surface. Remove 1 spring roll skin from under the kitchen towel, keeping the rest covered, and lay it flat on the work surface, with one corner pointing toward you. Place about 2 tablespoons of the filling on the corner of the skin nearest you, positioning it about 1/2 inch from the tip. Spread the filling out horizontally to within 3/4 inch of either side of the skin to form a log. Fold the corner nearest you over the filling, tucking it in as you go. The filling must not be simply covered but instead hugged very tightly. Continue rolling and tucking until the cylinder reaches the left and right corner, then fold in the side corners on a slight angle, so the remaining rolling path is slightly tapered instead of straight like an envelope. The angle is necessary, as the end of the spring roll skin tends to flare outward because of the pressure applied as you roll. Lightly brush the unrolled spring roll skin with water, then continue rolling tightly until you reach the corner farthest from you. Press down firmly on the seam to seal. Repeat until the spring roll skins and filling run out. There is no need to keep the finished rolls covered, but make sure they do not touch one another or they may stick together.

To fry the spring rolls, pour the oil to a depth of 3 inches into the wok, Dutch oven, or deep fryer and heat to 325°F to 350°F. To test if the oil is ready without a thermometer, stick an unvarnished wooden chopstick into the oil; when the oil is hot enough, a steady stream of tiny bubbles will rise from the tip of the chopstick. Line a baking sheet with paper towels and place it next to the stove.

continued

Using a slotted spoon, carefully lower 3 or 4 spring rolls into the hot oil and fry until crispy and golden brown, about 3 minutes. Using the slotted spoon, transfer the rolls to the towel-lined baking sheet. Repeat until all of the rolls are cooked.

Do not serve the rolls right out of the oil, as the filling will be much too hot to eat. Let them cool down to slightly warmer than room temperature. Line a platter with the lettuce leaves—which serve as both a decoration and a side vegetable, and arrange the rolls on top. Serve with a bowl of the chile sauce.

Baked Variation. Preheat the oven to 400°F. Arrange the assembled spring rolls, not touching, on a baking sheet, lightly brush the entire outside of each roll with vegetable oil, and then turn the rolls seam side down. (If baking frozen spring rolls, bake them directly from the freezer.) Bake until crispy, about 20 to 25 minutes for fresh spring rolls and 30 to 35 minutes for frozen spring rolls. Baked spring rolls will not be as thoroughly and evenly golden brown as deep-fried spring rolls and will lose their crispiness sooner. But when fresh out of the oven, they are crispy and delicious.

เมี่ยงคำ
LEAF-WRAPPED SALAD BITES
miang kham

Miang, which I like to call "leaf-wrapped salad bites," is a bit of an interactive dish: Various items—in this case, finely diced ginger, shallot, and lime; dried shrimp; flaked coconut; chopped peanuts—are assembled on a platter. Diners are invited to grab a palm-size leaf, pile on it a little bit of each component, top the whole thing with a drizzle of sauce, wrap it up into a small bundle, and then consume it in one perfect bite.

Miang kham, one of the best-known of these flavorful salad bites outside of Thailand, is dressed with a thick, sweet sauce and traditionally wrapped in *cha-phlu* leaves, which are known as *la lot* in Vietnamese and wild betel leaves in English (not to be confused with betel leaves). In their absence, you can use young deveined collard greens or tender leaves of Chinese broccoli; in the case of the latter, the dish is often called *miang khana* (เมี่ยงคะน้า). **SERVES 4**

Sauce

1 tablespoon meaty dried shrimp

½ cup hot water

1 stalk lemongrass

½ cup plus 2 tablespoons unsweetened dried coconut flakes

1 shallot, about 1 ounce, peeled and sliced thinly against the grain

2 (¼-inch-thick) slices galangal, coarsely chopped

2 tablespoons coarsely chopped peeled ginger

1 teaspoon shrimp paste

½ cup packed grated palm sugar plus ⅓ cup packed dark brown sugar (or substitute ⅔ cup packed dark brown sugar)

1 tablespoon fish sauce

¼ cup water

2 tablespoons finely chopped roasted peanuts

Salad

1 lime

1 (3-inch) piece fresh ginger, peeled and cut into ¼-inch dice

2 shallots, about 1 ounce each, peeled and cut into ¼-inch dice

½ cup roasted peanuts

5 or 6 fresh bird's eye chiles, sliced crosswise ¼ inch thick

⅓ cup meaty dried shrimp

20 to 30 *cha-phlu* leaves or 3-inch squares collard green or Chinese broccoli leaves

To make the sauce, soak the dried shrimp in hot water for 15 minutes. Meanwhile, trim off and discard the leafy parts of the lemongrass stalk, remove the tough outer leaves of the bulb portion until the smooth, pale green core is exposed, and trim off the root end. Working from the root end, cut the bulb crosswise into paper-thin slices, stopping once you reach the point at which the purple rings disappear. Set the slices aside and discard the remainder.

continued

Put the dried coconut flakes in a wok or 14-inch skillet and toast them on medium heat, stirring constantly, until medium brown, about 2 to 3 minutes. Reserve 2 tablespoons of the toasted coconut flakes for the sauce and set the remainder aside for the salad. Wipe out any toasted coconut sediment from the wok. Add the lemongrass slices, shallot, galangal, and ginger to the clean wok, then toast over medium-high heat, stirring constantly, until fragrant and the shallot slices are dry to the touch, about 5 minutes. Place the toasted mixture, drained dried shrimp, and shrimp paste in a mortar or a mini chopper and grind to a smooth paste.

Put the prepared paste, sugars, fish sauce, and water in a 1-quart saucepan and bring to a boil over medium-high heat, stirring constantly. When the sauce has thickened and reduced to about 1 cup, after 2 to 3 minutes, take the saucepan off the heat. Let the sauce cool completely. Once the dressing is cooled, stir in the chopped peanuts and the reserved 2 tablespoons toasted coconut flakes and transfer to a small serving bowl.

To prepare the salad, quarter the lime lengthwise and trim away the core. Cut the quarters into ¼-inch dice, leaving the rind intact. Alternatively, for those who are sensitive to the bitterness of the lime rind, cut the lime into wedges (as shown in the photograph) and invite diners to squeeze about ½ teaspoon lime juice onto each composed salad bite.

Arrange the lime, ginger, shallots, peanuts, chiles, dried shrimp, *cha-phlu* leaves, and the dressing on a large serving platter.

To eat, put a leaf on your palm, add a bit of each component to the center of the leaf, top with a small spoonful of dressing, gather up the corners of the leaf to form a bag, and eat the whole thing in one bite.

Note: If the diced ginger tastes too spicy hot, rinse it in cold water three or four times until the water runs clear and blot it dry.

ขนมปังหน้าหมู

PORK TOAST with CUCUMBER RELISH

khanom pang na mu

Pork toast is one of those perplexing things that seem so easy to make that you wonder why it is not easy to make well. When done right, these golden jewels are a delicacy: a beautiful paste spread over crunchy-on-the-outside, soft-on-the-inside toast. When done poorly, they are reduced to pieces of sponges soaked and softened with the oil in which you fried them.

The key is to dry out the bread before you spread the pork paste on it so it will not absorb too much oil. It is equally important not to pile too much pork on the bread, thinking that a higher pork-to-bread ratio will improve the flavor of the dish. Doing so will increase the frying time in order to cook the pork sufficiently, which usually results in the bread turning too dark and bitter. Too much pork also causes the finished pork toast to lose its crispiness more quickly. A thin layer of pork mixture, no thicker than half the thickness of a bread slice, ensures that the pork will be cooked through around the same time the bread becomes perfect, that is, golden and crispy—so crispy you hear a crackling, crunchy sound when you bite into it. **MAKES 40 PIECES**

10 slices white sandwich bread, each about 4 by 3 by ½ inch

8 ounces ground pork

1 tablespoon thin soy sauce

1 tablespoon cornstarch

½ teaspoon ground white pepper

1 large clove garlic

1 cilantro root, or 1 tablespoon finely chopped cilantro stems

40 fresh cilantro leaves

Vegetable oil, for deep-frying

2 eggs

Cucumber relish (page 191), or ½ cup Thai Sriracha sauce, homemade (page 186) or store-bought, for serving

Trim the crusts off the bread. Cut the bread slices in half horizontally and then vertically to create quarters. Leave the bread out to dry for at least 2 to 3 hours, flipping the pieces over once, or for up to overnight.

To make the pork topping, in a food processor, combine the pork, soy sauce, cornstarch, pepper, garlic, and cilantro root and process until a smooth paste forms.

Spread the pork paste evenly across the top surface of each square of bread. (The thickness of the pork paste should never exceed half the thickness of the bread. This ensures that the pork will be cooked through before the bread gets too brown.) Place 1 cilantro leaf on top of each piece and press down lightly to secure it in place.

To fry the pork toast, pour the oil to a depth of at least 2 inches into a wok or a small, deep skillet and heat to 325°F to 350°F. To test if the oil is ready without a thermometer, stick an unvarnished wooden chopstick into the oil; when the oil is hot enough, a steady stream of tiny bubbles will rise from the tip of the chopstick. Line a baking sheet with paper towels and place it next to the stove. Break the eggs into a wide, shallow bowl and beat lightly until blended, then place the bowl next to the stove.

One at a time, dip a square of bread, pork side down, into the eggs (the side without the pork should not be coated with the eggs) and quickly drop it, pork side down, into the hot oil. Fry the pork toast in batches, being careful not to crowd the pan. Once the pork side is golden brown, after about 1 to 2 minutes, flip the bread pieces over and fry until the other side is golden brown, about 1 minute. Using a slotted spoon, transfer the pork toast to the towel-lined baking sheet. Repeat with the remaining pork toast.

Do not serve the pork toast right out of the oil, as the topping will be too hot to eat. Let cool to slightly warmer than room temperature, then arrange on platters and serve with the cucumber relish.

กุ้งแช่น้ำปลา

FISH SAUCE-MARINATED FRESH SHRIMP with SPICY LIME DRESSING (Naked Shrimp)

kung chae nam pla

On behalf of the shrimp, I would like to point out that the name of this dish in Thai has nothing to do with nakedness. Literally, it means "shrimp soaked [or marinated] in fish sauce." The English moniker, naked shrimp, is something that many overseas Thai restaurants have adopted and popularized. It is a fun name, but it is neither fair to the shrimp nor entirely accurate, not to mention it damages the dignity and public image of the crustacean.

The livid shrimp would like you to know that they are not naked. True, the shells are off, but the tails are left on. That is way more than enough to avoid arrest. And even though the raw—*completely raw*—shrimp lie flat, spread open like a book on a bed of sliced cabbage, they are partially covered in a dressing and mint leaves. In other words, that is akin to someone lying around in public unclothed but with their socks on and partially covered in salad dressing and strategically placed herb sprigs. That is totally acceptable socially, isn't it?

It isn't? Oh.

Perhaps needless to say, since this dish *will* be consumed raw, make sure to buy the best shrimp you can find. Alternatively, use sashimi-grade raw salmon or tuna. **SERVES 4**

1 pound large shrimp in the shell

1 (4-ounce) wedge green cabbage, finely shredded

3 or 4 fresh bird's eye chiles, chopped finely

¼ cup freshly squeezed lime juice

1½ tablespoons fish sauce

1 teaspoon granulated sugar

5 large cloves garlic, sliced crosswise paper-thin

½ cup loosely packed fresh mint leaves

Peel the shrimp, pulling off the head, if attached, and the legs and leaving the tail shell on. To butterfly each shrimp, lay it on a cutting board and, using a sharp paring knife, make a cut along the outer curve of the body, cutting almost all of the way through. The cut must be deep enough to open the shrimp up flat without separating the halves. With the tip of the knife, lift out and discard the dark veinlike intestinal tract. Refrigerate the shrimp until ready to serve.

Line a serving platter with the cabbage. In a small bowl, combine the chiles, lime juice, fish sauce, and sugar, stirring to dissolve the sugar. Taste the dressing: it should be predominantly sour and hot followed by salty, with sweetness lurking in the background. Adjust as necessary and set aside.

Take the shrimp out of the refrigerator and arrange them, cut side up and spread open like a book, on the cabbage. Drizzle the dressing all over the shrimp. Scatter the garlic slices over the shrimp, followed by the mint leaves.

Serve the shrimp immediately and consume while they are still cold and shivering.

ทอดมันข้าวโพด

CORN FRITTERS

thot man khao phot

A street-cart vendor sells these crispy nuggets of gold a block away from my place in Bangkok. He makes them only once a year, however, during the Nine Emperor Gods festival when many Thais of Chinese descent abstain from meat. Not content with the fact that I can eat the vendor's corn fritters only when the festival is on, I have been making them at home.

If you like the flavor of the classic Thai fish cakes (page 41), you will like the flavor of these little corn fritters because both of them are seasoned with red curry paste and perfumed with kaffir lime leaves. You will not get the bouncy, elastic texture of the traditional fish cakes in these fritters. Instead, you will be rewarded with crispy edges, slightly chewy centers, and the textural contrast between pureed and whole corn kernels. **MAKES ABOUT 30 (2-INCH) FRITTERS**

½ cup sweet chile sauce, homemade (page 187) or store-bought

½ cup Thai Sriracha sauce, homemade (page 186) or store-bought

Kernels from 4 medium ears corn, or 2 cups frozen corn kernels, thawed and patted dry

1 tablespoon red curry paste, homemade (page 175) or store-bought

1 egg

¾ cup rice flour (preferred) or ½ cup plus 1 tablespoon all-purpose flour

2 teaspoons baking soda

2 teaspoons salt

3 fresh kaffir lime leaves, deveined and cut lengthwise into very thin strips (optional)

Vegetable oil, for deep-frying

To make the dipping sauce, stir together the sweet chile sauce and Sriracha sauce; set aside.

In a blender or food processor, combine 1 cup of the corn kernels with the curry paste, egg, flour, baking soda, and salt and process until smooth. Transfer the mixture to a bowl; fold in the remaining 1 cup corn kernels and the lime leaves.

To fry the fritters, pour the oil to a depth of 2 inches into a wok, Dutch oven, or deep fryer and heat to 325°F to 350°F. To test if the oil is ready without a thermometer, stick an unvarnished wooden chopstick into the oil; when the oil is hot enough, a steady stream of tiny bubbles will rise from the tip of the chopstick. Line a baking sheet with paper towels and place it next to the stove.

Gently drop the batter into the hot oil by the tablespoonful, being careful not to crowd the pan. (Don't worry about forming a perfectly round ball. The crispy, jagged edges are delicious.) When the fritters float to the top, in less than 1 minute, begin to flip them around to ensure even browning. Cook for 1 to 2 minutes longer, until they are golden brown and start to darken around the edges. Using a slotted spoon, transfer them to the towel-lined baking sheet. Repeat until the batter runs out.

Arrange the warm fritters on a platter and accompany with the dipping sauce.

Grilled Steaks with Roasted Tomato
Dipping Sauce (Crying Tiger), page 112

กับข้าว
RICE ACCOMPANIMENTS
kap khao

The recipes in this chapter are all known as *kap khao*, literally "[that which is eaten] with rice," a term used for dishes that form a *samrap*, or full family meal. The term's meaning reflects the prominence of rice in Thai eating culture: it is the center of the meal—the sun in the solar system—around which everything else orbits. The opposite is often true in Western meals, where meat is typically the main focus and rice, potatoes, or another starch is a side dish.

There are no hard-and-fast rules on how to compose a *samrap*, whether preparing the meal at home or eating out. In general, however, Thais try to include a variety of flavors and textures, always striving to avoid repetition within the same meal. For example, if a red curry is part of a *samrap*, serving a green curry would be superfluous. In this case, a vegetable stir-fry, a spicy salad, or a fried or grilled meat with a dipping sauce would be a better choice. Likewise, if a spicy salad is part of a *samrap*, a hot-and-sour soup, essentially a spicy salad in wet form, would repeat the same flavor. A braised meat, a coconut-based curry, or a clear soup would be a more complementary pairing.

Color is yet another consideration when putting together a menu. Unlike the traditional Western meal, which is served in courses, all of the dishes of a Thai meal are served at the same time. Ideally, the table reflects a healthy mix of colors,

including red, such as a red chile–based dish; green, such as a vegetable soup or a stir-fry; and yellow, such as a golden deep-fried dish.

Understanding how the Thai people compose a meal not only helps you understand how to enjoy eating Thai food but also how to season it when you are cooking. The concept that rice is the main dish and everything in the *samrap* is there to accompany it cannot be overstated. That means that a dish must always be seasoned in anticipation of its role alongside the bland rice. If a recipe is seasoned just enough to be good as a stand-alone dish, by the time it is mixed with the rice, the dish will taste much too mild. So do not be afraid to use a heavier hand with the seasoning of *kap khao* dishes than you may be used to—and do not be surprised when you discover that the recipes in this chapter are seasoned to accompany rice.

I should also note that the serving sizes I have suggested here assume that the dishes will be served as part of a *samrap*—in other words, part of a meal rather than a meal unto itself.

Stir-Fried and Deep-Fried Dishes

Thanks to the arrival of Chinese immigrants in Thailand centuries ago, dishes that call for stir-frying and deep-frying are common in the Thai daily diet, and a wok has become an essential Thai cooking tool. Stir-frying is one of the simplest Thai cooking techniques to master. With the exception of a few Chinese-influenced dishes that call for cooking over high heat, Thai-style stir-frying is done in a wok over medium-high heat, making it easier for home cooks. One rule remains the same regardless of the intensity of the heat, however: always prepare all of your ingredients before you start cooking and arrange them next to the stove. Once the wok is on the fire, you will be stir-frying nonstop.

Deep-frying suffers from a reputation of being both messy and difficult. But with the correct equipment and a few tips, such concerns quickly fade. Just as with stir-frying, the bowl-shaped, flare-sided wok is the ideal pan for deep-frying. It easily accommodates oil to a depth of a couple inches, the amount typically needed for deep-frying most foods, without the risk of it splashing over the rim. Its shape even cuts down on the number of tiny droplets that will soil your stove top when you add foods to the hot oil. The shape and size also allow you to cook a small amount of food without having to use a large amount of oil, which cuts down on both mess and cost. Most worries about the difficulty of deep-frying are reduced if you follow three rules: allow sufficient time for the oil to reach the temperature indicated in the recipe, allow the oil to return to the original temperature after each batch is removed from the pan before adding the next batch, and never crowd the foods in the pan. Follow this trio of tips and your foods will absorb very little oil and be wonderfully crisp.

If you do not already own a wok, I have provided guidelines on how to select a good-quality one on page 6. I have also included information on which pans can be used for stir-frying and deep-frying in place of a wok. Choosing the correct oil for stir-frying and deep-frying is important, as well. It must have a high smoke point and be flavorless. I call for generic vegetable oil in the recipes, and have specified which types are the best to use on page 212.

Salads

Of all of the different types of Thai food, *yam* (pronounced "yum"), or salads, form one of the largest and, according to my observation, the fastest-growing realm. They are also, in my opinion, the most enjoyable to eat and to make.

One of the reasons for the popularity of salads among Thais is that they carry the taste that Thai people prefer, namely, a combination of sour, salty, and sweet, with sour being the dominant flavor. While too much coconut-based curry or fried fatty cuts of meat can be *lian* (rich to the point of sickening), the refreshing, bright, tart flavors of *yam* make them something that can be enjoyed quite liberally any time of the day—with rice as part of a meal or as a stand-alone between-meal snack—or even as a late-night drinking snack.

A second reason is because street vendors love selling them. The *yam* cart is a fuss-free undertaking: it requires no special equipment and rarely relies on any specialized cooking skills or long-guarded family recipes. All it needs is an ice box to keep meats and vegetables fresh in the hot weather and a portable picnic stove for keeping the blanching liquid simmering. With the seasoning ingredients prepared in advance and within reach, a *yam* vendor can make a salad to order in just a few minutes.

Salads are also enjoyable and practical to make. The anything-but-the-kitchen-sink approach that the Thai people have exuberantly adopted—not unlike the way modern salads are made elsewhere in the world—opens up a world of possibilities. Thai supermarkets are now flooded with locally grown nonnative produce. You can foresee how in the next few decades these newly introduced fruits and vegetables will give birth to new dishes or new takes on old dishes that will someday become classics, just as the once-foreign chile (which, you will recall, was brought to Thailand from the New World by European traders) is at the heart of countless dishes recognized as resolutely Thai.

There are, of course, the classics that must be revered and, for the most part, are revered (at least nominally). The players in these iconic dishes are kept constant, and the way the salads are presented typically adhere closely to what has always been done, just as you can apply only so much creativity to a classic Caesar salad before it becomes unrecognizable.

Some classics are more forgiving than others, of course. These are often the salads that are favored by overseas Thai cooks. For example, *som tam* (page 79) is often made with nontraditional fruits and vegetables not because cooks are on a mission to overturn custom but rather because the closest Asian grocery store is twenty miles away, it is snowing, the grocery store just a block away has really fresh carrots on sale right now, and, hey, this rutabaga is crunchy and mild when raw and costs less than a dollar a pound . . . you get the idea.

In my experience, Thais living outside Thailand who are deprived of traditional ingredients are among the most imaginative *yam* creators I know. The fewer options they have and the more dependent they are on the locally available and affordable ingredients, the more innovative they are when attempting to re-create the taste of home.

That said, when you first make these recipes I encourage you to stick to the ingredients lists and instructions as closely as possible. That will help you understand what makes Thai salads what they are, and armed with that knowledge, you will soon be making them as if you had been doing it for years.

But before you make that first recipe, here are a few fundamentals. In its most basic form, the dressing—the heart of any Thai salad—consists of lime juice, fish sauce, and sometimes sugar. Opinions vary on whether chile is a core ingredient (in other words, without it, a *yam* ceases to be a *yam* and must immediately relinquish its ID badge) or an accent ingredient (that is, the *yam* is still a *yam* but it may need to apologize for its bland character). I do not have a strong opinion on this.

Grating Papaya, Green Mango, and Other Vegetables for Thai Salads

When it comes to grating green papaya or green mango for salads, I do not recommend a box grater or washboard-style grater that requires you to push the papaya hard against the holes and apply pressure constantly as you grate. That is a lot of work that unfortunately yields a lackluster result: limp, bruised strands that are much too short. In contrast, a hand grater (see page 7) is easier on your wrist and produces more strands of the correct length in far less time. A mandoline can also be used.

In the absence of a hand grater or a mandoline, the next best tool for grating green papaya or green mango is a food processor with the grater blade attached. To use a food processor, first, peel the fruit with a paring knife or a vegetable peeler. Then, if using a papaya, halve it lengthwise, remove all of the seeds, cut each half crosswise, then lengthwise into long wedges slim enough to fit through the feeding tube, and shred away. If using a mango, hold the mango horizontally with the stem pointing toward you. Then, with the blade of a sharp knife parallel with the wide surface of the pit and positioned just above the stem, cut downward to remove the flesh in a single slab. Cut the flesh from the opposite side of the pit the same way. Cut each slab into long pieces slim enough to fit through the feeding tube and shred them in the processor.

Nowadays, some Asian markets sell preshredded green papaya, which is a good option if you want to leave the shredding step to someone else.

My favorite ratio for *yam* dressing is one part fish sauce and one and a half parts lime juice. I like to rely on the natural sweetness of the fresh ingredients, so I generally do not add sugar, even though sugar is the ingredient that makes a Thai salad palatable to many people. I also think that sour should be the predominant flavor of a *yam*. Experiment with the dressing ingredients to come up with a ratio that you like.

In the following salad recipes, I often instruct the cook to season to taste. I know that this presents a problem for anyone who is attempting to make a dish that he or she has never eaten before. But the direction becomes more doable if you consider these three points:

- The same ingredient can vary in flavor. The sweetness of palm sugar is different from batch to batch and brand to brand. The brand of fish sauce I use may be saltier than the one you use. A high-quality tomato at the height of the season may provide a *yam* with enough natural sweetness to forgo the addition of sugar. An out-of-season tomato, on the other hand, may need help from a pinch of sugar.

- Some ingredients are intrinsically salty, sour, or sweet. That means that when I use any of these ingredients, I cannot stick blindly to my favorite fish sauce–lime juice ratio. Instead, I will have to adjust it accordingly. A salad of tart green mango, for example, requires very little or no lime juice. Likewise, a salad of preseasoned cooked meat will not need much fish sauce.

- A salad is traditionally eaten as a rice accompaniment, which means that it needs to be seasoned in anticipation of the bland rice.

In the end, of course, you must determine what tastes good to you. My directions are based on what I consider the norm, namely, sour first, then salty, and finally a little bit of sweet. If you are new to making Thai salads, start with my suggestions and you will soon discover your own way to season salads.

Soups

Even though many overseas Thai restaurants have adopted the Western soup course, a Thai soup, just like a Thai salad, is typically eaten with rice as part of a meal, not as a stand-alone dish. You should think of a Thai soup as simply a main dish that comes with lots of liquid.

To give your soups a true Thai flavor, use the Thai-style homemade stock on page 178. Store-bought stocks or homemade stocks used for Western cuisines will not yield the same results because they often contain aromatics and herbs not associated with Thai food. Thai cooks traditionally make soups with bone-in meats, which require long cooking but become the main source of the savory flavor, or umami, that makes the soups taste so good. Because the soups in this book are made with boneless meat, they need some help from a good homemade stock. Try to make stock whenever you have a little extra time, so that you have some on hand when you want to make a pot of soup.

If you do not have homemade Thai stock on hand, and do not have time to make stock, you can use a sodium-free commercial product. Make sure that it does not contain tomato in any form or any root vegetables or herbs that are not typically used in Thai cuisine, such as parsley root, rosemary, and sage.

Curries

Two components are at the heart of every coconut-based curry: coconut milk and curry paste, and their quality helps to define the success of the finished dish.

Every coconut-based curry begins with frying the curry paste in coconut cream, the thick, fat-rich layer that rises to the top of coconut milk. Different Thai cooks have different ways of doing this: some heat the coconut milk and coconut cream together until the mixture "cracks" (the fat separates from the liquid), scoop out the coconut fat, fry the paste in the fat, and return the fried paste to the coconut milk; others fry the paste and coconut cream together until the fat separates, then add the milk later. I have tried both methods and cannot taste a difference in the finished curry. If you extract your own coconut milk (see page 172), you may want to try both methods to see which one works the best for you.

However, most American cooks purchase coconut milk in cans (or aseptic boxes), which has a slightly different taste and texture than freshly made coconut milk. The biggest issue with using store-bought coconut milk is not how to crack the coconut cream but whether you can crack it at all. Canned coconut milk can fluctuate dramatically in quality, even among the reliable brands, so you never know exactly what you will get when you open a can. Sometimes you will find a thick layer of cream on top and sometimes you will not. Sometimes the thick cream is the result of fat and sometimes it is due to the presence of thickeners. (See page 198 for tips on shopping for coconut milk.)

When making curry, never shake a can of coconut milk before you open it, or you will disturb the cream layer. If you do scoop off the layer of cream and fry it and it still does not crack, add some coconut oil or vegetable oil to help it along. In this book, I take the preemptive measure of having you add some oil at the frying stage, assuming that you use canned coconut milk. If you use freshly extracted coconut cream, you can omit the oil.

Homemade curry paste is better than a commercial paste, of course, but only if the correct ingredients are used to make it. In general, Thai curries are not very forgiving when necessary ingredients are missing and are even less forgiving when ingredients are used that have no business being there. For example, a homemade curry paste that is made with ginger when galangal is called for, or with lemon in lieu of lemongrass, will create an

off taste that is readily noticeable to anyone familiar with Thai food. Also, if a cook tries to make the classic Thai red curry with fresh red chiles instead of the usual dried red chiles—perhaps thinking that if something is dried, it must be inferior to the equivalent fresh ingredient—then the curry will not be the classic. If the goal is to create a Thai-*inspired* curry made from wholesome, fresh ingredients, it is okay to swap in an ingredient or two. But if the goal is to replicate the taste of a traditional Thai curry, and if a key ingredient, such as lemongrass or galangal, is unavailable, a commercial curry paste is the better option. See page 3 for advice on selecting commercial brands.

Always keep a couple of things in mind when using commercial curry pastes. Commercial products, especially those imported from Thailand, tend to be saltier and spicier than the homemade paste recipes in this book. So if you want your curry to have a more pronounced herbal flavor but not be hotter or saltier, you need to start out with less curry paste than you think you will need. That is why some recipes call for a smaller amount of ready-made paste than homemade paste.

Not all curries are coconut-based; there are some that do not contain any coconut at all. I have included some of the most popular in this book. Although these curries may seem more souplike, the Thai people consider them curries because they have curry paste as their foundation.

Miscellaneous

The dishes at the end of this chapter represent a random sampling of restaurant favorites that come with too few friends in their category to form a large team of their own, the way the salads, soups, and curries do. But that does not mean that they are not special or delicious, because they are. Like the other recipes in this chapter, they are accompaniments to rice, so do not be shy with the seasoning.

ไก่ผัดขิง
CHICKEN-GINGER STIR-FRY
kai phat khing

This dish is as down-home as they come: comfort food for grown-ups who love ginger. It can be served as part of a full-meal ensemble or as a one-plate meal on top of rice with a crispy fried egg on the side. I call for a lot of ginger, and I specify young ginger, which is milder but harder to find in the United States. If you have to use mature ginger, take the edge off the heat by pouring cold water over the ginger matchsticks and stirring them around to help release some of the juice. Rinse and repeat until the water runs clear, then drain well. The ginger will be milder.

Dried wood ear mushrooms are the traditional choice for this dish. If you cannot find them, you can use any type of mild-flavored fresh mushroom instead. I find shiitakes too strong for this dish, but you can certainly use them if you like. **SERVES 4**

½ cup dried wood ear mushrooms, or 8 ounces fresh white button or cremini mushrooms

1 pound boneless, skinless chicken thighs or breasts

3-ounce piece fresh young ginger, about 5 inches long and 1½ inches in diameter

3 green onions

2 large cloves garlic

2 tablespoons vegetable oil

2 tablespoons fish sauce

1 tablespoon oyster sauce

½ teaspoon granulated sugar

¼ cup sodium-free chicken stock, homemade (page 178) or store-bought

If using dried mushrooms, put them in a bowl of hot water, stir, and let soak for at least 20 minutes while you prepare the chicken and vegetables.

Cut the chicken against the grain and on the diagonal (30- to 40-degree angle) into thin, bite-size pieces; set aside. Peel the ginger and cut it on the diagonal into slices about 2 inches long and ⅛ inch thick. Stack 3 or 4 slices and cut them lengthwise into thin matchsticks. Repeat until all of the ginger slices are in matchsticks. Cut the green onions into 1½-inch lengths, keeping the white and green parts separate. Mince the garlic.

By this time, the mushrooms should be fully hydrated. Remove them from the water, give them a good rinse (sometimes they come with lots of gritty dirt), and pat them dry. If the mushrooms have hard, knobby ends, trim them off. Then slice the mushrooms into ½-inch-wide strips. If using fresh mushroom, slice them ¼ inch thick.

Heat the oil in a wok or a 14-inch skillet over medium-high heat. When the oil is hot, add the garlic and stir for about 30 seconds, until fragrant. Add the chicken, fish sauce, oyster sauce, and sugar and stir-fry for about 1 minute, until the chicken starts to turn opaque. Add the mushrooms, the ginger, the white and light green parts of the onions, and the stock and stir-fry until the chicken is cooked through, about 1 to 2 minutes. Add the remaining dark green parts of the onions and stir-fry for about 30 seconds, until the onions are wilted. Remove from the heat and serve.

ผัดฟักทองใส่ไข่

STIR-FRIED PUMPKIN with EGGS

phat fak thong sai khai

Here is a perfect weeknight meal that calls for just seven easy-to-find ingredients and goes together quickly. If possible, use kabocha squash, also known as Japanese pumpkin, or Red Kuri squash, also known as Potimarron. They have a mild, sweet flavor and a low moisture content that gives them a texture that is dense and starchy, yet soft and fluffy—almost like a chestnut. When the kabocha or Red Kuri is cooked, the skin becomes soft enough to eat and is quite delicious. Buttercup (not to be confused with butternut) squash and Fairy Tale pumpkin are two other great choices, though these two need to be peeled. Do not use sugar pie pumpkin for this dish, as it becomes too soft and watery when cooked. **SERVES 4**

1 kabocha squash, about 2½ pounds

3 tablespoons vegetable oil

3 large cloves garlic, minced

1 tablespoon fish sauce, or 2 tablespoons thin soy sauce

1 tablespoon oyster sauce

4 eggs, lightly beaten

¼ teaspoon ground white or black pepper

Cut the squash into quarters and scrape out the seeds and fibers with a spoon. If you like, you can peel the quarters, although as noted above, the skin is edible. Cut the quarters into 1-inch cubes.

Heat the oil in a wok or a 14-inch skillet set over medium-high heat. When the oil is hot, add the garlic and fry until fragrant, about 30 seconds. Add the squash, fish sauce, and oyster sauce to the wok, then add just enough water to cover the squash. Bring to a boil and cook, stirring occasionally, until the squash is soft enough to pierce easily with the tip of knife and the water has evaporated, about 10 to 15 minutes.

Make a well in the center of the squash. Pour the beaten eggs directly into the well and scramble them with a wok spatula until they are barely set, about 1 to 2 minutes. Stir everything together so the scrambled egg bits are evenly dispersed among the pumpkin pieces. Remove the wok from the heat, dust the stir-fry with the pepper, and serve.

ทอดมันปลา

FISH CAKES with CUCUMBER-PEANUT RELISH

thot man pla

Thai fish cakes are different from fish cakes or crab cakes in other cuisines because of five defining factors: First, they have a soft and smooth, yet bouncy texture. In other words, even though they are not so rubbery that you hear squeaky noises when you chew them, they are not flaky like New England–style crab cakes either. Second, they are usually not coated with anything—no bread crumbs, no flour, no cornmeal. Third, they are seasoned with curry paste and perfumed with kaffir lime leaves—a heady combination that is difficult to match. Fourth, they are deep-fried or at least shallow fried, rather than seared in a lightly oiled pan. If fat is a concern, you can definitely pan-fry them, though you will need to adjust your expectations. And finally, even though they can be enjoyed as a stand-alone snack, Thai fish cakes are usually eaten as an accompaniment to rice. Knowing that rice is on the table will help you determine how to season your fish cakes.

Unless you live in the same area as the clown featherback fish, the traditional choice for Thai fish cakes, you will have to use another type of fish. I recommend fresh halibut or trout fillets. Either one, plus a couple of tricks and a couple of ingredients to act as binders, will yield the same bouncy fish cakes found on Thai dinner tables. **MAKES 24 (2-INCH) CAKES**

1½ pounds skinless halibut or trout fillets (preferably fresh), cut into small cubes and well chilled

1 teaspoon salt

1 teaspoon granulated sugar

¼ cup crushed ice

2 egg whites

2 tablespoons tapioca flour or cornstarch

2 to 4 tablespoons red curry paste, homemade (page 175) or store-bought

Vegetable oil, for deep-frying

4 ounces long beans or green beans, sliced crosswise ⅛ inch thick

4 fresh kaffir lime leaves, deveined and cut lengthwise into very thin strips

1 small pickling cucumber, or ¼ English cucumber, halved lengthwise and thinly sliced crosswise

¾ cup sweet chile sauce, homemade (page 187) or store-bought

3 tablespoons finely chopped roasted peanuts

In a food processor, combine the fish, salt, sugar, ice, egg whites, tapioca starch, and 2 tablespoons red curry paste and process, stopping to scrape down the sides of the bowl a few times, until smooth, about 2 minutes. The mixture must be ground to a smooth, sticky paste, rather than finely chopped. With a rubber spatula, scrape every bit of the fish paste into a bowl.

To test for seasoning, scoop up a teaspoonful of the fish paste and cook it briefly in a microwave (10 to 15 seconds on medium power) or sear it in a small pan on the stove

continued

top, then taste to see if it is flavorful enough. I have you start out with 2 tablespoons of the curry paste because you need at least that much to keep the fish cakes from being tasteless. But if you like your fish cakes as spicy as I like mine, you will use all 4 tablespoons. So, add more curry paste, cook, and taste until the fish paste tastes spicy enough for you, then cover the bowl and refrigerate the fish paste until well chilled.

To fry the fish cakes, pour the oil to a depth of 2 inches into a wok or a small, deep skillet and heat to 325°F to 350°F. To test if the oil is ready without a thermometer, stick an unvarnished wooden chopstick into the oil; when the oil is hot enough, a steady stream of tiny bubbles will rise from the tip of the chopstick. Line a baking sheet with paper towels and place it next to the stove. Fill a small bowl with water and place it next to the stove, as well.

Remove the fish paste from the refrigerator and fold in the long beans and lime leaves.

Dampen your hands with the water, scoop up some fish paste, form it into a cake about 2 inches in diameter and ½ inch thick, and carefully drop it into the oil. Working quickly, repeat to make 3 more cakes.

Once the first side of the cakes is golden brown, after 30 to 40 seconds, flip them over to the second side. When the cakes have puffed up and are golden brown all over, after 30 to 40 seconds longer, using a slotted spoon, transfer them to the towel-lined baking sheet to drain. Repeat to cook the remaining fish paste the same way.

Arrange the fish cakes on a serving platter. Mix the cucumber slices into the chile sauce and sprinkle the peanuts on top. Serve the fish cakes and the relish immediately.

ไก่ผัดน้ำพริกเผา

STIR-FRIED CHICKEN with CHILE JAM

kai phat nam phrik phao

I could wax poetic all day about the versatility of Thai chile jam (see page 4) and about how this flavorful condiment makes a weeknight Thai dinner at home a breeze. It allows you to create a complexly flavored dish with an astonishingly small number of ingredients, as this recipe illustrates. If you are new to cooking with *nam phrik phao*, start with this recipe to get accustomed to the flavor of this powerhouse. Soon you will be hit with a barrage of ideas on what else you can do with it. **SERVES 4**

12 ounces boneless, skinless chicken breasts

2 tablespoons vegetable oil

2 yellow, white, or red onions, cut into 1-inch-wide wedges

2 fresh red or green Thai long chiles, seeded and deveined, if desired, and cut on the diagonal into long strips

¼ cup chile jam, homemade (page 184) or store-bought

1 tablespoon oyster sauce

1 teaspoon fish sauce

Cut the chicken against the grain and on the diagonal (30- to 40-degree angle) into thin, bite-size pieces.

Place a wok or a 14-inch skillet over high heat. When the wok is hot, add the oil and onion and stir-fry for about 1 minute, until the onion begins to soften a little. Add the chicken, chiles, chile jam, oyster sauce, and fish sauce and stir-fry until the chicken is cooked through, about 5 minutes. Remove from the heat and serve.

น่องไก่ทอด
FRIED CHICKEN DRUMSTICKS
nong kai thot

Thai-style fried chicken gets its flavor from a paste-based marinade and its crunch from being deep-fried at a low temperature for a long period of time. It also tends to be drier than American-style fried chicken, and although the chicken is sometimes coated—as it is here—greater emphasis is put on the flavorful marinade that goes all of the way to the bones than on the crunchy coating.

This is a basic recipe that calls for the most commonly used marinade ingredients: garlic, peppercorns, and cilantro roots. But I often embellish it, depending on what I have on hand and whether I am in the mood to experiment. For example, if I add ground turmeric to the marinade and serve the chicken topped with fried shallots (page 183), the dish resembles the fried chicken popular in southern Thailand. If I want to spice up the chicken, I add red chile powder (page 181) to the marinade. Or sometimes I add lots of lime juice, finely chopped cilantro, minced shallots, red chile powder, and a tablespoon or so of toasted rice powder (page 182) to the marinade, which mimics the flavors of *lap* (page 74).

Try this base recipe first, then go crazy with whatever idea comes into your mind. Serve the drumsticks with long-grain rice (page 168) or glutinous rice (page 169). **MAKES 6 DRUMSTICKS**

2 tablespoons packed basic aromatic paste (page 179)	6 small chicken drumsticks, about 1½ pounds total
1 teaspoon ground coriander	½ cup rice flour or all-purpose flour
1 tablespoon fish sauce	Vegetable oil, for deep-frying
1 tablespoon thin soy sauce	½ cup sweet chile sauce, homemade (page 187) or store-bought
2 tablespoons oyster sauce	
1½ tablespoons packed grated palm sugar, or 3 tablespoons packed light or dark brown sugar	

In a large bowl, mix together the aromatic paste, ground coriander, fish sauce, soy sauce, oyster sauce, and sugar. Add the drumsticks and mix well, coating them evenly. Cover and refrigerate for at least 8 hours or up to overnight. If you cannot wait that long, make 2 or 3 diagonal slashes around each drumstick, all of the way to the bone, then marinate the drumsticks in the refrigerator for 2 to 3 hours.

Spread the flour on a plate and, one at a time, coat the drumsticks with the flour, shaking off the excess. Arrange the coated drumsticks, not touching, on a large platter or baking sheet and allow them to sit for 10 minutes. This resting period is important because it allows the coating to absorb the moisture on the drumsticks and form a crust, which will become very crunchy when the chicken is fried.

To fry the drumsticks, pour the oil to a depth of 5 inches into a wok, Dutch oven, or deep fryer and heat to 300°F. To test if the oil is ready without a thermometer, stick an unvarnished wooden chopstick into the oil; when the oil is hot enough, tiny bubbles will rise slowly from the tip of the chopstick. If the bubbles rise up in a steady stream rapidly, turn down the heat a little, as the oil is too hot. Line a baking sheet with paper towels and place it next to the stove.

Carefully drop the drumsticks into the hot oil and fry, stirring occasionally, until they are deep golden brown and have shrunk a bit, about 25 to 30 minutes. Using tongs or a slotted spoon, transfer them to the towel-lined baking sheet. Repeat until all of the drumsticks are fried.

Let the drumsticks cool slightly before serving, then accompany with the chile sauce.

ไข่ลูกเขย

SON-in-LAW EGGS

khai luk khoei

Many theories exist regarding the origin of the odd name of this dish, but two stand out as the most plausible. Okay, maybe they are not the most plausible. I just like them better than the rest. One maintains that the name has to do with the color of the hard-boiled eggs that have been deep-fried and thoroughly doused in a deep golden sauce. Thai culture is rich in symbolism, and the color gold is traditionally linked with wealth, something the parents of a daughter naturally hope for in their future son-in-law. As much sense as this theory makes, I reject it, solely because it fails to amuse me sufficiently.

The second theory paints a much grimmer, more gruesome picture. But that is precisely what makes it appealing. The Thai word for egg (as in the egg laid by the female in various species) is the same as the informal word for the male reproductive glands that come in pairs. Now, visualize an egg—and I am being intentionally ambiguous here as to which of the two above meanings should be applied—boiled, deep-fried until blistered and browned all over, whacked in half with a cleaver, and topped with a hot, sticky sauce. Apparently, the message that the parents of a daughter want to send to their future son-in-law is, "This is what's going to happen to you, boy, if you mistreat our daughter." After seeing that, if the guy does not run away in terror, he is probably worthy of the daughter.

But those are just theories. What we know for sure is that Thais across all age groups and socioeconomic strata are head over heels in love—and have been for ages—with these sweet-and-sour son-in-law eggs.

If you are pressed for time or do not feel up to hard boiling and then deep-frying the eggs, you can do what I do when the purists are not around: replace hard-boiled and deep-fried eggs with crispy fried eggs (page 194), preferably with runny yolks. They are just as great as the traditional version, if not better. The oozing yolks mixed with sweet-and-sour sauce form something quite memorable. **SERVES 4**

Vegetable oil, for deep-frying

8 hard- or medium-boiled eggs (page 195), peeled

½ cup fried shallots (page 183), plus 1 tablespoon of their cooking oil

½ cup packed grated palm sugar, or ¼ cup packed light or dark brown sugar

¼ cup fish sauce

2 tablespoons tamarind pulp, homemade (page 171) or store-bought

3 tablespoons water

2 fresh red Thai long chiles, or ½ red bell pepper, seeded and slivered lengthwise, for garnish

Fresh cilantro leaves, for garnish

Pour the vegetable oil to a depth of 3 inches into a wok or deep skillet and heat to 325°F to 350°F. To test if the oil is ready without a thermometer, stick an unvarnished wooden chopstick into the oil; when the oil is hot enough, a steady stream of tiny

continued

bubbles will rise from the tip of the chopstick. Line a baking sheet with paper towels and place it next to the stove.

When the oil is ready, gently drop in 4 eggs and fry, stirring them as needed to ensure even browning, until they are thoroughly and evenly browned, about 3 minutes. Using a slotted spoon, transfer the eggs to the towel-lined baking sheet and let them cool down. Repeat with the remaining 4 eggs. Let them cool down to room temperature.

To make the sauce, in a 1-quart saucepan, combine the shallot oil, sugar, fish sauce, tamarind, and water over medium heat. Bring the mixture to a gentle boil, stirring constantly. Once the sugar has fully dissolved, check the consistency of the mixture. It should have the consistency of warm pancake syrup. If it is too thin, reduce it a bit more. If it is too thick, add a little more water. When the desired consistency is achieved, remove the pan from the heat.

Working quickly while the sauce is still warm, slice the deep-fried eggs in half lengthwise and arrange the halves, cut sides up, on a serving platter. Pour the warm sauce over the eggs and sprinkle the shallots over the top. Garnish with the chiles and cilantro and serve.

กุ้งผัดผงกะหรี่

SHRIMP CURRY STIR-FRY

kung phat phong kari

This dish of jumbo shrimp stir-fried in Chinese-style creamy, eggy curry sauce is a classic Chinese-Thai dish that you cannot miss whenever you dine at a family-style seaside restaurant or at certain spots in Bangkok known for high-quality seafood dishes. The far more prevalent version, however, uses whole crab cut into large chunks. I prefer jumbo shrimp; it's easier to eat. **SERVES 4**

2 eggs

½ cup whole milk

1 tablespoon chile jam, homemade (page 184) or store-bought

1 tablespoon curry powder, homemade (page 180) or store-bought (see note)

1 teaspoon salt

1 teaspoon granulated sugar

¼ cup sodium-free chicken stock, homemade (page 178) or store-bought

1 tablespoon vegetable oil

1 tablespoon oil from chile jam or vegetable oil

2 large cloves garlic, minced

1 small yellow or white onion, cut into ½-inch-wide wedges

1 pound jumbo shrimp in the shell, peeled and deveined

1 fresh red or green Thai long chile, seeded, deveined, and cut lengthwise on the diagonal into ½-inch-wide strips

1 cup packed Chinese or regular celery leaves

In a small bowl, whisk together the eggs, milk, chile jam, curry powder, salt, sugar, and stock just until blended. Set aside.

Heat the vegetable oil and oil from the chile jam in a wok or 14-inch skillet over high heat. When the oil is hot, add the garlic and onion and fry until the garlic is fragrant and the onion slightly softened, about 1 minute. Add the shrimp and stir-fry until just starting to turn opaque, about 30 seconds. Add the egg mixture and chile strips and stir-fry until the egg sauce curdles just a bit and the shrimp is cooked through, about 1 to 2 minutes. Remove from the heat, stir in the celery leaves, and serve.

Note: If you use homemade or store-bought curry powder that has been sitting on your shelf for more than a month, toast it in a dry skillet over low heat just until it becomes fragrant before using it in this stir-fry. This extra step, which takes less than a minute, will make a huge difference in the taste of the finished dish.

ไข่เจียวหมูสับ
GROUND PORK OMELET
khai jiao mu sap

Ask a random Bangkokian to name five ultimate comfort foods, and I am willing to bet all of my money on one of the answers being *khai jiao*. Golden and fluffy, with soft inner layers and crispy edges, this deep-fried omelet is both a sight to behold and an absolute joy to consume. One thing must be made clear about this omelet, however: it is not meant to be eaten by itself in the manner of a French or American omelet. *Khai jiao* is a rice accompaniment and seasoned accordingly.

The dish is good enough unembellished, but cooks sometimes add ingredients to their omelet to make it more special or substantial. Ground pork is one of the classic mix-ins. You can replace it with ground chicken, ground turkey, shrimp, crabmeat—nearly anything. Try making *khai jiao* with shucked oysters, cut into ½-inch dice, and see if you like it as much as I do. Vegetarians like onion wedges, thinly sliced shallots, or tomato chunks in their omelet.

Whenever jungle curry (page 102) or sour curry (page 177) is part of a meal ensemble, or *samrap*, an omelet on the table is a must—at least it was on my family's table when I was growing up. When preparing a *samrap* to be eaten family-style, *khai jiao* is the last dish to be cooked because it is best when it is hot out of the wok. It helps that the dish is so quick and easy to make, which means that one family member can make the omelet in the time that it takes the other members to set the table and plate other dishes. Once the table is ready and everyone is seated, the arrival of *khai jiao* is a nonverbal equivalent of the jubilant "Dig in!"

I instruct you to fry the egg mixture in two batches because the omelet is easier to flip and you get a higher crispy-to-soft ratio, which my recipe testers liked. You can fry it all in one go, if you prefer; simply use the entire 2 cups of vegetable oil at once. (This may seem like an excessive amount of oil, but when prepared correctly, the omelet will not absorb too much of it.) If you have a hard time flipping the omelet in one perfect piece, do not worry; *khai jiao* does not have to form a perfect round to be good. The key is to get an omelet with crispy edges and multiple soft inner layers.

Serve this classic omelet as part of a *samrap*, or serve it over rice drizzled with Sriracha sauce (page 186)—a classic combo. **SERVES 2**

4 duck or chicken eggs

4 ounces ground pork

1 tablespoon fish sauce

2 teaspoons freshly squeezed lime juice

1 tablespoon cornstarch, rice flour, or all-purpose flour (optional)

1 tablespoon water

1 to 2 cups vegetable oil

Crack the eggs into a bowl big enough to hold twice their volume, then beat with a fork until frothy. Beat in the pork, fish sauce, lime juice, cornstarch, and water. Divide the egg mixture evenly between 2 small bowls.

Heat 1 cup of the oil in a wok over high heat. Grab a large plate and place it near the stove; that is where your omelet will land. Wait until the oil smokes (this is important!), then, holding a bowl of egg mixture about 12 inches above the wok, pour the contents of the bowl into the hot oil. No hardcore splattering should occur. But, to be on the safe side, you may want to stand back.

After 30 seconds, flip the omelet once. You should see the omelet has turned golden on one side. Cook the other side for another 30 seconds. The omelet should be thoroughly golden on both sides and its jagged edges crispy. Now, using a wok spatula or a wire-mesh skimmer, scoop the omelet out of the oil, shake off the dripping oil, and place it on the plate. Check to see how much oil is left in the wok; add more to the pan as needed to restore the volume to 1 cup. Repeat the process with the second portion of the egg mixture. Serve piping hot.

ผัดวุ้นเส้น

STIR-FRIED GLASS NOODLES with CHICKEN

phat wun sen

It may seem strange that Thais regard this noodle stir-fry as a rice accompaniment rather than as a one-plate noodle dish, such as pad thai (page 123) or *phat si-io* (page 120). You will not see it offered at any made-to-order noodle shop in Thailand, but you will see it at a casual family meal at home or at most rice-curry shops, where different dishes are served atop a plate of rice.

The choices of vegetables and aromatics for this dish vary from place to place and from cook to cook. Some people add everything from baby corn to cabbage to broccoli; others keep it simple. Some use green onions or yellow onions as the aromatics; others use Chinese celery. The meat choices vary as well. Although pork is by far the most common, shrimp or chicken is often used.

I am sticking to this simple version, which I like the best. **SERVES 4**

3 ounces glass noodles

8 ounces boneless, skinless chicken thighs or breasts

3 tablespoons vegetable oil

2 large cloves garlic, minced

2 Roma tomatoes, cut into 1-inch-wide wedges

2 yellow or white onions, cut into 1-inch-wide wedges

1 teaspoon fish sauce

2 tablespoons thin soy sauce

2 tablespoons oyster sauce

1 teaspoon granulated sugar

½ teaspoon ground white or black pepper

½ cup sodium-free chicken stock, homemade (page 178) or store-bought

3 eggs

1 cup packed Chinese celery or regular celery leaves

Immerse the glass noodles in a bowl of room-temperature water and soak for 20 minutes, until pliable. Drain and cut into 6-inch lengths with kitchen shears. Set aside.

Cut the chicken against the grain and on the diagonal (30- to 40-degree angle) into thin, bite-size pieces; set aside.

Heat the oil in a wok or a 14-inch skillet set over medium-high heat. When the oil is hot, add the garlic and fry until fragrant, about 30 seconds. Add the chicken, tomatoes, onions, fish sauce, soy sauce, oyster sauce, sugar, and pepper and stir-fry until the chicken is half-cooked, about 2 minutes. Add the noodles and stock and continue to stir for about 1 minute, until the noodles have softened a bit. Create a well in the center of the mixture and crack the eggs directly into the well. Using the tip of a wok spatula, stir the eggs just to break them up. Let the eggs cook for 30 to 40 seconds, just until they are no longer liquid but are not yet quite cooked. Add the celery leaves, stir everything together, and continue to cook until the celery has wilted, about 30 to 40 seconds. Remove from the heat and serve.

ปีกไก่ทอดซอสสามรส

CRISPY WINGS with THREE-FLAVORED SAUCE

pik kai thot sot sam rot

The so-called three-flavored sauce is one of the most versatile sauces in Thai cooking. Although it is usually served over fried fish, it can also be used in other ways. Grilled or pan-seared scallops, grilled or baked lobster tails, grilled jumbo shrimp, batter-fried fish, and even tempura-style vegetables are all amazing when anointed with three-flavored sauce. When I was a hungry, busy, cash-challenged student, this benevolent sauce saw me through. All I needed was a jar of it, a pot of rice, and whatever was on sale at the market—chicken wings, most of the time. I have always told people that once they have learned how to make this sour, sweet, and salty sauce, they can create many modern dishes with a traditional Thai flavor profile. I still stand by that.

In this recipe, the three-flavored sauce is reduced until thicker and stickier than it usually is, then used to coat hot, crispy deep-fried chicken wings the moment they come out of the oil.

SERVES 2 OR 3

Wings

1½ pounds chicken wings, tips removed and separated into drummettes and flats

1 tablespoon oyster sauce

1 tablespoon fish sauce

½ cup rice flour or all-purpose flour

Vegetable oil, for deep-frying

Three-Flavored Sauce

10 fresh bird's eye chiles, or 2 fresh Thai long chiles

5 large cloves garlic

1 large shallot, about 1 ounce

3 cilantro roots, or ¼ cup chopped cilantro stems

2 tablespoons vegetable oil

½ cup packed grated palm sugar, or ⅓ cup packed light or dark brown sugar

2 tablespoons granulated sugar

¼ cup water

¼ cup fish sauce

¼ cup tamarind pulp, homemade (page 171) or store-bought

¼ cup coarsely chopped fresh cilantro leaves, for garnish

To marinate the chicken, combine the chicken, oyster sauce, and fish sauce in a large bowl and mix well. Cover and refrigerate for at least 4 to 5 hours or up to overnight.

To make the sauce, in a food processor, combine the chiles, garlic, shallot, and cilantro roots and pulse into a coarse paste with bits the size of a match head. Heat the oil in a 2-quart saucepan over medium-high heat. Add the paste and fry just until fragrant, about 1 minute. Add the palm sugar, granulated sugar, water, fish sauce, and tamarind pulp and bring to a boil, stirring constantly. Lower the heat to maintain a simmer and cook, stirring often, until reduced to about ¾ cup. This will take about 5 to 8 minutes. Remove from the heat and transfer to a bowl large enough to hold the chicken. Let cool completely.

continued

Spread the flour on a plate. One at a time, coat the chicken pieces with the flour, shaking off the excess. Arrange the coated pieces, not touching, on a baking sheet and allow them to sit for 10 minutes. This resting period is important because it allows the coating to absorb the moisture on the chicken and form a crust, which will become very crunchy when the chicken is fried.

To fry the chicken, pour the oil to a depth of 3 inches into a wok, Dutch oven, or deep fryer and heat to 300°F. To test if the oil is ready without a thermometer, stick an unvarnished wooden chopstick into the oil; when the oil is hot enough, tiny bubbles will slowly rise from the tip of the chopstick. If you see a steady stream of bubbles rise up rapidly, lower the heat a bit. Line another baking sheet with paper towels and place it near the stove.

Add the chicken pieces (in batches if necessary, so as not to crowd the wok) to the hot oil and fry, turning the pieces as needed for even browning, until deep golden brown, about 20 to 25 minutes. Using a slotted spoon or tongs, transfer the pieces to the towel-lined baking sheet.

Put the fried chicken into the sauce bowl and toss to coat evenly. Arrange the chicken on a large platter, sprinkle the cilantro over the top, and serve immediately.

ไข่ยัดไส้

STUFFED EGG CREPES

khai yat sai

"O, Cilantro, you enhance the inner value of anything you adorn," says *"Phak Chi Roi Na"* (Garnished with Cilantro), a megahit song from the late 1980s by Asanee and Wasan Chotikul, two of Thailand's most famous rockers. Even though nobody likes to eat cilantro, the song asserts, nobody will eat anything without this useless garnish. The catchy tune also goes on to suggest—winking, of course—that, likewise, if we want our work to be found acceptable by society, we need constantly to look for some cilantro to put on top of it.

It reminds me of this childhood favorite of mine (and of every kid I knew growing up), for I have never seen this dish without a cilantro sprig garnish. It is almost as if people think the yellow, eggy pouches would look unappealing without something green perching on top. I think everyone sells this well-loved modern Thai dish short because it certainly tastes and looks good enough to forgo adornment. **SERVES 4**

Egg Crepes

8 eggs

4 tablespoons vegetable oil

Filling

1 tablespoon vegetable oil

2 large cloves garlic, minced

8 ounces ground pork or chicken

1 small yellow or white onion, cut into ¼-inch dice

1 tablespoon oyster sauce

2 teaspoons thin soy sauce

½ cup frozen mixed peas and carrots, thawed

1 (8-ounce) can tomato sauce

¼ teaspoon ground white or black pepper

4 sprigs cilantro, for garnish

To make the crepes, in a small bowl, beat 2 of the eggs with a fork just until blended. Arrange 4 large dinner plates near the stove. Put 1 tablespoon of the oil in a 14-inch nonstick skillet or a wok, set over medium-high heat, and with a heatproof rubber spatula, spread the oil evenly over the bottom.

When the pan is hot, pour in the beaten eggs and tilt the pan in a circular motion so the eggs form a round crepe about 12 inches across, making sure the center of the crepe is not too thin. Cook until the bottom turns light brown and the top is somewhat firm yet still moist and glossy, about 1 minute. Gently slide the egg onto a dinner plate. Repeat to make 3 more crepes with the remaining 6 eggs and 3 tablespoons oil. You should have four 12-inch crepes, one on each dinner plate.

To make the filling, return the pan to medium-high heat and add the 1 tablespoon oil. When the oil is hot, add the garlic and fry until fragrant, about 30 seconds. Add the pork, onion, oyster sauce, and soy sauce and cook, stirring, until the pork is almost cooked through and the onion is translucent, about 2 minutes. Add the peas and carrots and tomato sauce and cook, stirring, until the mixture thickens, about 5 minutes. At this point, the filling should look moist but there should be no runny tomato sauce bubbling in the pan. Stir in the pepper and remove the pan from the heat.

Immediately spoon the filling onto the center of each crepe, dividing it evenly and forming a round mound about 4 inches in diameter. Fold the 4 sides of each crepe over the filling, forming a square pocket. Carefully flip each pocket over onto a serving platter, so the seams are on the underside. If desired, cut a large X across the surface of the pocket and peel back the petals to reveal the filling. Place a cilantro sprig on top of each crepe—because you must—and serve.

STIR-FRIED BEEF with BANANA PEPPERS

nuea phat phrik yuak

When I was in grade school, this was my favorite school lunch because I was able to eat not just a little bit of chile, but bite after bite of chile, which made me feel like a grown-up. This is akin to riding a bike without the training wheels. For a while, I reveled in my ability to eat peppers without running to my mommy, crying, until I found out that banana peppers are not hot at all. Bummer.

Banana peppers taste like a sweet, mild vegetable. The green long chiles are added for both color (the light green and dark green look pretty together) and heat (though not too much, since the chiles are seeded and deveined). If you are making this dish for children or for folks who prefer it completely mild, forget the long chiles.

This dish is also great with pork and chicken. I like to use boneless country-style rib pork meat or boneless, skinless chicken thighs. Cut the pork the same way you cut the beef. For the chicken thighs, I prefer to cut the slices about ½ inch thick. **SERVES 4**

12 ounces rib-eye or chuck steak

8 ounces banana peppers (about 5)

2 fresh green Thai long chiles (optional)

2 tablespoons vegetable oil

2 large cloves garlic, minced

1 tablespoon thin soy sauce

1 yellow or white onion, cut into ½-inch-wide wedges

1 tablespoon fish sauce

1 teaspoon granulated sugar

Cut the beef against the grain and on the diagonal into very thin, bite-size pieces. Stem and halve the banana peppers and long chiles lengthwise. Remove and discard the veins and seeds, then cut them on a slight diagonal into ½-inch-wide strips.

Heat the oil in a wok or a 14-inch skillet over medium-high heat. When the oil is hot but not smoking, add the garlic and fry until fragrant, about 30 seconds. Add the beef, spreading it across the bottom of the pan in a single layer. Quickly drizzle the beef evenly with the soy sauce and then stir-fry until the beef is almost cooked through, about 1 minute. Add the pepper slices, chile slices, onion wedges, fish sauce, and sugar, and stir-fry until the beef is cooked through and the chiles and onions slightly softened, about 2 minutes. Remove from the heat and serve.

เห็ดผัดน้ำมันหอย

MUSHROOM–OYSTER SAUCE STIR-FRY

het phat nam man hoi

This is one of my top meatless—well, almost meatless—dishes. The absence of meat is not even a factor for me. The mushrooms taste great not only because their meaty texture makes a wonderful meat substitute—though that is true—but also because they are flavorful, especially when combined with oyster sauce, the other main ingredient of this dish. If you use an assortment of only wild mushrooms, this chinese-style stir-fry tastes even better.

To make this dish truly meatless, use vegetarian "oyster" sauce, which is made from mushrooms and is available at many health food stores and online. If you cannot find sodium-free stock, reduce the soy sauce by 1 tablespoon. **SERVES 4 TO 6**

⅓ cup oyster sauce

¼ cup thin soy sauce

2 teaspoons sesame oil

¼ cup Chinese rice wine or dry sherry

¾ cup sodium-free chicken or vegetable stock, homemade (page 178) or store-bought

3 tablespoons cornstarch

3 large cloves garlic, minced

3 pounds assorted wild and domestic mushrooms (such as oyster, chanterelle, cremini, and white button), cut into bite-size pieces

¼ cup water

5 green onions, white and green parts, cut crosswise into 1-inch pieces, with white and green parts kept separate

To make the sauce, in a bowl, whisk together the oyster sauce, soy sauce, sesame oil, wine, stock, cornstarch, and garlic until no cornstarch lumps remain.

Place a wok or a 14-inch skillet over high heat. When the pan is hot, add the mushrooms, the water, and the white parts of the onions and stir for 1 minute. Whisk the sauce mixture again briefly (the cornstarch may have sunk to the bottom), pour it into the pan, and stir for about 2 minutes, until the mushrooms have softened and the sauce has thickened. Stir in the green parts of the onions, then immediately remove the pan from the heat and serve.

ผัดเปรี้ยวหวานไก่

SWEET-and-SOUR VEGETABLE STIR-FRY with CHICKEN

phat priao wan kai

Although the Chinese influence in this dish is undeniable, the Thai-style sweet-and-sour stir-fry is traditionally quite different from the sweet-and-sour dishes you may have enjoyed at Chinese restaurants, though Thai restaurants outside Thailand tend to make their sweet-and-sour stir-fries almost identical to their Chinese counterparts. In Thailand, however, these dishes use no starch for thickening the sauce and do not include the extra step of batter-frying the meat. The Thai version is simpler, with a lighter, thinner sauce and with the emphasis on the vegetables. **SERVES 4**

8 ounces boneless, skinless chicken thighs or breasts

1 English cucumber, or 3 pickling cucumbers

1 banana pepper, or ½ red bell pepper

2 tablespoons vegetable oil

3 large cloves garlic, minced

3 green onions, white and green parts, cut crosswise into 1½-inch lengths, white and green parts kept separate

3 Roma tomatoes, cut into ½-inch-wide wedges

1 tablespoon fish sauce

1 tablespoon thin soy sauce

2 teaspoons oyster sauce

2 teaspoons distilled white vinegar or cider vinegar

2 teaspoons packed grated palm sugar, or 1 teaspoon granulated sugar

¾ cup 1-inch-cubed fresh pineapple

¼ teaspoon ground white pepper

Cut the chicken against the grain and on the diagonal (30- to 40-degree angle) into thin, bite-size pieces; set aside. Peel the cucumber(s) and halve lengthwise. Place the halves cut side down and cut crosswise on the diagonal into ½-inch-thick pieces. Halve the banana pepper lengthwise, remove the seeds, and slice lengthwise on the diagonal into ½-inch-wide strips (or seed the bell pepper and slice as directed).

Place a wok or a 14-inch skillet over medium-high heat. Add the oil to the wok. When the oil is hot, add the garlic and fry until fragrant, about 30 seconds. Add the white part of the onions and one-fourth of the tomato wedges and stir-fry for 30 seconds. Add the chicken, fish sauce, soy sauce, oyster sauce, vinegar, and sugar, turn up the heat to high, and stir-fry until the chicken is half-cooked, about 1 minute. Add the cucumber, pepper, pineapple, and the remaining tomato wedges and stir-fry until the chicken is cooked through and the vegetables have softened, about 1 to 2 minutes. Taste the sauce; it should be equally sweet, sour, and salty. Fresh tomatoes and pineapple vary in tartness and sweetness, so you may need to adjust the seasoning to achieve this balance.

Remove the pan from the heat, add the ground pepper and the green part of the onions, and stir briefly just to wilt the onions in the residual heat in the pan. Transfer the stir-fry to a platter and serve.

ไก่ผัดเม็ดมะม่วงหิมพานต์

CHICKEN-CASHEW STIR-FRY

kai phat met mamuang himma-phan

This is a dish with one name and a thousand faces. In the past ten years, I have eaten dozens of different versions of it at Thai restaurants around the globe. Sometimes it was made with a large amount of thick gravy and lots of vegetables; other times it included a Chinese-style sweet-and-sour sauce and the cashews were sprinkled on top. That wild range makes me wonder if it is even possible to convince folks who have never eaten this dish in Bangkok that what is generally labeled chicken-cashew stir-fry in Thailand is dramatically different from what they may be used to.

By saying this, I do not mean to suggest that my version is the only correct one. Instead, I want to prepare you in case this recipe does not meet your expectations. What I am offering here is what I remember eating as a child at home and elsewhere in Bangkok. This recipe produces a light mahogany–colored, smoky stir-fry with a somewhat sticky sauce that coats, rather than drowns, the cashews, thus preserving their crunch.

Timing and the control of heat are crucial in the success of this dish. Try to follow the instructions as closely as possible. **SERVES 4**

1 pound boneless, skinless chicken breasts or thighs	2 teaspoons packed dark brown sugar
3 tablespoons cornstarch	½ cup water
1 yellow or white onion	¾ cup vegetable oil
3 green onions	1¾ cups (8 ounces) whole roasted cashews
2 tablespoons oyster sauce	3 dried Thai long chiles, seeded and cut crosswise into ¾-inch-wide pieces
2 tablespoons thin soy sauce	2 large cloves garlic, finely chopped

Cut the chicken against the grain and on the diagonal (30- to 40-degree angle) into thin, bite-size pieces. Place the chicken in a bowl, sprinkle the cornstarch over it, and stir well, making sure each piece of chicken is coated with the cornstarch; set aside.

Cut the yellow onion through the stem end into ½-inch-thick slices. Cut the green onions crosswise into 2-inch lengths. Add the white parts to the yellow onion slices. Keep the green parts separate.

In a small bowl, stir together the oyster sauce, soy sauce, sugar, and water, mixing well. Set aside.

Line 2 plates with paper towels and place them near the stove. Heat the oil in a large wok or a 14-inch skillet over medium heat. When the oil is hot, add the cashews and fry, stirring constantly, until golden brown, about 1 minute. Using a slotted spoon,

continued

immediately transfer the nuts to a towel-lined plate. Do your best to keep as much oil in the pan as possible, as we need to fry two more ingredients in it.

With the pan still over medium heat, add the chiles and fry, stirring constantly, until crisp, about 1 minute, taking care not to burn them. Using the slotted spoon, transfer the chiles to the cashew plate and set the plate aside.

Turn up the heat to high. When the oil is very hot, add half of the chicken, gently lowering each piece into the oil and leaving room between the pieces. After 1 to 2 minutes, one side of the chicken should feel firm when you touch it with the end of the spatula. This is your cue to flip the chicken pieces. Do not go by color, because the oil has taken on the color of the dried chiles and the chicken will look golden brown when it is still uncooked. Also, do not stir the chicken around, as you want each piece to develop a soft crust. Once that has been achieved, using the slotted spoon, transfer the chicken to the second towel-lined plate. Repeat with the remaining half of the chicken.

Discard nearly all of the oil in the pan, leaving only a thin film to coat the pan bottom, and return the pan to high heat. Immediately add the garlic, the yellow onion, and the white parts of the green onions and stir them around. When the onions have softened a bit, after about 1 minute, add the chicken to the pan along with the oyster sauce mixture (be sure to use a small rubber spatula to get every bit of the sauce out of the bowl) and stir everything around constantly. The sauce should evaporate quickly, without turning the coating of the chicken soft and gummy.

Immediately add the green parts of the green onions and the fried cashews and chiles and stir-fry for about 30 seconds. At this point, everything should be heated through and the green onion tops should be wilted. Remove from the heat, transfer to a platter, and serve.

Note: It is imperative that you use either a large wok or a 14-inch skillet, unless you halve the recipe. At the frying stage, using a cooking vessel that is too small may not present a problem. But at the stir-frying stage when we want the liquid ingredients to form a glistening sauce quickly, fast evaporation is crucial. If at any point the chicken looks like it is taking its sweet time stewing gently in a bubbling sauce, either the pan is too small or the heat is too low. Follow the instructions as closely as you can, and at any time that there appears to be a difference between your stove's output and my stove's output, use your instinct.

เนื้อแดดเดียว

FRIED SUN-DRIED BEEF

nuea daet diao

Often called Thai beef jerky, this sun-dried beef actually is not nearly as dry as most beef jerky products commonly found in the United States. While Western-style jerky is seasoned and dehydrated until it is fully dried and then is eaten without further cooking, this dish is made by sun-drying beef strips just until they are dry to the touch, with much of the moisture still inside the dehydrated exterior "walls," and then the meat is deep-fried briefly.

If you crave this addictive beer snack—which also happens to be one of the most delicious sticky rice accompaniments—but the weather is not cooperating, fret not. You can dehydrate the beef in the oven or in a dehydrator. **SERVES 4**

1½ pounds top round or sirloin steak

2 large cloves garlic, minced

¼ teaspoon ground white or black pepper

1 teaspoon coriander seeds, coarsely cracked (optional)

2 tablespoons fish sauce

2 tablespoons thin soy sauce

2 tablespoons packed grated palm sugar, or 1 tablespoon packed light or dark brown sugar

Vegetable oil, for deep-frying

Dried chile dipping sauce (page 190; optional)

Slice the beef into strips about 4 inches long, ½ inch wide, and ¼ inch thick. It is important that the grain of the beef runs perpendicular to the length of the beef strips. If it does not, you will have a hard time biting off or chewing a piece. Arrange the beef strips, not touching, in a single layer on 2 large baking sheets.

Place the baking sheets outdoors in a sunny spot well protected from the wind and any curious pets. Dry the beef strips, flipping them over once when the first side is just dry to the touch, until both sides are just dry to the touch and the texture is still somewhat soft and elastic. This could take from 15 to 40 minutes or more, depending on the day's humidity level and intensity of the sun.

To dehydrate the beef strips in the oven, set the oven temperature to 120°F (if your oven does not go as low as 120°F, set it at the lowest temperature it allows and prop the door open with a wooden spoon) and dehydrate the beef strips, flipping them once at the midway point, for 45 to 60 minutes, until the strips are dry to the touch. If you use a dehydrator, depending on the type and make of the appliance, plan on 15 to 30 minutes. Do not go by the time, however; use the description as your guide. (The beef can be dehydrated in advance and frozen for 2 to 3 months. Thaw the strips and then marinate them as directed before frying.)

Transfer the dehydrated beef to a bowl, add the garlic, pepper, coriander, fish sauce, soy sauce, and sugar, and mix well, making sure that every strip is evenly coated with the marinade. Let the beef marinate for 10 minutes.

To fry the beef strips, pour the oil to a depth of 3 inches into a wok, Dutch oven, or deep fryer and heat to 325°F to 350°F. To test if the oil is ready without a thermometer, stick an unvarnished wooden chopstick into the oil; when the oil is hot enough, a steady stream of tiny bubbles will rise from the tip of the chopstick. Line a baking sheet with paper towels and place it next to the stove.

Working in small batches, fry the beef strips, flipping them around constantly, for about 1 minute, just until they turn dark brown. Using a slotted spoon, transfer the beef to the towel-lined baking sheet. Allow it to cool to slightly above room temperature.

Serve the beef warm with the dipping sauce.

ปลาทอดยำมะม่วง

FRIED FISH and GREEN MANGO SALAD

pla thot yam mamuang

The Thai saying *ot priao wai kin wan*, literally "withhold [your desire for a fruit] when [it is] tart; eat [it] when [it is] sweet," is one of those expressions that resonate with people across cultures. Simply put, you should refrain from taking something when it has not yet reached its full potential, and instead wait for the fullness of time to reap maximum benefits. In other words, "good things come to those who wait."

One exception to this rule is the mango, which offers two clear choices. Mangoes at their sourest are perfect for savory dishes like this salad. But those same super-tart mangoes, if left to ripen, become the extraordinarily sweet ones that we love to eat.

Every year Mom and I would look at the green mangoes swinging in Bangkok's summer breeze in our backyard and experience this quandary together. For some reason, the greed for tart mangoes often won out. This salad proves that we were correct: it is best not to delay gratification. **SERVES 4**

1 small tart green mango, 3 to 4 ounces, or 1 large Granny Smith apple

2 to 3 tablespoons freshly squeezed lime juice or distilled white vinegar, if using apple

12 ounces skinless halibut fillet (trout or salmon also works well), cut into 1-inch cubes

½ teaspoon salt

½ cup rice flour or all-purpose flour

Vegetable oil, for deep-frying

1 tablespoon freshly squeezed lime juice

1 tablespoon fish sauce

2 teaspoons packed grated palm sugar or light brown sugar

2 fresh bird's eye chiles, minced

1 large shallot, about 1 ounce, thinly sliced lengthwise

¼ cup packed fresh cilantro leaves

¼ cup packed fresh mint leaves

½ cup roasted whole or halved cashews

If using the mango, peel it and grate into thin strips about 3 inches long (see box on page 35). If using the apple, there is no need to peel it. Halve and core it, then place each half cut side down and cut into slices ¼ inch thick. Stack 3 or 4 slices and cut lengthwise into ¼-inch-wide matchsticks. Repeat until all of the apple slices are in matchsticks. Immerse the apple matchsticks in water mixed with the lime juice until needed.

In a bowl, combine the fish and salt and mix well. Spread the flour on a plate and coat the fish cubes with the flour, shaking off the excess. Arrange the fish cubes, not touching, on a large plate. Let the fish sit for 10 minutes to allow the flour coating to absorb the moisture on the surface of the fish and form a crunchy crust when fried.

continued

To fry the fish, pour the oil to a depth of 2 inches into a wok or a small, deep skillet and heat to 325°F to 350°F. To test if the oil is ready without a thermometer, stick an unvarnished wooden chopstick into the oil; when the oil is hot enough, a steady stream of tiny bubbles will rise from the tip of the chopstick. Line a large plate with paper towels and place it next to the stove.

Add about one-third of the fish cubes to the hot oil and fry until light golden brown and crispy, about 8 to 10 minutes. Using a slotted spoon or a wire-mesh skimmer, transfer the fish to the towel-lined plate. Repeat to fry the remaining fish in two batches.

If using the apple, drain and pat dry. In a bowl, stir together the lime juice, fish sauce, and sugar until the sugar dissolves. Add the chiles, shallot, and mango or apple and toss well. Taste and correct the seasoning as needed. It should be predominantly sour, then salty, with some sweet in the background. Once the salad tastes right to you, add the cilantro and mint and toss well.

Keep the fried fish, the mango salad, and the cashews separate until the moment you are ready to eat, then add the fish and cashews to the salad, toss everything together, and enjoy before the fish gets soggy and the cashews lose their crunch. Alternatively, you can arrange the fried fish on a serving platter and top it with the mango salad just before serving.

ยำเนื้อย่าง

SPICY GRILLED BEEF SALAD

yam nuea yang

This is one of the most popular meat salads at overseas Thai restaurants. It is not difficult to see why. Who can resist a salad of charred tender steak, fresh tomatoes, crunchy, refreshing cucumber, a gentle bite of shallots, and a tart dressing with a hint of smokiness from red chile powder?

It is easy, too. Marinate the beef before you leave for work. When you get home, cook some rice and throw the steak on a grill pan. The rest of the ingredients take only minutes to prepare. Once all that is done, dinner is only seconds away—or however long it normally takes you to toss a salad. This is one of my favorite weeknight meals. **SERVES 2 OR 3**

1 tablespoon thin soy sauce

½ teaspoon ground white or black pepper

1 tablespoon vegetable oil

12 ounces rib-eye steaks

2 shallots, 1 ounce each, or ½ red onion, thinly sliced lengthwise

½ English cucumber or 2 pickling cucumbers, peeled, halved lengthwise, and thinly sliced crosswise on the diagonal

1 Roma tomato, about 4 ounces, cut into ½-inch-wide wedges

2 tablespoons freshly squeezed lime juice

2 teaspoons fish sauce

½ teaspoon packed grated palm sugar or light brown sugar (optional)

1 teaspoon red chile powder (page 181)

¼ cup packed fresh cilantro leaves

In a bowl large enough to accommodate the steaks, stir together the soy sauce, pepper, and oil. Prick the steaks all over with a fork, add them to the soy mixture, and turn them to coat well. Cover and refrigerate for at least 3 to 4 hours or up to 10 hours.

Prepare a hot fire in a charcoal or gas grill. If using charcoal, allow the charcoal to develop a gray ash before you start grilling. Oil the grate with vegetable oil. Alternatively, heat a well-oiled stove-top grill pan over high heat until hot or preheat the broiler and oil a broiler pan. Cook the steaks, turning them once halfway through the cooking, until they are medium-rare to medium. The timing will vary depending on which cooking method you are using. If possible, test if they are ready with an instant-read thermometer, which should register 140°F to 150°F, the ideal level of doneness for this dish. Transfer the steaks to a cutting board, tent with aluminum foil, and let rest for 10 to 15 minutes.

Meanwhile, ready the shallots, cucumber, and tomato. In a salad bowl, stir together the lime juice, fish sauce, sugar, and chile powder.

Cut the steaks against the grain and on the diagonal (30- to 40-degree angle) into thin slices, capturing any juices. Add the steak slices and their juices to the salad bowl along with the shallots, cucumber, and tomato and toss to mix evenly. Taste the salad and correct the seasoning as needed. It should be predominantly sour, then salty, with some sweet in the background. Once everything tastes right, sprinkle the cilantro on top and serve immediately.

PORK in SPICY DRESSING with ICED BROCCOLI STEMS

mu manao

Warm, tender pork in a tart, spicy dressing served with a plate of ice-cold uncooked broccoli stems is a thing of beauty—the perfect interplay of spicy and clean flavors, soft and crunchy textures, warm and ice-cold temperatures. I just love this dish. Eating it with rice is common in Thailand, but you can certainly enjoy it as a stand-alone plate, too.

The type of broccoli traditionally used in this dish is Chinese broccoli, sometimes labeled with its Chinese name *gai lan* or *kai lan*. If you can find Chinese broccoli easily, you may want to use it. I have found the stems of regular supermarket broccoli to be a perfect—actually better and less expensive—substitute. Although nontraditional, I have even found fresh asparagus to be a great substitute when I do not have broccoli stems around. You do not even need to peel them. Simply snap off the tough, woody part toward the bottom and they are good to go.

In this recipe, I have employed a trick commonly used by Chinese cooks, which is to marinate the pork with baking soda, resulting in extra tender and juicy meat just like in Chinese-restaurant dishes. I suspect that many restaurants in Bangkok where I have had this dish also use this trick. This step can be skipped, however, if desired. **SERVES 4**

1 pound lean pork loin or tenderloin or boneless, skinless chicken breasts

2 teaspoons baking soda

12 ounces Chinese broccoli or regular broccoli stems

3 tablespoons freshly squeezed lime juice

2 tablespoons fish sauce

1 teaspoon packed grated palm sugar, or ½ teaspoon granulated sugar

4 large cloves garlic, minced

3 fresh bird's eye chiles, minced

8 cups water

2 teaspoons salt

1 cup crushed ice

¼ cup packed fresh mint leaves (optional)

Cut the pork against the grain and on the diagonal (30- to 40-degree angle) into thin, bite-size pieces. Put the pork in a bowl, sprinkle the baking soda over the top, and mix well (this is best done with your hands). Cover and chill while you ready the other ingredients.

If using Chinese broccoli, test to see if the stems are tender enough to eat without peeling them. If they are, trim about 1 inch off the bottom of each stalk end and any leaf stems, leaving just the main stem, which will look like an asparagus spear but thicker. If they are not, trim them as directed and then lightly peel them with a vegetable peeler. If using stems of regular broccoli, peel off the fibrous skin with a vegetable peeler until the inner core is exposed. Cut the Chinese or regular broccoli stems into sticks 5 inches long and ¾ inch thick. Arrange the stems on a plate, cover, and refrigerate.

continued

In a bowl, stir together the lime juice, fish sauce, sugar, garlic, and chiles until the sugar dissolves. Place the bowl next to the stove.

Pour the water into a 4-quart saucepan and bring to a boil over high heat. Stir in the salt. Lower the heat until the water is barely bubbling. Immediately add the pork to the water and stir. The temperature of the water will drop to the point that it is no longer bubbling; increase the heat just a little so the water is barely bubbling again. Stir the pork gently until it is no longer pink, about 1 to 2 minutes. Using a wire-mesh skimmer or a slotted spoon, lift out the pork, shaking off the excess water, and add it to the dressing in the bowl. Toss the pork with the dressing and transfer the mixture to a serving platter.

While the pork is still warm, remove the plate of broccoli stems from the refrigerator and scatter the crushed ice over the stems. Serve the pork salad and the iced broccoli stems together, instructing diners to enjoy a bite of the pork alternately with a bite of ice-cold broccoli stem. Garnish with mint leaves.

ยำมะเขือยาว

BROILED EGGPLANT SALAD with SHRIMP

yam makhuea yao

This salad is special to me because it was a dish that my great-grandfather and I used to enjoy together while getting to know each other. And by getting to know each other I mean talking about everything in each other's vastly different worlds and actually enjoying it—at least as much as a ninety-six-year-old man and a four-year-old girl could. For some reason, every time my family and I visited my great-grandfather, this grilled eggplant salad was always—yes, *always*—on the menu.

I do not remember much about my great-grandfather, but I do remember loving him. I also remember loving this salad with its creamy eggplant—a vegetable that, looking back, I would never have imagined discovering and liking so early in my life. **SERVES 4**

2 pounds long, purple Chinese or Japanese eggplants or other long, slender eggplants, split lengthwise	3 tablespoons fish sauce
	3 tablespoons freshly squeezed lime juice
¼ cup vegetable oil	1 teaspoon packed grated palm sugar or light brown sugar
1 tablespoon salt	
4 ounces medium shrimp in the shell, peeled and deveined	1 large shallot, about 1 ounce, thinly sliced lengthwise
4 hard- or medium-boiled eggs (page 195), peeled and quartered lengthwise	2 or 3 fresh bird's eye chiles, thinly sliced crosswise
	½ cup loosely packed fresh cilantro leaves

Position an oven rack in the middle of the oven and preheat the broiler.

Arrange the eggplant halves, cut sides up, in a single layer on a baking sheet. Brush the cut surface of the eggplants with the oil and slide under the broiler. Broil the eggplants on one side until soft and lightly charred, about 12 to 15 minutes. Remove from the oven and let cool.

Half fill a 4-quart saucepan with water and bring to a boil. Stir in the salt. Lower the heat until the water is barely bubbling. Add the shrimp and stir. When the shrimp turn opaque, after about 1 minute, using a wire skimmer or a slotted spoon, transfer them to a bowl.

Cut the cooled eggplants crosswise into 1-inch-wide pieces and arrange the pieces in a single layer on a large serving platter. Scatter the warm shrimp and eggs evenly over the eggplant. In a small bowl, stir together the fish sauce, lime juice, and sugar until the sugar dissolves. Drizzle the dressing evenly over the eggplant, shrimp, and eggs. Scatter the shallot, chiles, and cilantro evenly over the top and serve.

ลาบไก่
NORTHEASTERN MINCED CHICKEN SALAD
lap kai

Lap (pronounced "laap," with a long α sound) is a verb denoting the mincing of meat. The word is also used as a noun to refer to the preparation of this warm minced meat salad indigenous to northern and northeastern Thailand. The way *lap* is made varies from province to province, and it is hard to nail down a normative version—if there is one. But this version is the most common in Bangkok and at Thai restaurants outside Thailand. It also happens to be one of the simplest. I call for chicken in this recipe, but you can make it with other types of meat. Ground pork, coarsely chopped chuck steak, and skin-on, boneless duck meat are all good choices.

You may be used to seeing this salad served in little lettuce cups as a cocktail-party appetizer, but try enjoying *lap* with steamed sticky rice (page 169), which is how it is commonly eaten in the north and northeastern regions of Thailand. Take a chunk of warm rice about the size of your thumb in one hand and squeeze it lightly with just the tips of your fingers to form a compact, oblong shape. Now, dip the rice into the *lap*, pressing a bit of the salad against the rice, and put the whole package into your mouth—a perfect bite. If you are not used to eating this way, it will take some practice. But that only means that you will be eating this delicious salad more often so that you can get in enough practice. What is the downside of that? **SERVES 4**

1 (¼-inch-thick) slice galangal, minced (optional)

2 large shallots, about 1 ounce each, sliced lengthwise paper-thin

2 tablespoons red chile powder (page 181)

1½ tablespoons fish sauce

3 tablespoons freshly squeezed lime juice

12 ounces ground chicken

⅓ cup water

2 teaspoons toasted rice powder (page 182)

10 blades fresh sawtooth coriander, coarsely chopped, or ½ cup fresh cilantro leaves

½ cup loosely packed fresh mint leaves

3 or 4 (1-inch-wide) wedges green cabbage

Place a dry wok or 14-inch skillet over medium-low heat, add the galangal, and toast, stirring constantly, until dry to the touch and fragrant, which should take about 1 minute. Transfer to a bowl.

Add the shallots, chile powder, fish sauce, and lime juice to the bowl with the galangal, stir to mix, and set aside.

Return the pan to medium heat. When the pan is hot, add the chicken and water and cook, stirring and breaking up the meat with the edge of the spatula, just until the chicken is cooked through, about 5 to 8 minutes. Transfer the chicken and its juices to the bowl with the dressing.

Stir everything together well, then taste to see if the seasoning needs correcting. The salad should be predominantly sour, then salty. Adjust the seasoning as needed. When the salad tastes right, stir in the rice powder, sawtooth coriander, and mint. Serve immediately with the cabbage on the side.

ยำวุ้นเส้น
GLASS NOODLE SALAD

yam wun sen

Just as the stir-fried glass noodle dish on page 52 is a rice accompaniment, rather than a stand-alone noodle dish, so too is this noodle salad, even though you may see it in the appetizer section of many Thai restaurant menus.

This is my favorite salad. I can eat it warm, cold after it has been sitting at room temperature for a few hours, or even chilled from the refrigerator. The ingredients list may be a bit long, but most of these items are easy to find and the preparation is not complicated. Roadside street vendors can make this salad for you in less than five minutes while you wait. The key is to have your ingredients prepared, organized, and ready to go. **SERVES 4**

¼ cup dried wood ear mushrooms

2 ounces glass noodles

1 tablespoon dried shrimp (optional)

Boiling water, to cover the dried shrimp

¼ cup vegetable oil

4 ounces ground pork or chicken

⅓ cup cold water

1½ tablespoons freshly squeezed lime juice

1 tablespoon fish sauce

½ teaspoon granulated sugar

2 fresh bird's eye chiles, finely chopped

1 teaspoon red chile powder (page 181)

8 ounces medium to large shrimp in the shell, peeled and deveined, or fresh cleaned squid tubes, cut into ½-inch-wide rings

1 large shallot, about 1 ounce, thinly sliced lengthwise

1 Roma tomato, cut into ½-inch-wide wedges

½ cup packed Chinese or regular celery leaves

¼ cup roasted peanuts or cashew halves (optional)

You need to rehydrate the mushrooms, noodles, and shrimp. First, immerse the mushrooms in a bowl of hot water to cover for about 20 minutes, until soft. Remove them from the water, give them a good rinse (sometimes they come with lots of gritty dirt), and pat them dry. If the mushrooms have hard, knobby ends, trim them off. Then slice the mushrooms into ½-inch-wide strips. At the same time, immerse the glass noodles in a bowl of room-temperature water and soak for about 20 minutes, until pliable. Drain and cut into 6-inch lengths with kitchen shears. Finally, in a small heatproof bowl, combine the dried shrimp with boiling water to cover for about 20 minutes, until soft, then drain and pat dry.

Heat the oil in a small skillet over medium heat. Line a small plate with a paper towel and place it next to the stove. When the oil is hot, add the dried shrimp and fry until golden brown and crispy, about 2 minutes. Using a slotted spoon, transfer the shrimp to the towel-lined plate.

In a small saucepan, combine the pork and cold water over medium-high heat. Cook the pork, breaking it up into tiny bits with a wooden spatula, until thoroughly cooked, about 2 to 3 minutes. Remove from the heat and set the undrained pork aside.

In a large bowl, whisk together the lime juice, fish sauce, sugar, fresh chiles, and chile powder until the sugar dissolves to form a dressing. Place the bowl next to the stove.

Half fill a 3-quart saucepan with water and bring to a boil. While waiting for the water to boil, grab a wire-mesh skimmer or slotted spoon and keep it handy. Once the water is boiling, add the glass noodles and the mushrooms and stir them around. Within less than 1 minute, the noodles should become translucent and soft. Do a strand test to see if the noodles are cooked through; they should be soft yet still chewy. The mushrooms should also be ready. Using the skimmer, scoop the noodles and the mushrooms out of the water, shaking off the excess water, and drop them into the bowl containing the dressing.

Add the shrimp to the boiling water and immediately turn down the heat to low so the water is steaming instead of boiling. Stir the shrimp around until they turn opaque, about 1 to 2 minutes. Using the skimmer, scoop the shrimp out of the water, shaking off the excess water, and add them to the bowl with the dressing.

Quickly add the shallots to the bowl, so the heat from the noodles, mushrooms, and shrimp will wilt them slightly. Then add the cooked pork and its liquid, tomatoes, and celery leaves and toss everything together.

Take a bite to see if you like the way the salad tastes. If not, add more lime juice and fish sauce as needed. The salad should taste predominantly sour, followed by salty. The sweetness should come from the tomatoes and the little bit of sugar in the dressing. Once the taste is right, plate the salad, sprinkle the fried dried shrimp and peanuts on top, and serve.

ส้มตำมะละกอ

GREEN PAPAYA SALAD

som tam malako

Of all of the dishes that I have been making since I first came to the United States, *som tam* is the one that has given me the most fun. It seems as if every year I discover a new fruit or vegetable to use in this classic dish. Years ago, green papaya supplies at my local Asian grocery store were not as reliable as they are now, and I ended up making *som tam* with whatever raw, crunchy, bland vegetables I could find (and afford) at a mainstream grocery store. That means everything from grated carrots, sliced purple and green cabbage, frenched green beans, and julienned radishes or turnips to raw and cooked corn kernels. My current favorite is *som tam* made with grated raw rutabaga and raw golden and candy-striped beets.

In case you are thinking that I am tiptoeing dangerously at the edge of *som tam* sacrilege, I want to point out that even though green papaya is the most popular main ingredient in *som tam*, it is by no means the definitive ingredient. *Som* (an archaic regional word for "sour") *tam* ("to pound") is essentially a salad made in a mortar; it can be and has long been routinely made with various ingredients, that is, all kinds of vegetables and fruits. In fact, papaya is actually native to the New World and is a relative latecomer to Thailand.

If I were in Thailand, I would probably make my fruit *som tam* with such local fruits as pineapple, green and semiripe mangoes, guava, dragon fruit, pomelo, or rose apple. Here in the United States, I could mourn the lack of tart tropical fruits, especially the absence of the fresh, juicy, tart homegrown star gooseberries (*mayom*) that I enjoyed several times a week year-round when I lived in Thailand. But there are many wonderful possibilities here, too. When I first made fruit *som tam* in the States, I used pineapple, grapes, and tart apples. Then I began to go beyond those choices. Just recently, I discovered that fresh sour cherries are good for more than making jam. They also make delicious, beautiful deep garnet *som tam*. I know that as new fruits and vegetables show up at the farmers' market or local grocer, I will continue to experiment.

Meanwhile, on the other side of the globe, *som tam* has also been undergoing changes. In fact, of all of the dishes that have gone through changes since I last lived in Bangkok full time, I think *som tam* has spawned more variations in ingredients and preparation methods than any other classic Thai dish, including one that calls for batter-frying individual green papaya strands before tossing them with the dressing.

Cuisine has never been static and I hope it never will be, so take advantage of the fresh produce from your garden or local market and have fun experimenting with this dish. But first, so you know what *som tam* is like before you start deconstructing it, here is a base recipe.
SERVES 4

continued

2 large cloves garlic

Fresh bird's eye chiles, seeded if desired, for seasoning

1 tablespoon packed grated palm sugar, or 2 teaspoons packed light brown sugar

2 tablespoons dried shrimp (optional)

½ cup roasted peanuts

12 ounces grated green papaya (see box, page 35), from a 2-pound whole papaya

4 ounces cherry tomatoes, halved crosswise

4 ounces green beans, cut into 1½-inch lengths

2 tablespoons fish sauce

3 tablespoons freshly squeezed lime juice

For this recipe, you can use a clay mortar and a wooden pestle (ideal and traditional), or you can pound the ingredients inside a large plastic food storage bag with a rolling pin or other heavy object. If you only have a granite mortar, you can use it, too; just be careful not to pound too hard.

If you are using a clay mortar, put the garlic, chiles, and sugar in the mortar and pound until they form a paste. Add the shrimp and pound until they disintegrate. Add the peanuts and pound until they are broken up into tiny pieces. Add the papaya, tomatoes, and green beans and pound until the papaya is softened and the tomatoes and the green beans smashed, about 30 seconds. Add the fish sauce and lime juice and mix well. Taste and adjust the seasoning as needed. Transfer the salad from the mortar to a plate and serve immediately.

If you do not have a mortar, mince the garlic and chiles until they form a smooth paste. Put the paste in a small bowl along with the sugar, fish sauce, and lime juice; stir to dissolve the sugar to form a dressing. Chop the peanuts coarsely. Set the dressing and peanuts aside. Put the dried shrimp in a gallon-sized plastic food-storage bag and pound the shrimp with a heavy object until they are falling apart. Add the green beans to the bag and pound them until they are bruised and broken up. Put the papaya strands in the bag along with the tomatoes and the dressing; seal the bag closed, pressing out all of the air. Squeeze the bag until the papaya is soft and the tomatoes bruised and everything is blended together. Taste and adjust the seasoning as needed. Add the chopped peanuts to the bag and stir them into the salad with a large spoon. Transfer the salad to a plate and serve immediately.

MIXED FRUIT SALAD, SOM TAM STYLE

som tam phonlamai

Although green papaya *som tam* can be served as part of a family meal or by itself as a snack, I think that fruit *som tam* is best served as a stand-alone snack. Refreshing, light, and accommodating to most fruits in season, this is one of my favorite Thai salads.

You can use one type of fruit or a combination of fruits of varied textures and tastes (fruits that hold their shape are best in this salad). Notice that I do not specify the amount of sugar, lime juice, or even salt (which I prefer over fish sauce here) in this recipe. I cannot because it is not possible, as it all depends on the fruit. **SERVES 4**

2 large cloves garlic, finely minced

1 fresh red or green bird's eye chile, minced

2 tablespoons dried shrimp (optional)

½ cup roasted peanuts, finely chopped

4 ounces cherry tomatoes, quartered

4 ounces green beans, cut crosswise on the diagonal ¼ inch thick and bruised with a heavy object

¾ cup loosely packed grated carrots

1½ cups 1-inch-cubed sweet or tart fruit (such as apple, pineapple, cantaloupe, honeydew melon, or pear, or a mixture)

Freshly squeezed lime juice, for seasoning

Granulated sugar, for seasoning

Salt, for seasoning

In a bowl, combine the garlic, chile, shrimp, peanuts, tomatoes, beans, carrots, and fruit(s) and toss to mix well. Add 1 tablespoon lime juice, 2 teaspoons sugar, and ¼ teaspoon salt to start and toss gently to combine. Taste and adjust the seasoning as needed. The salad should be sweet and sour with a little bit of saltiness in the background. Serve immediately.

พล่าปลาแซลมอน

HERBAL SALMON SALAD

phla pla salmon

This light, flavorful, and fragrant salad is all about freshness. The dressing is also simple. Because I want the natural sweetness of the lightly poached fish to come through, I do not even add any sugar to it. The fresh herbs and the fresh fish are what make the salad. Whenever I go camping by the river in Thailand, this is what I make with the fresh prawns or cockles I can get there. But here I have been making my *phla* with salmon, which is not a traditional Thai ingredient, and loving it.

Before you think there is nothing special about this salad, consider this. When President Barack Obama kicked off his first post-reelection Asian tour with a visit to Thailand in November 2012, the government of Thailand hosted a state dinner in his honor. *Phla pla salmon* was served as the very first item on the twelve-course dinner. **SERVES 4**

4 stalks lemongrass

2 large shallots, about 1 ounce each

3 fresh bird's eye chiles, finely chopped

¼ cup freshly squeezed lime juice

3 tablespoons fish sauce

1½ pounds skinless salmon fillet

1 cup loosely packed fresh mint leaves

4 fresh kaffir lime leaves, deveined and cut lengthwise into very thin strips (optional but highly recommended)

Trim off and discard the leafy parts of the lemongrass stalk, remove the tough outer leaves of the bulb portion until the smooth, pale green core is exposed, and trim off the root end. Working from the root end, cut the bulb crosswise into paper-thin slices, stopping once you reach the point where the purple rings disappear. Put the lemongrass in a large bowl.

Halve the shallots lengthwise. Place each half, cut side down, on a cutting board and slice lengthwise into paper-thin slices. Add them to the bowl with the lemongrass. Then add the chiles, lime juice, and fish sauce and mix well. Set aside.

Half fill a 4-quart saucepan with water and bring to a boil. While waiting for the water to boil, cut the salmon fillet into 1½-inch cubes. When the water is boiling, add the salmon and turn down the heat to medium, so the water is steaming rather than boiling. Cook until the salmon turns opaque, about 1 to 2 minutes. Using a wire-mesh skimmer or a slotted spoon, lift out the salmon, shaking off the excess water, and add to the bowl holding the dressing.

Toss everything together gently. Taste the salad and correct the seasoning if necessary. It should be predominantly sour, followed by salty and hot (for this salad, I prefer no sweetness at all). Once the salad tastes right, transfer it to a serving platter and sprinkle with the mint and lime leaves. Serve immediately.

แกงจืดเต้าหู้ไก่สับ

CLEAR SOUP with SILKEN TOFU and CHICKEN DUMPLINGS

kaeng juet taohu kai sap

Lest you think all Thai soups must be hot and sour and spicy, here is one from a family of stock-based soups oddly (and unfairly) named *kaeng juet* or *tom juct*, literally "bland soup." They are not infused with herbs or with spice-rich pastes but are instead seasoned simply with fish sauce or thin soy sauce. This type of soup is typically part of a meal ensemble that consists of a spicy salad or a spicy stir-fry—in other words, a menu in which a spicy soup such as *tom yam* (page 86) would throw off the balance of the *samrap*. **SERVES 4**

Dumplings

8 ounces ground chicken

2 cloves garlic

2 cilantro roots, chopped, or 2 tablespoons chopped cilantro stems

1 egg white

4 teaspoons fish sauce

½ teaspoon ground white pepper

4 cups chicken stock, homemade (page 178) or store-bought, or water

1 tablespoon thin soy sauce

2 green onions, white and green parts, cut crosswise into 1-inch lengths, white and green parts kept separate

1 (12-ounce) package soft or firm silken-style tofu, drained and cut into 1-inch cubes

¼ cup loosely packed fresh cilantro leaves, for garnish

Ground white pepper, for garnish

To make the dumplings, in a food processor, combine the chicken, garlic, cilantro roots, egg white, 2 teaspoons of the fish sauce, and pepper and process until smooth and sticky. Transfer to a bowl.

In a 2-quart saucepan, combine the stock, soy sauce, remaining 2 teaspoons fish sauce, and the white parts of the onions and bring to a boil over high heat. Turn down the heat until the stock is at a gentle boil. Drop the dumpling mixture by the teaspoonful into the gently bubbling stock. Cook the dumplings until all of them have floated to the surface, about 1 to 2 minutes.

Gently add the tofu to the pan, bring the liquid back to a gentle boil, and then remove the pan from the heat. Taste and correct the seasoning. Stir in the green parts of the green onions and ladle into individual serving bowls. Garnish with the cilantro and a sprinkle of pepper and serve piping hot.

ต้มข่าไก่

COCONUT-GALANGAL CHICKEN SOUP

tom kha kai

Tom kha kai is easy to make. If you can smash things, cut things, and boil water, you can pull off this classic on the first try. The hardest part? Getting your hands on the essential fresh seasonings. Galangal (the *kha* in *tom kha kai*), kaffir lime leaves, and lemongrass have come to define *tom kha kai*. Although I do offer substitutions for harder-to-find Thai ingredients for most of the recipes in this book, that is not possible here. Some people will tell you that you can substitute ginger for the galangal, but that is not the case. In fact, the two ingredients are not even *close* to being interchangeable in the minds of Thai cooks.

If you cannot find the fresh galangal and kaffir lime leaves, either locally or through mail order, you can use *tom kha* paste, which comes in small glass jars. Any brand from Thailand will do. Just follow the directions on the label. Most of the time, making the broth involves dissolving the paste in the coconut milk. **SERVES 4**

1 pound boneless, skinless chicken thighs or breasts

1 stalk lemongrass

2 cups sodium-free chicken stock, homemade (page 178) or store-bought

1½ cups coconut milk

2-inch piece galangal, thinly sliced

4 kaffir lime leaves, torn into pieces and bruised

8 ounces oyster or white mushrooms

¼ cup fish sauce

⅓ cup freshly squeezed lime juice

4 or 5 fresh bird's eye chiles, bruised

½ cup packed fresh cilantro leaves

Cut the chicken against the grain and on the diagonal (30- to 40-degree angle) into thin, bite-size pieces. If using oyster mushrooms, separate them into individual pieces. If using white mushrooms, halve the small ones and quarter the bigger ones.

Trim off and discard the leafy parts of the lemongrass stalk, remove the tough outer leaves of the bulb portion until the smooth, pale green core is exposed, and trim off the root end. Quarter the bulb portion crosswise and smash the pieces with a heavy object until they are bruised and split.

In a 2-quart saucepan, combine the stock and coconut milk and bring to a boil over high heat. Immediately turn down to heat so the liquid is barely bubbling. Add the galangal, lemongrass, and lime leaves and steep for 1 minute. Add the chicken, mushrooms, and fish sauce, stir, and increase the heat slightly so the liquid is simmering gently. Once the chicken is no longer pink, after about 2 minutes, remove the pan from the heat.

Add the lime juice and chiles and stir. Taste and correct the seasoning as needed. The soup should be sour and salty with natural sweetness from the coconut milk. Sprinkle the cilantro on top just before serving. Thai cooks do not usually remove the chunky herbs from food when they serve it, as it is understood that they are not to be eaten. But you can fish out the lemongrass, galangal, and lime leaves before serving, if you like.

ต้มยำกุ้ง

HOT-and-SOUR PRAWN SOUP with CHILE JAM

tom yam kung

Nailing down an "authentic" *tom yam* is at once an exciting challenge and an exercise in futility. First, there are the questions that never end. Should the soup contain galangal? Should it have chile jam in it? What about shallots? Mushrooms—yes or no? And if yes, what kind? Dried chiles or fresh chiles? Tomatoes or no tomatoes? What did *tom yam* look like when it was first invented?

Next come the statements of absolute certainty. *Tom yam* must be made this way because my grandmother made it this way. That is wrong because my grandmother is older than your grandmother and she cooked it this way. But my family got this recipe from someone who used to cook for someone important, and in that kitchen it was made this way. And on and on.

I do not know what the original *tom yam* looked like or how it tasted. But I do know that most Thai restaurants, both at home and abroad, tend to make *tom yam* as I have in this recipe. So, if you like the herbal broth, the vibrant flavor of lime against the sweet, smoky taste of chile jam, and the fresh, plump prawns of a *tom yam* that you ate either along the Chao Phraya River or at a neighborhood Thai restaurant in the States, this recipe will help you re-create that experience.

Like the Coconut-Galangal Chicken Soup on page 84, this recipe calls for some hard-to-find ingredients—galangal and kaffir lime leaves—for which there are no substitutes. If you do not live near an Asian grocery, you might have to mail-order them (see page 217). **SERVES 4**

1 stalk lemongrass

4 cups sodium-free chicken stock, homemade (page 178) or store-bought

3-inch piece galangal, thinly sliced

4 or 5 fresh kaffir lime leaves, torn into pieces and bruised

1 large shallot, about 1 ounce, smashed

1 pound white button, straw, or oyster mushrooms, cut into bite-size pieces

2 tablespoons chile jam, homemade (page 184) or store-bought

¼ cup fish sauce

2 or 3 small dried red chiles, broken in half and seeds reserved

1 pound large river prawns or jumbo shrimp in the shell, peeled and deveined, with heads and tails intact if desired

3 fresh bird's eye chiles, stemmed and bruised

¼ cup freshly squeezed lime juice

¼ cup packed fresh cilantro leaves

Trim off and discard the leafy parts of the lemongrass stalk, remove the tough outer leaves of the bulb portion until the smooth, pale green core is exposed, and trim off the root end. Cut the bulb portion into 3-inch lengths and smash the pieces with a heavy object until they are bruised and split.

In a 2-quart saucepan, bring the stock to a boil over high heat. When it is boiling, add the lemongrass, galangal, lime leaves, and shallot, turn down the heat to medium, and let the broth infuse for 1 minute. Add the mushrooms and stir in the chile jam. Then add the fish sauce, followed by the dried chiles. Lower the prawns into the broth and stir gently. The temperature will drop slightly at this point, so turn up the heat just enough to return the liquid to a gentle simmer. Within 2 minutes, the shrimp will turn opaque. At that point, remove the pan from the heat.

Stir in the fresh chiles and lime juice. Taste for seasoning and correct if needed. The flavor of the broth should be sour first, then salty, with mild sweetness from the chile jam. Stir in the cilantro, ladle into bowls, and serve piping hot. Thai cooks do not usually remove the chunky herbs from this soup, as it is understood that they are not to be eaten. But you can fish out the lemongrass, galangal, and lime leaves before serving, if you like.

ซุปหางวัว
OXTAIL SOUP
sup hang wua

This flavorful, comforting soup is a mainstay at any restaurant offering Thai Muslim food in Thailand but is virtually nonexistent at Thai restaurants overseas, which is all the more reason to make it at home. It takes a little longer than most of the recipes in this book because the oxtail requires long cooking to tenderize, but the results are well worth the time. If you start a pot of this soup just after lunch on a weekend, it will be ready—without much babysitting—by dinnertime.

This recipe is my take on the version served at a halal restaurant in the heart of Bangkok where my parents, two non-Muslims who shared an intense love of Thai Muslim food, used to eat when they were dating. I never asked them exactly when they fell in love, but if they had told me that it was between sips of this soup, I would not have been surprised. **SERVES 4**

3½ pounds meaty oxtail, in 3-inch pieces

4 or 5 Thai or green cardamom pods

2 cinnamon sticks

2 teaspoons white or black peppercorns

1 tablespoon salt

1 large yellow onion, cut into 1-inch-wide wedges

4 Roma tomatoes, quartered lengthwise

2 or 3 small Yukon gold or other waxy potatoes, peeled and cut into 1-inch cubes

2 green onions, white and green parts, cut into 1-inch lengths, with white and green parts kept separate

5 or 6 bird's eye chiles, stemmed and bruised

¼ cup freshly squeezed lime juice

¼ cup fried shallots (page 183)

½ cup loosely packed fresh cilantro leaves

In a large pot, combine the oxtail with water to cover by 1½ to 2 inches. If you like, tie the cardamom pods, cinnamon sticks, and peppercorns in a small cheesecloth satchel, which will make it easier to fish them out at the end of cooking, and add the satchel to the pot along with the salt, or just toss in the spices loose. Bring the water to a boil over high heat, turn down the heat to a gentle simmer, cover, and cook for 1 hour. Check the water level periodically and replenish the water as needed to maintain the original level, adjusting the heat each time as well to maintain the simmer.

After 1 hour, check the water level again, replenish the water and restore the simmer as needed, re-cover, and continue to cook until the oxtail is tender when pierced with a fork but is not falling apart, which should take about 2 more hours.

Using a large spoon, skim off as much fat as possible from the surface of the broth, then add the yellow onion, tomatoes, potatoes, and the white parts of the green onions. Add more water if needed to keep everything submerged, then simmer, covered, for 20 to 25 minutes, until the potatoes are fork-tender.

Remove from the heat and stir in the chiles, lime juice, and the green parts of the green onions. Taste and correct the seasoning. The flavor should be sour first, then salty. Once that is done, ladle the soup into individual serving bowls and top each serving with one-fourth each of the shallots and the cilantro. Serve piping hot.

แกงเลียง

SPICY VEGETABLE SOUP with SHRIMP and LEMON BASIL

kaeng liang

Sometimes you can pretty accurately guess the origin of a dish just by looking at its ingredients. This down-home soup is a good example. I suspect that the inventor of it did not even leave home to look for ingredients. The aromatics are common kitchen staples, and as for the vegetables, you can imagine the cook telling one of her children to go outside and bring back whatever is growing on the vines that trail along the fence, shooting up young leaves, or sprouting from the soil.

Everyday cooking in the old days was like that in tropical Thailand, where gardens produced year-round. My paternal grandmother ran her household and kitchen that way, and how I have imagined the origin of this dish is influenced by my experience helping her around the kitchen when I was a child. My days with her were full of trips to the yard to gather whatever was growing there. I did not see it as a privilege at the time, but my heart aches for it now. Everything about this old-fashioned, traditional Thai soup whispers "home" and "family"—a vegetable soup for the Thai expat's soul, as one of my friends describes it.

This dish is the main reason—no, the sole reason—I started growing lemon basil, which is impossible to find at regular or Asian grocery stores. I could make *kaeng liang* without it, but it would never be as good. If you have fresh lemon basil around, this is the dish to make. When I do not have any on hand, I omit the basil altogether, instead of using another type. That said, you may want to experiment with Thai or Mediterranean sweet basil.

Luffa gourds, which belong to the cucumber family, have green skin, sometimes ridged, sometimes smooth, and pale flesh with a mild flavor. They can be found in Asian grocery stores and at some farmers' markets. Zucchini are a good, readily available substitute. **SERVES 4 TO 6**

8 ounces oyster or white button mushrooms

1 pound large shrimp in the shell, peeled and deveined

2 large shallots, about 1 ounce each

2 teaspoons ground white pepper

1 teaspoon shrimp paste (optional)

4 cups sodium-free chicken stock, homemade (page 178) or store-bought

8 ounces low-moisture winter squash or pumpkin (such as kabocha or Buttercup squash or Fairy Tale pumpkin), peeled and cut into 1-inch cubes

1 smooth-skinned chayote, halved, cored, and cut into 1-inch cubes

1 pound fresh baby corn, trimmed and halved on the diagonal, or 1 (14-ounce) can baby corn, drained, rinsed, and halved on the diagonal

1 luffa gourd, about 1 pound, peeled and cut into 1-inch cubes, or 2 to 3 zucchini, about 1 pound total, halved lengthwise, then sliced crosswise 1 inch thick

3 tablespoons fish sauce, or ¼ cup if not using shrimp paste

1 cup loosely packed fresh lemon basil leaves

If using oyster mushrooms, separate them into individual pieces. If using white mushrooms, halve the small ones and quarter the bigger ones. Set aside.

continued

Separate out one-fourth of the shrimp and keep the rest in the refrigerator for now. Half fill a 1-quart saucepan with water and bring to a boil. Add the shrimp and cook until they turn opaque, about 1 to 2 minutes. Drain and transfer the shrimp to a blender.

Add the shallots, white pepper, shrimp paste, and stock to the blender and blend until smooth. Pour the contents of the blender into a 4-quart saucepan, place over high heat, and bring to a boil. Add the pumpkin and chayote and cook for 3 minutes. Add the corn and cook for another 3 minutes. Add the luffa, mushrooms, and the reserved whole shrimp and continue cooking until the shrimp turn opaque and all the vegetables are tender, about 2 minutes. Stir in the fish sauce and remove the pan from the heat. Taste; add more fish sauce, if needed.

Stir in the basil, ladle into individual serving bowls, and serve piping hot.

ไก่ต้มขมิ้น

SOUTHERN HOT-and-SOUR TURMERIC-CHICKEN SOUP

kai tom khamin

I do not think there has ever been any cold or flu in my adult life that has not been cured by this southern Thai herbal chicken soup. There is something about its bright golden color that makes me feel like I am sipping liquid sunshine. This underrated regional Thai dish deserves as much recognition internationally as its more famous central cousin, *tom yam* (page 86).

This recipe is from the southern-born mother of a friend of mine. She allows for the use of boneless, skinless chicken as long as chicken stock is used. When she makes this classic at home, however, she always makes it with a *kai ban*, a small, less voluptuous free-range chicken that is cut into small bone-in pieces and simmered until tender. The innards, including the delicious ovaries of the bird, go into the pot, too.

If you cannot find fresh turmeric, she agrees that ground turmeric is an acceptable substitute. The only thing that she is adamant about is that salt must be used and not fish sauce.
SERVES 4

1 stalk lemongrass

6 cups sodium-free chicken stock, homemade (page 178) or store-bought

3 inches fresh turmeric, peeled and smashed, or 3 teaspoons ground turmeric

1-inch piece fresh galangal, thinly sliced

4 fresh kaffir lime leaves, torn into pieces and bruised

1 teaspoon salt, or to taste

1½ pounds boneless, skinless chicken thighs, cut into 1½-inch cubes

3 green onions, white and green parts, cut crosswise into 1-inch pieces, white and green parts kept separate

5 fresh bird's eye chiles, stemmed and bruised

3 tablespoons freshly squeezed lime juice

½ cup packed fresh cilantro leaves, for garnish

Trim off and discard the leafy parts of the lemongrass stalk, remove the tough outer leaves of the bulb portion until the smooth, pale green core is exposed, and trim off the root end. Quarter the bulb portion crosswise and smash the pieces with a pestle, the side of a cleaver, or a heavy object until they are bruised and split.

In a 2-quart saucepan, combine the stock and turmeric and bring to a boil over high heat. Turn down the heat until the stock is at a gentle boil. Add the lemongrass, galangal, lime leaves, and salt and simmer for 1 minute. Add the chicken and the white parts of the green onions, stir, and turn up the heat slightly to return the liquid to a gentle boil. Once the chicken is cooked through, after about 5 minutes, add the green parts of the green onions and remove the pan from the heat.

Stir in the chiles and lime juice. Taste for seasoning and correct if needed. The soup should be predominantly sour, then salty. Ladle into individual serving bowls, garnish with the cilantro, and serve piping hot.

แกงเผ็ดเป็ดย่าง

DUCK RED CURRY with PINEAPPLE and TOMATOES

kaeng phet pet yang

Here is one of those dishes that is a staple at Thai restaurants overseas, yet is not nearly as common in Thailand, though I am not sure why. This rich curry is balanced by the presence of a sweet-and-sour element, usually in the form of pineapple and tomatoes or sometimes lychees. I strongly recommend using only fresh fruits here. Canned pineapple and canned lychees in light syrup, which many restaurants use, lack the necessary acidity—not to mention freshness—that this dish needs. Instead, they add a cloying sweetness to a curry that is already rich.

For the duck, the most convenient choice is a ready-made roasted duck. If you live near a Chinatown or a place where Chinese-style roasted ducks are sold—either a shop or a restaurant—take advantage of the proximity and buy a roasted duck. If you cannot find a roasted duck, use two 6-ounce skin-on duck breasts. Score the skins and sear the breasts skin side down in a skillet just to crisp up the skin, then slice the partially cooked meat against the grain into thin bite-size pieces before using.

The duck meat does not need a long cooking time. If you use store-bought roasted duck, you only need to heat it through. If you use seared and sliced duck breasts, which should not be cooked too long, you only need to heat them briefly toward the end of the cooking time.
SERVES 4

½ cup coconut cream (the thick layer at the top of a can of coconut milk)

1 tablespoon coconut oil or vegetable oil

¼ cup homemade red curry paste (page 175), or 2 tablespoons store-bought red curry paste

1 cup coconut milk

4 ounces cherry tomatoes

1 cup 1-inch-cubed fresh pineapple

12 ounces roasted duck (meat and skin only), cut into bite-size pieces (about 2 cups)

Fish sauce, for seasoning

½ cup packed fresh Thai sweet basil or regular sweet basil leaves

In a 2-quart saucepan, combine the coconut cream, oil, and curry paste over medium-high heat and stir until the paste is fragrant and the coconut fat separates, about 2 minutes. Add the coconut milk, tomatoes, and pineapple and bring to a gentle boil. Lower the heat to a simmer and cook for 3 minutes. Add the duck and cook until the duck is heated through, about 2 minutes.

Taste the curry and then season with the fish sauce. It is impossible to know how salty the duck is, so it is also impossible to specify an amount of fish sauce. Once the seasoning is good, remove from the heat, stir in the basil, and serve.

แกงเขียวหวานเนื้อ

BEEF GREEN CURRY with THAI EGGPLANTS

kaeng khiao wan nuea

If you have purchased the fresh ingredients for homemade curry pastes and wonder how to take the fullest advantage of your investment, this classic green beef curry with round Thai eggplants is one of my top recommendations. That is because I find that a greater chasm of quality exists between homemade green curry paste and commercial green curry paste than with other curry pastes. This chasm is not so great between homemade and store-bought red curry paste, for example, perhaps because the dried red chiles used in the red paste are more forgiving than the fresh chiles that go into the green paste. **SERVES 4**

½ cup coconut cream (the thick layer at the top of a can of coconut milk)

2 tablespoons coconut or vegetable oil

¼ cup homemade green curry paste (page 176), or 2 tablespoons store-bought green curry paste

1½ cups coconut milk

12 ounces chuck steak, cut against the grain and on the diagonal into bite-size pieces

8 ounces Thai round eggplants, stemmed, quartered through the stem, and immersed in water with a squeeze of lemon juice

2 fresh Thai long chiles, cut lengthwise on the diagonal into ¼-inch-wide strips

2 tablespoons fish sauce

2 teaspoons packed grated palm sugar, or ½ teaspoon granulated sugar

½ cup packed fresh Thai sweet basil or regular sweet basil leaves

In a 2-quart saucepan, combine the coconut cream, oil, and curry paste over medium-high heat and stir until the paste is fragrant and the coconut fat separates, about 2 minutes. Add the coconut milk and beef and bring to a gentle boil, stirring occasionally. Cover, lower the heat to a simmer, and cook for about 15 minutes, stirring occasionally.

Drain the eggplants and add them to the pan along with the chiles, fish sauce, sugar, and, if necessary, just enough water to keep everything submerged. Turn up the heat just enough to return the curry to a simmer, re-cover, and continue to cook until the eggplants are tender, about 5 to 7 minutes.

Taste for seasoning. No more sugar should be added, but more fish sauce may be needed. When the taste is good, remove the pan from the heat, stir in the basil leaves, and serve.

VEGETABLE SOUR CURRY with SHRIMP

kaeng som phak ruam sai kung

Every Thai food expert to whom I have spoken expresses the same sentiment, very passionately, on the subject of sour curry: it is both one of the easiest curries to make and one of the most difficult to master. At first glance, this seems perplexing. The souplike curry requires a relatively small number of ingredients, most of which are common. And the procedure? I can summarize it so briefly that you can sneeze and miss it. It contains no coconut, so it does not even require that you fry the curry paste in coconut cream. What makes it so difficult? I have decided that the issue has less to do with the level of difficulty than it does with the lack of consensus on what constitutes a good bowl of sour curry.

This dish, in which no flesh of land animals is ever used (at least not in Bangkok or central Thailand), is so deeply connected to the primitive river- or ocean-dependent Thai lifestyle that it runs in your veins. It is such a common home dish that a family's version has inevitably become the standard by which that family judges every other sour curry. Throw in the fact that every region has its own way of making it, and you understand the profound passion and sense of ownership that surrounds this dish. In other words, when people say that nobody makes a good sour curry these days, what they mean is nobody except their mother makes a good sour curry.

This recipe is a version of the central-style sour curry that I grew up eating at home. The vegetables that the recipe calls for are only suggestions. Most nonstarchy, mild-flavored vegetables are appropriate in this curry. In addition to the ones included here, I also like chayote, carrot, napa cabbage, bok choy, daikon, zucchini, and yellow summer squash. Although some of these are not traditional sour curry vegetables, all of them are delicious. For a single-vegetable sour curry, you may want to try green papaya, peeled and cut into small, thin slices. It is a traditional ingredient for this curry. Watermelon rinds, peeled and cut into bite-size chunks, are also a favorite of mine.

If you decide to use commercial sour curry paste, read the ingredients list carefully before purchasing it. Some include fish or shrimp meat, which will throw off the flavor of the finished dish. If this is the case, follow the instructions on the curry paste label, instead of pureeing shrimp and adding it to the stock as directed in the method. **SERVES 4 TO 6**

1 pound shrimp in the shell, peeled and deveined

¼ cup sour curry paste, homemade (page 177) or store-bought

2 cups store-bought fish stock

¼ cup packed grated palm sugar, or 3 tablespoons packed light brown sugar

2 tablespoons fish sauce

¼ cup tamarind pulp, homemade (page 171) or store-bought

4 ounces long beans or green beans, cut into 1-inch lengths

4 ounces cauliflower florets (about 1 cup)

1 (4-ounce) wedge green cabbage, cut into 1½-inch pieces

4 ounces baby bok choy, halved lengthwise, cored, and halved crosswise

Half fill a 2-quart saucepan with water and bring to a boil. Measure out one-fourth of the shrimp to use now and cover and refrigerate the remaining shrimp. When the water is boiling, drop in the shrimp and cook until they turn opaque, about 2 minutes. Using a wire-mesh skimmer or slotted spoon, lift out the shrimp, shaking off the excess water, and put them in a food processor along with the curry paste and the fish stock; blend until you get a smooth curry base.

Rinse out the saucepan, add the curry paste and fish stock to it, and bring to a boil over high heat. Add the sugar, fish sauce, and tamarind pulp and stir until everything dissolves. Taste for seasoning and correct as needed with more fish sauce, sugar, and tamarind. The flavor should be sour first, then sweet and salty.

Add the green beans, cauliflower, cabbage, and as much additional water as necessary to keep the vegetables barely submerged (they will release more moisture once cooked), then cook for 2 minutes. Add the bok choy and the reserved shrimp and cook until all the vegetables are tender and the shrimp turn opaque, about 2 minutes. Remove the pan from the heat and serve.

ผัดพริกขิง

SWEET DRY CURRY of PORK and LONG BEANS

phat phrik khing

The Thai name of this dish, literally chile (*phrik*) and ginger (*khing*) stir-fry (*phat*), has confused many. People assume based on the name that ginger must be a main ingredient—but, believe it or not, there is not a smidgen of ginger in the dish.

So then why is it called chile and ginger stir-fry? Most food experts, including veteran food journalist Polsri Kachacheewa, believe that the use of *phrik khing* (พริกขิง) here is the colloquially shortened form of the phrase *thueng phrik thueng khing* (ถึงพริกถึงขิง), which in the context of cooking can mean "seasoned to the nth degree." Cooking instructor and cookbook author Sisamon Kongpan has a different opinion. The ginger, she suggests, represents the maximum level of chile heat this dish is supposed to pack. In other words, the heat from the chiles (*phrik*) must not exceed that of ginger (*khing*). This, says Kongpan, explains both the puzzling name and the noticeably milder, sweeter flavor of this dry curry.

I cannot decide which of these theories is more plausible. The only thing of which I am utterly confident is this: when done correctly, this dish is one of the most delicious classic Thai dishes ever.

Some people may prefer a leaner dish, in which case you can substitute pork loin or boneless, skinless chicken meat for the pork shoulder. Others may prefer to go the opposite direction, in which case I suggest using pork cracklings or fried pork belly for a decadent alternative. **SERVES 4**

8 ounces pork shoulder

2 tablespoons dried shrimp (optional)

2 tablespoons vegetable oil

2 tablespoons homemade red curry paste (page 175), or 1 tablespoon store-bought red curry paste

2 teaspoons fish sauce

3 tablespoons packed grated palm sugar, or 2 tablespoons packed light or dark brown sugar

½ cup sodium-free chicken stock, homemade (page 178) or store-bought, or water

8 ounces long beans or green beans, cut into 1½-inch pieces

4 fresh kaffir lime leaves, deveined and cut lengthwise into thin strips (optional but highly recommended)

Cut the pork against the grain and on the diagonal into thin, bite-size pieces. If using dried shrimp, grind the shrimp in the mortar or mini chopper until flaky.

Heat a wok or a 14-inch skillet over medium-high. When the pan is hot, add the oil and curry paste and stir to break up the paste. When the paste is fragrant, after about 2 minutes, add the pork, fish sauce, sugar, and stock and stir well. Turn up the heat to high and stir until the pork is almost cooked through and most of the moisture has evaporated, about 5 to 7 minutes. Add the beans and continue to stir just until the pork is fully cooked and the moisture has evaporated, about 5 minutes. This dish is not supposed to be saucy. When it looks like a dry curry that glistens with deep orange oil, you know it is done. Also, you want the beans to be tender-crisp when the dish is served, so do not cook them until they are soft and mushy. Transfer to a platter, add the kaffir lime leaves, and serve immediately.

แกงกะหรี่ไก่

CHICKEN KARI "YELLOW" CURRY

kaeng kari kai

Milder than red or green curry, kari or "yellow" curry, as it is often called, is one of the training curries that some Thai parents—mine included—use to build up their kids' ability to eat spicy food. Most Asian markets carry two types of Thai "yellow" curry paste. One is a southern-style sour curry, similar to its central-style cousin *kaeng som phak ruam sai kung* (page 96). That one is *not* appropriate for this dish. Instead, look for the word *karee* or *kari* on the label. Alternatively, if the label on the container includes a picture of a finished dish, use that as your guide: if potatoes are visible, that is a good sign, as *sour* yellow curry does not usually include potatoes. **SERVES 4**

¼ cup kari or "yellow" curry paste, homemade (page 177) or store-bought

1 tablespoon coconut or vegetable oil

½ cup coconut cream (the thick layer at the top of a can of coconut milk)

1 cup coconut milk

¾ cup sodium-free chicken stock, homemade (page 178) or store-bought

1 pound Yukon gold or waxy potatoes, peeled and cut into 2-inch cubes

1 pound yellow or white onions, quartered through the stem end

2 tablespoons fish sauce

1 pound boneless, skinless chicken thighs or breasts, cut into 2-inch cubes

Cucumber relish (page 191)

In a 2-quart saucepan, combine the curry paste, oil, and coconut cream over medium-high heat and fry until fragrant and the coconut fat separates, about 2 minutes. Add the coconut milk, stock, potatoes, onions, and fish sauce, stir well, and simmer, covered, for about 15 minutes, until the potatoes have softened.

Add the chicken to the pan, then add water if necessary to keep everything submerged. Turn up the heat to bring the mixture to a gentle boil, then lower the heat to a simmer, and cook until the chicken is cooked through and the potatoes and onions are tender, about 5 to 8 minutes. Taste for seasoning and add more fish sauce if needed.

Remove from the heat and serve, with the cucumber relish on the side.

ฉู่ฉี่ปลา

FISH in RED CURRY SAUCE

chuchi pla

Chuchi is a type of thick curry that is usually made with seafood, freshwater fish, or quick-cooking cuts of meat. Once the paste is fried and the coconut fat "cracks," the fish or meat goes in. After just few a minutes of cooking and listening to the hissing *chuuu* and *chiii* noises (the source of the Thai name), you have dinner on the table.

I recommend salmon fillets in this recipe, though halibut or trout fillets would work as well. In fact, you can use a total of 1½ pounds of any fish, shellfish, or tender cut of meat you like. I also sometimes use small whole fish, such as mackerel or sardines: make a few diagonal slashes all the way down to the bones, on both sides of the fish, and they will cook more quickly.

SERVES 4

1½ tablespoons coconut or vegetable oil

2 tablespoons homemade red curry paste (page 175) or 1 tablespoon store-bought

¼ cup coconut cream (the thick layer at the top of a can of coconut milk)

½ cup coconut milk

½ cup water

2 teaspoons fish sauce

2 teaspoons packed grated palm sugar, or 1 teaspoon packed light or dark brown sugar

4 (6-ounce) skinless salmon fillets

1 fresh red or green Thai long chile, halved, seeded, and cut lengthwise into long slivers

2 fresh kaffir lime leaves, deveined and cut lengthwise into very thin strips (optional but highly recommended)

In a wok or a 14-inch skillet, combine the oil, curry paste, and coconut cream over medium-high heat and fry until the paste is fragrant and the coconut fat separates, about 2 minutes. Stir in the coconut milk, water, fish sauce, and sugar, then arrange the fish fillets in the pan in a single layer, leaving space between them. Turn down the heat to medium-low, cover, and cook the fish for 2 minutes. Turn the fillets over, add the chile, re-cover, and continue to cook until the fish flakes easily with a fork, about 2 minutes.

Sprinkle the lime leaves over the top and serve immediately.

แกงป่าเนื้อสับ

BEEF and VEGETABLE CURRY, JUNGLE STYLE

kaeng pa nuea sap

Jungle-style curry is made with different herbs and spices in different provinces. Some versions employ both fresh and dried chiles in the paste, some are scented by herbs specific to the region, some are accented with fresh cumin leaves instead of holy basil, and the list goes on. What they all have in common is the absence of coconut milk and a heavy use of herbs and spices designed to offset the smell of wild game or of freshly caught fish pulled from a body of muddy water—ingredients used in the past or in remote rural areas today.

If you want to experience Thai curry without the usual coconut milk, this is a good one to try.

I consider this version typical of the central region, especially Bangkok, and of what you most commonly find at Thai restaurants around the world. It features ground beef and a mélange of vegetables, most notably Thai round eggplants, and is accented with fingerroots, whole bunches of young peppercorns, and a generous fistful of fresh holy basil. In other words, this recipe calls for a lot of produce that is not readily found in markets in the States. That means you will need access to a well-stocked Thai grocery, or you must plan ahead and mail order the ingredients (see page 217). **SERVES 4**

8 bunches fresh or brined young green peppercorns (optional)

2 (3-inch) fresh or brined fingerroots (optional but highly recommended)

5 Thai round or long green eggplants or Chinese or Japanese long purple eggplants

2 tablespoons red curry paste, homemade (page 175) or store-bought

¼ cup water

8 ounces ground beef chuck, preferably coarsely ground

3 cups sodium-free chicken stock, homemade (page 178) or store-bought

4 ounces long beans or green beans, cut into 1-inch lengths

1 (8-ounce) can sliced bamboo shoots, drained and rinsed

1½ tablespoons fish sauce

1 teaspoon packed grated palm sugar or light brown sugar

2 fresh Thai long chiles, quartered lengthwise

2 fresh kaffir lime leaves, deveined and torn into quarters (optional but highly recommended)

½ cup packed fresh holy basil leaves (Thai sweet basil or regular sweet basil will do in a pinch)

If using brined peppercorns, rinse well under running water and drain. If using fresh fingerroots, cut lengthwise into slivers about ⅛ inch thick. If using brined fingerroots, rinse well before cutting (unless it comes already sliced). Stem the eggplants and set them aside for now. Thai eggplants oxidize quickly once they are cut, so it is best not to cut them until just before adding them to the curry.

In a 3-quart saucepan, combine the curry paste and water over medium-high heat and stir for about 1 minute, until the curry paste dissolves and becomes fragrant. Add the beef and sauté, breaking it up with a wooden spoon, until cooked through. Add the stock, beans, bamboo shoots, fish sauce, and sugar and stir well. If using fresh young peppercorns, add them to the pan now; if using brined peppercorns, reserve them for adding later. Bring the curry to a boil, cover, turn down the heat to a simmer, and cook for 2 minutes.

In the meantime, quarter the round eggplants or cut the long eggplants into 2-inch chunks and immediately add them to the pan along with the chiles, fingerroots, and lime leaves. Increase the heat to high and bring the curry back to a boil. Re-cover, immediately lower the heat to a simmer, and cook until the eggplants are tender, about 2 minutes.

Remove the pan from the heat, taste for seasoning, and add more fish sauce if needed. Stir in the basil and the brined peppercorns, if using, and serve.

ผัดเผ็ดปลาดุกทอดกรอบ

SPICY CRISPY CATFISH with FRIED BASIL

phat phet pla duk thot krop

This dry curry features a concept that can easily be lost in translation: bone-in catfish steaks fried until dried and crispy and then thoroughly coated in a spicy yet sweet mixture that falls somewhere between a sauce and a paste. Despite its unique character, this assertive yet harmonious dish has over the years crept onto the menus of many overseas Thai restaurants, especially those in big cities. Look for it slyly wedged between green curry and red curry.

This recipe is a slightly simplified version of the classic, which calls for bone-in catfish steaks. Using catfish fillets allows you to cut the frying time down by almost half. Still, the fish needs to be fried until dried and brittle—so dried and brittle that if you were to put a piece of it on the ground and crush it with the heel of your stiletto (or leather loafer), it would be reduced to little fishy shards rather than a squishy blob. Think fish crackers.

If you prefer to skip deep-frying the basil leaves, you can simply stir them into the dish just before you take it off the heat. **SERVES 4 TO 6**

2 fresh Thai long chiles

2 tablespoons red curry paste, homemade (page 175) or store-bought

¼ cup packed grated palm sugar, or 3 tablespoons granulated sugar

2 tablespoons fish sauce

1 tablespoon oyster sauce

3 large cloves garlic, minced

1 tablespoon vegetable oil, plus more for deep-frying

¾ cup water

2 pounds skinless catfish fillets

About 20 fresh Thai sweet basil or regular sweet basil leaves, patted thoroughly dry

2 (3-inch) fresh fingerroots, julienned, or ¼ cup well-drained brined fingerroot slivers (optional)

1 fresh kaffir lime leaf, deveined and sliced lengthwise into very thin strips (optional)

Cut 1 chile lengthwise on the diagonal into ½-inch-thick slices; set aside. Seed and mince the second long chile. In a small bowl, stir together the minced chile, curry paste, sugar, fish sauce, oyster sauce, garlic, 1 tablespoon oil, and water until the sugar dissolves.

Halve the catfish fillets lengthwise along the natural seam that runs down each piece. Cut each half crosswise into ½-inch-thick slices. Pat the catfish slices as dry as possible with paper towels to minimize the inevitable splattering of the hot oil and—if you are anything like me—the undignified dodging and shrieking.

To fry the basil and catfish, pour the oil to a depth of 3 inches into a wok, Dutch oven, or deep fryer and heat to 325°F to 350°F. To test if the oil is ready without a thermometer, stick an unvarnished wooden chopstick into the oil; when the oil is hot enough, a steady stream of tiny bubbles will rise from the tip of the chopstick. Line a baking sheet with paper towels and place it next to the stove. Keep a wire-mesh skimmer or slotted spoon handy.

Add the basil leaves to the hot oil and immediately stand back. Even if the leaves have been thoroughly dried, there will be some serious splattering, so watch out. Once the popping and spitting subside, after about 15 seconds, the basil is ready. Using the skimmer or slotted spoon, transfer the basil to one side of the towel-lined baking sheet.

Now, to fry the catfish, carefully lower the pieces, one at a time, into the hot oil, then stir them around a bit to keep them from sticking to one another. Fry the catfish pieces until they have turned golden brown and taken on a crackerlike texture, about 30 minutes. Using the skimmer or slotted spoon, transfer the fish to the baking sheet, arranging them next to the fried basil leaves. Remove the pan from the heat.

Remove the oil and any residue left from deep-frying from the wok, leaving just a thin film of oil on the surface. If using a Dutch oven or deep fryer, bring out a 14-inch skillet and add 1 tablespoon of the deep-frying oil to it. Set the wok or skillet over medium-high heat. When the oil is hot, add the sauce mixture and stir well. Let the sauce boil gently until it is reduced by nearly half, forming a thicker, more syrupy consistency. Add the fried fish to the pan, followed by the prepared chile slices, fingerroots, and lime leaves and stir well. Once the fish pieces are thoroughly coated with the sauce, remove the pan from the heat and transfer its contents to a large platter.

Strew the fried basil leaves over the crispy catfish and serve.

Note: If you do not want to deep-fry the basil, you may not want to deep-fry the fish either. You can instead lightly coat a skillet with vegetable oil and sear the catfish pieces over medium-high heat just until a crust has formed on all sides, then remove it from the pan. This creates a nice texture and will keep the fish from disintegrating when you return it to the pan to coat it with the sauce. You can then stir in the basil leaves just before the dish comes off the stove. Although the texture of the fish will be different, you will have a good idea of the sublime flavor of this dish. If you do opt to sear the fish, rather than deep-fry it, you will need to drop the *thot krop*—"crispy fried"—from the Thai name, for it no longer applies.

แกงพะแนงไก่กับฟักทอง

PHANAENG CURRY with CHICKEN and KABOCHA SQUASH

kaeng phanaeng kai kap fak thong

In our household when I was growing up, phanaeng curry was always made with tough and sinewy cuts of beef or bone-in, skin-on chunks of chicken. We cooked it in a barely simmering curry-coconut milk mixture until the meat was tender and the liquid became a thick, glistening sauce. Topped with even more fresh coconut cream, the finished dish was so rich and intense that you'd only need two or three spoonfuls of it for a cup of rice.

This recipe is a quick and easy version that takes less than thirty minutes to prepare. It is not as thick and intense as the version I grew up with, but those who like their sauce thicker and more intense can strain out the liquid into another saucepan once the chicken is cooked through then reduce the liquid by half. **SERVES 4 TO 6**

½ cup coconut cream (the thick layer at the top of a can of coconut milk)

1 tablespoon coconut oil or vegetable oil

¼ cup homemade red curry paste (page 175) or 2 tablespoons store-bought

½ of a small kabocha or Buttercup squash, halved, seeded, and cut into 1-inch cubes, 1½ to 2 pounds total

1 cup coconut milk

2 tablespoons fish sauce

1 pound boneless, skinless chicken breasts or thighs, cut on the diagonal (30- to 40-degree angle) into thin, bite-size pieces

½ cup sodium-free chicken broth

2 tablespoons packed grated palm sugar, or 1 tablespoon light brown sugar

1 long red Thai chile, stemmed, seeded, and cut lengthwise into thin strips

3 kaffir lime leaves, deveined and thinly sliced lengthwise

½ cup Thai sweet basil (or Mediterranean basil) leaves (optional, especially if kaffir lime leaves are used)

In a 2-quart saucepan, combine the coconut cream, coconut oil, and curry paste over medium-high heat and stir until the paste is fragrant and the coconut fat separates, about 2 minutes.

Add the squash to the saucepan along with the coconut milk and 1 tablespoon of the fish sauce; stir lightly to make sure every piece of squash is submerged. Turn the heat to high. Once the liquid comes to a boil, reduce the heat to medium, cover the saucepan, and cook the squash until tender, about 5 to 7 minutes. The squash should still hold its shape, yet is tender enough that you can pierce it easily with the tip of a paring knife.

Add the chicken to the saucepan along with the chicken broth, sugar, and the remaining 1 tablespoon fish sauce. Turn the heat up to medium-high; bring the curry back to a boil, stirring occasionally. Once the chicken firms up and turns opaque, about 2 to 3 minutes, remove the saucepan from the heat. Stir in the red chile strips as well as the kaffir lime leaves and/or basil leaves. Serve with rice.

แกงมัสมั่นเนื้อน่องลาย
BEEF SHANK MATSAMAN CURRY

kaeng matsaman nuea nong lai

This version of *matsaman* (sometimes spelled *massaman*) curry represents what I grew up eating and making at home, which is only one of the many interpretations of the dish. Although *matsaman* is one of the milder curries in the Thai repertoire, it is unabashedly rich, with specks of orange oil on top. It is also perfumed with toasted whole spices that are traditionally included in the presentation though not eaten.

This recipe calls for a tough cut of meat that takes a long time to tenderize, which means that it is perfect for a weekend supper when you are more likely to have time to linger in the kitchen. **SERVES 4 TO 6**

½ cup matsaman curry paste, homemade (page 176) or store-bought

1 tablespoon coconut or vegetable oil

½ cup coconut cream (the thick layer at the top of a can of coconut milk)

1½ cups coconut milk

2 pounds boneless beef shank, cut into 1½-inch cubes

1 pound Yukon gold or other waxy potatoes, peeled and cut into 1½-inch cubes

½ teaspoon salt

2-inch piece cassia bark, or 1 cinnamon stick

3 Thai or green cardamom pods

2 star anise pods

2 tablespoons tamarind pulp, homemade (page 171) or store-bought

3 tablespoons fish sauce

⅓ cup packed grated palm sugar, or ¼ cup packed light or dark brown sugar

8 ounces small yellow or white onions, quartered with the root end intact

2 bay leaves

¼ cup roasted peanuts

In a large, heavy saucepan, combine the curry paste, oil, and coconut cream over medium-high heat and fry until the paste is fragrant and the coconut fat separates, about 2 minutes. Add the coconut milk, beef and enough water just to cover the meat, turn up the heat to high, and bring to a boil. Immediately lower the heat so the mixture is at a gentle simmer, cover, and cook until the meat is tender, about 3 to 3½ hours. Check the level of the liquid periodically and replenish with water as needed to maintain the original level, adjusting the heat each time as needed to maintain a gentle simmer.

While the beef is cooking, in a saucepan, combine the potatoes with water to cover by 2 inches and bring to a boil over high heat. When the water is boiling, add the salt, lower the heat to a simmer, and cook until the potatoes are tender but still firm and retain their shape, about 10 to 12 minutes. Drain and set aside.

In a small, dry skillet, toast the cassia bark, cardamom pods, and star anise pods over low heat until fragrant, about 1 minute. Set aside.

When the beef is tender but not falling apart (check after 3 hours), add the tamarind, fish sauce, sugar, onions, bay leaves, and toasted spices and stir well. Continue to simmer for 10 minutes, until the onions have softened and become translucent. Gently stir in the cooked potatoes and peanuts and cook for 1 minute more, then serve.

SHRIMP-COCONUT RELISH with VEGETABLE CRUDITÉS

lon kung mu sap

Most people who did not grow up in a Thai household or live with Thai people are unfamiliar with the various coconut milk–based relishes called *lon*. That is because these dishes are not the type of food you usually buy from a street vendor. Instead, you eat them either on home dining tables or at restaurants that serve old-fashioned, traditional Thai dishes.

Not surprisingly, Thai restaurants overseas rarely include *lon* on their menus, probably because most of their customers do not know the dishes or how they are eaten. Even though the word *lon* is translated as coconut "relish," which implies a condiment of sorts, it is as much of a rice accompaniment as any of the other recipes in this chapter, plus it comes with an entourage of raw vegetables.

This is how I eat *lon*: I take a piece of the vegetable crudités, put it on a bite's worth of rice on my plate, top it with a dollop of the *lon*, transport the whole assembly on a spoon, and eat it in one big bite. As you eat, flitting from one vegetable to another is encouraged, as it allows you to experience different flavors and textures. **SERVES 4**

1 stalk lemongrass

4 ounces fatty pork cut, such as shoulder

8 ounces shrimp in the shell, peeled and deveined

1 cup coconut milk

2 tablespoons packed grated palm sugar or light brown sugar

1 teaspoon salt

2 tablespoons tamarind pulp, homemade (page 171) or store-bought

1 large shallot, about 1 ounce, thinly sliced lengthwise

1 fresh red or green Thai long chile, sliced crosswise ½ inch thick

2 fresh kaffir lime leaves, deveined and cut lengthwise into very thin strips (optional)

Assorted crunchy and mild-flavored raw vegetables (such as cucumber, zucchini, and carrot slices; 1-inch-long green bean and celery pieces; thin green cabbage and iceberg lettuce wedges; 2-inch napa cabbage pieces; quartered Thai round eggplants; halved or quartered radishes; cauliflower florets; small red or yellow bell pepper squares)

Trim off and discard the leafy parts of the lemongrass stalk, remove the tough outer leaves of the bulb portion until the smooth, pale green core is exposed, and trim off the root end. Working from the root end, cut the bulb crosswise into paper-thin slices, stopping once you reach the point where the purple rings disappear. Set aside.

Cut the pork into small pieces, roughly the size of the shrimp. Put the shrimp and pork in a food processor and pulse to grind coarsely. (Alternatively, chop the shrimp and pork with a cleaver on a large, sturdy cutting board, my preferred method.)

continued

In a 2-quart saucepan, combine the coconut milk and the shrimp-pork mixture over medium-high heat. Using a wooden spoon, stir and cook the shrimp-pork mixture, breaking it up with the spoon into a fine mince as you go, until the meat mixture is cooked, about 3 to 5 minutes. Add the palm sugar, salt, tamarind, and shallot, turn down the heat to medium, and continue to cook, stirring, until the sugar has dissolved. Taste for seasoning and correct as needed. The mixture should be predominantly sweet-and-sour first, then salty. Keep in mind that it will be eaten with mild-flavored vegetables and bland rice and season accordingly.

Add the lemongrass and chile and continue to cook over medium heat, stirring occasionally, for 2 to 3 minutes, to blend all of the flavors. Remove from the heat, transfer to a serving bowl, and sprinkle the lime leaves on top. Let cool.

While the dish cools, prepare the raw vegetables, cutting them into roughly bite-size pieces as directed. Arrange the crudités on a large serving platter, and put the bowl of *lon* in the middle. Serve the *lon* at room temperature or slightly warmer.

ปลานึ่งมะนาว

FISH with LIME-CHILE-GARLIC DRESSING

pla nueng manao

Some of the best Thai dishes are the ones that are the simplest to make and call for the most basic of ingredients. This is one of them. Steamed fish with lime-chile-garlic dressing is a restaurant classic for good reason.

But for many home cooks, steaming seems like a bit more trouble than it is worth. I can sympathize, which is why I prefer to bake the fish. It is more convenient and leaves me with fewer things to wash. As long as you keep the baking dish covered and do not overcook the fish, the end result is just as good. I have provided directions for both methods here.

Steamed fish is usually served whole at restaurants in Thailand. The dressing and the liquid released from a bone-in whole fish during steaming combine to form a broth that is so delicious it could be a dish on its own. But to keep things simple here, I am using skinless fish fillets. I prefer to use fillets that have been cut into one large piece instead of smaller individual portions because the fish stays moister. Although I cannot think of any fish that will not work here, my top favorites for this dish are trout, salmon, and halibut. **SERVES 4**

¼ cup freshly squeezed lime juice

2 tablespoons fish sauce

½ teaspoon granulated sugar

¾ cup chicken stock, homemade (page 178) or store-bought

2 whole skinless fish fillets, about 1½ pounds each

4 large cloves garlic, coarsely chopped

4 fresh bird's eye chiles, coarsely chopped

1 cup loosely packed fresh cilantro leaves

If you plan to steam the fish, assemble your steamer and get the water boiling. If you plan to bake the fish, preheat the oven to 350°F.

In a small bowl, stir together the lime juice, fish sauce, sugar, and stock until the sugar dissolves; set aside.

Place the fillets in a large baking dish, or in any heatproof dish suitable for use in your steamer, positioning them so that the tapered ends point in opposite directions to allow both fillets to fit nicely in the dish. Fold the thin tail ends under to allow the entire fillets to cook more evenly. Pour the dressing over the fish fillets and sprinkle the garlic and chiles over the top.

Steam the fish over boiling water, checking for doneness at the 10-minute mark. Depending on the steamer, this could take from 10 to 20 minutes. Play it by ear. To bake the fish, cover the baking dish tightly with a piece of aluminum foil and bake until the fish is opaque and flakes easily at the thickest part when pierced with a fork, about 20 minutes.

Remove the fish from the steamer or oven. Sprinkle the cilantro leaves on top and serve.

Put the cherry tomatoes, garlic, and shallot on a baking sheet and broil, turning often, until charred in spots and softened, about 5 to 7 minutes. Remove from the broiler and let cool until they can be handled. Peel the garlic and shallot but leave the tomatoes unpeeled. Put the garlic in a bowl and press with the back of a spoon until reduced to a paste. Add the shallot and mash with the spoon until it breaks down into small pieces. Add the tomatoes and cut into chunks with edge of the same spoon. Stir in the fish sauce, lime juice, pepper flakes, sugar, chopped cilantro, and sawtooth coriander; set aside.

Prepare a hot fire in a charcoal or gas grill. If using charcoal, allow the charcoal to develop a gray ash before you start grilling. Oil the grate with vegetable oil. Alternatively, heat a well-oiled stove-top grill pan over high heat until hot or leave the broiler on and oil a broiler pan. Cook the steaks, turning them once halfway through the cooking, until they are medium-rare to medium. The timing will vary depending on which cooking method you are using. If possible, test if they are ready with an instant-read thermometer, which should register 140°F to 150°F, the ideal level of doneness for this dish. Transfer the steaks to a cutting board, tent with aluminum foil, and let rest for 10 to 15 minutes.

Transfer the sauce to a small serving bowl and place it on the center of a large platter. Cut the steaks against the grain into slices ¼ to ½ inch thick and arrange them around the sauce bowl. Arrange the cucumber and tomatoes on the side of the platter. Sprinkle the whole cilantro leaves over the beef and serve immediately.

CURRIED FISH CUSTARD

ho mok

According to Mrs. Gump, life is like a box of chocolates, and you never know what you're gonna get. On the other side of the globe, far away from Greenbow, Alabama, life is kind of like a bunch of *ho mok* in banana-leaf packets: you never know if what you are going to get is sweet, bitter, or something in between.

When I was a kid, my mother would buy a bunch of individual packets of curried fish custard wrapped in banana leaves. Each was folded into either a triangular prism or a rectangular pyramid, then held together with a coconut-leaf blade and secured with a toothpick-thin stick of bamboo. There were always three types of *ho mok* packets in the refrigerator: one with napa cabbage underneath, one with Thai sweet basil leaves, and one with *noni* (Indian mulberry) leaves. On the outside, all of the packets looked identical—at least to me. On the other hand, my feelings about each type were very different.

The ones with napa cabbage were delicious, sweet, mild, and kid-friendly. The ones with basil were sometimes okay and sometimes just tolerable. The ones with *noni* leaves were monstrously bitter, and it seemed the more I hated them, the more they popped up. As far as I was concerned, nobody should ever have to approach a bunch of fish custard packets praying that they be saved from the evil ones.

Life with *ho mok* remained a game of minesweeper until two things happened, both around the same time: First, I grew up and learned not only to appreciate but also to look forward to the herbal basil leaves and the bitter *noni* leaves. Second, I finally figured out that just as a chocolate manufacturer has its own designs to let you know what is inside every bonbon, each *ho mok* vendor has a way of cutting the ends of the coconut blade that binds each banana-leaf packet to let you know which "flavor" is inside.

This recipe—and I am telling you now so you will not have to guess—has sweet basil leaves underneath the custard, making the flavor neither too mild nor too bitter. In other words, it is a Goldilocks-approved *ho mok*. **SERVES 6**

1½ pounds skinless trout or salmon fillets

2 to 4 tablespoons red curry paste, homemade (page 175) or store-bought

2 cups coconut milk

3 eggs

1 teaspoon packed grated palm sugar or light brown sugar

2 teaspoons fish sauce

2 teaspoons rice flour or all-purpose flour

1 cup loosely packed fresh Thai basil or sweet basil leaves

3 or 4 kaffir lime leaves, deveined and cut lengthwise into very fine strips (optional but highly recommended)

1 large red Thai long chile, seeded and cut lengthwise into 12 long strips

Cut the fish into 2-inch cubes, transfer the cubes to a bowl, and freeze just until the fish is frosty but not frozen, about 10 to 15 minutes.

Put half of the fish in a food processor bowl and return the other half to the freezer. Add 2 tablespoons of the curry paste, 1½ cups of the coconut milk, the eggs, the sugar, and the fish sauce to the processor and process until velvety smooth.

With a rubber spatula, scrape every bit of the fish paste into the bowl of a stand mixer fitted with the paddle attachment, then add the fish from the freezer to the bowl. Beat on the lowest speed for 10 minutes, stopping to scrape down the sides of the bowl occasionally. After 10 minutes, the custard mixture should be thick and viscous.

While the mixer is running, preheat the oven to 350°F. In a small saucepan, combine the remaining ½ cup coconut milk and the flour over medium heat and cook, stirring, until thickened. Remove the pan from the heat and set aside.

Put a kettle of water (at least 8 cups) on to boil. Place six ¾-cup ramekins, not touching, in a large roasting pan or 2 smaller baking pans. Divide the basil leaves evenly among the ramekins, placing them on the bottoms. Cut six 6-inch squares of aluminum foil.

Cook a tablespoonful of the fish custard in a small skillet over medium heat or in a microwave, taste it, and adjust the seasoning with more curry paste or other seasonings as needed. Keep in mind that this will be served with bland rice, so season accordingly.

Fold in half of the lime leaves and spoon the fish custard into the ramekins, dividing it evenly and smoothing the tops. Spoon a dollop of the thickened coconut milk on top of each custard. Sprinkle the remaining lime leaves, followed by the red chile strips, on top. Cover each ramekin tightly with a foil square. Pour the boiling water into the pan(s) to come halfway up the sides of the ramekins.

Carefully transfer the pan(s) to the oven and bake until the custards are firm all the way to the center and do not jiggle when tapped, about 30 to 40 minutes. Let the custards cool down to slightly warmer than room temperature before serving in the ramekins.

GRILLED PORK NECK with DRIED CHILE DIPPING SAUCE

kho mu yang

Pork neck, sometimes called pork collar, is one of the favorite pork cuts among Thais. This part of the pig has just the right combination of lean meat, muscle, and fat, making it so flavorful that it does not require an elaborate preparation.

I keep the marinade simple here, because the dried chile dipping sauce that accompanies the pork has an intense flavor. The inclusion of whiskey in the marinade may surprise you. It is there because whenever one of my uncles prepares this dish at a family gathering, he sips on his favorite Thai spirit and accidentally spills a couple of tablespoons—maybe three—of it into the marinade. This uncle is known within our family as the grill master, so if the master accidentally spills some booze into the pork marinade, who am I not to accidentally follow suit?

You can serve grilled pork neck as an appetizer or as a rice accompaniment. If you opt for the latter, steamed glutinous rice (page 169) is the best choice. **SERVES 4**

2 pounds pork neck

3 tablespoons packed grated palm sugar, or 1 tablespoon packed brown sugar

2 tablespoons oyster sauce

2 tablespoons thin soy sauce

2 tablespoons whiskey, rum, or brandy

½ English cucumber, or 2 pickling cucumbers, peeled and sliced on a slight diagonal ¼ inch thick

2 Roma tomatoes, sliced crosswise ¼ inch thick

Dried chile dipping sauce (page 190)

Slice the pork into large slabs about ½ inch thick. Put the pieces in a large bowl, add the sugar, oyster sauce, soy sauce, and whiskey, and mix well. Cover and refrigerate for 3 to 4 hours.

Prepare a hot fire in a charcoal or gas grill. If using charcoal, allow the charcoal to develop a gray ash before you start grilling. Oil the grate with vegetable oil. Alternatively, heat a well-oiled stove-top grill pan over high heat until hot or preheat the broiler and oil a broiler pan. Cook the pork pieces, turning them once halfway through the cooking, for 10 to 12 minutes total, until just cooked through and slightly charred on the outside. (The timing will vary depending on which cooking method you are using.) Transfer the pork to a cutting board, tent with aluminum foil, and let rest for 10 to 15 minutes.

Cut the pork against the grain into ¼- to ½-inch-thick slices. Arrange the slices on a serving platter and place the cucumber and tomato on the side. Serve with the dipping sauce.

ไก่ย่างขมิ้น
TURMERIC GRILLED CHICKEN

kai yang khamin

This is a simplified version of the so-called train grilled chicken sold at major railway stations on the route between Bangkok and the south. Whole marinated chickens are secured with partially split bamboo and grilled over moderate-hot coals until golden, tender, and smoky.

There is no need to split any bamboo here. In place of the traditional whole chicken, I have cut boneless, skinless chicken thighs into chunks and threaded the chunks onto skewers for easy grilling. **SERVES 4**

¼ cup packed basic aromatic paste (page 179)

2 teaspoons ground coriander

3 tablespoons fish sauce

2 tablespoons oyster sauce

1 tablespoon ground turmeric

2 tablespoons packed light or dark brown sugar

3 pounds boneless, skinless chicken thighs, cut into 1-inch cubes

In a large bowl, stir together the aromatic paste, ground coriander, fish sauce, oyster sauce, turmeric, and sugar, mixing well. Add the chicken and stir until evenly coated with the marinade. Cover and refrigerate for 1 to 2 hours.

While the chicken is marinating, soak 12 to 16 bamboo skewers in water to cover for at least 30 minutes.

To grill the chicken, prepare a medium-hot fire in a charcoal or gas grill. If you are using charcoal, allow time for the charcoal to develop a gray ash before you start grilling. Oil the grate with vegetable oil. Alternatively, heat a well-oiled stove-top grill pan over medium heat until hot or preheat the broiler and oil a broiler pan.

While the grill is heating, remove the chicken from the marinade and the skewers from the water. Thread the chicken pieces onto the skewers, pushing them firmly against one another to form a tight, compact body of meat on the skewers and leaving the bottom one-fourth empty to use as a handle.

Grill the chicken, turning the skewers occasionally, until thoroughly cooked through and slightly charred, about 8 to 10 minutes. Transfer the skewers to a platter and serve.

Spicy Basil Chicken and
Fried Eggs on Rice (page 147)

อาหารจานเดียว
ONE-PLATE MEALS
ahan jan diao

Ahan jan diao (อาหารจานเดียว) is the term used for a one-plate meal or, in many cases, a one-bowl meal, in contrast to the traditional *samrap*, or ensemble meal (see chapter 2). The majority of these one-plate meals are easily found everywhere in Thailand, but especially on the streets of Bangkok.

Because these one-dish meals are assembled quickly and are often consumed with much less ceremony than a *samrap*, you may think that they are also quick to make. Most of the time, however, this is not the case. The reason a vendor can make a bowl of noodles for you in less than two minutes is because he or she woke up before dawn that day to prepare the ingredients and ready them for quick assembly. Replicating this whole process at home can be time-consuming. However, I have streamlined the process for all the recipes in this section to make things as easy and quick as possible for home cooks.

For ease of reference, the recipes are separated into two categories: noodles dishes and rice dishes.

ผัดซีอิ๊วไก่

RICE NOODLES with CHICKEN and CHINESE BROCCOLI

phat si-io kai

With a well-seasoned wok (I do not recommend a nonstick skillet, but if you must use one, that is fine, just make sure that it is 14 inches in diameter) and the right ingredients, you can make this Thai restaurant favorite easily. This is my recipe, which just happens to be similar to the *phat si-io* (often spelled *pad see-ew, pad si-ew*, or similar romanizations) commonly found at Thai restaurants in the States or other countries. The addition of salted soybean paste is what makes it taste like the version I grew up eating in Bangkok, but the ingredient is optional. **SERVES 2**

1 pound fresh wide rice noodles, or 8 ounces dried wide rice noodles, prepared according to instructions on page 212

12 ounces Chinese broccoli or regular broccoli florets

8 ounces boneless, skinless chicken thighs or breasts

2 tablespoons vegetable oil

2 eggs

2 large cloves garlic, minced

2 teaspoons salted soybean paste (optional)

3 tablespoons dark sweet soy sauce

2 tablespoons thin soy sauce

2 teaspoons distilled white or cider vinegar

½ teaspoon granulated sugar

Table Condiments and Seasonings

Ground white pepper, for dusting

Granulated sugar

Fish sauce

Red chile powder (page 181)

Vinegar with pickled chiles (page 192)

If the noodles are in sheet form, rather than precut, cut them lengthwise into 1-inch-wide strips and separate the layers into singles.

If using Chinese broccoli, trim about 1 inch off the bottom of each stalk end. Cut the stalks on the diagonal (about a 45-degree angle) into ¼-inch-thick pieces, and cut the green leafy parts crosswise into 2-inch pieces. Keep the stalks and leafy parts separate.

Slice the chicken against the grain into thin, bite-size pieces.

Heat the oil in a wok or a 14-inch skillet over high heat. When the oil is hot, crack the eggs into the oil, add the garlic, and stir until the eggs are partially cooked. Add the chicken and Chinese broccoli stalks (if using broccoli florets, reserve them for adding later) and stir-fry until the chicken is cooked through, about 2 minutes.

Add the noodles, soybean paste, sweet soy sauce, thin soy sauce, vinegar, sugar, and the broccoli florets, if using, and stir for about 1 minute, until the noodles have softened and absorbed some of the sauce. Stop stirring and let the noodles sit undisturbed over high heat until the underside starts to brown and more of the sauce has been absorbed, about 1 minute. Flip the noodles over and again let sit undisturbed until the underside starts to brown and all of sauce has been absorbed, about 1 to 2 minutes. Add the leaves of Chinese broccoli (the broccoli floret people do not get to add anything here), stir to wilt, and remove from the heat.

Plate the noodles. Dust the top with the white pepper and serve with the sugar, fish sauce, chile powder, and pickled chiles for adding as desired.

Note: It is important that you not crowd the wok, so do not try to cook more than two servings at a time. If you need to feed more than two people, cook the dish in batches.

ผัดไทยกุ้งสด

PAD THAI with SHRIMP

phat thai kung sot

No introduction is needed for this iconic Thai dish. Even those with only a passing interest in Thai cuisine know pad thai. Unfortunately, when it comes to making this familiar dish, you must work your way through a long list of instructions if you want to end up with the kind of pad thai that you find on the streets of Bangkok. The combination of an intimidating ingredients list and a high number of things that can go wrong is why most Bangkokians are happy to leave the making of this dish to skilled street vendors. **SERVES 2**

4 ounces dried rice sticks, 3 millimeters (about ⅛ inch) wide

3 tablespoons packed grated palm sugar, or 2 tablespoons packed dark brown sugar

2 tablespoons tamarind pulp, homemade (page 171) or store-bought

2 tablespoons fish sauce

5 tablespoons vegetable oil

1 large shallot, about 1 ounce, minced

2 large cloves garlic, minced

¼ cup finely chopped preserved radish (optional)

6 ounces extra-firm tofu (use the firmest one you can find), cut into matchsticks 1 inch long and ¼ wide and thick

2 tablespoons shell-on small dried shrimp (optional)

8 ounces large raw shrimp in the shell, peeled and deveined

2 eggs, lightly beaten

6 Chinese chives or green parts of 3 green onions, cut into 1-inch lengths

4 ounces mung bean sprouts (about 2 cups)

Table Condiments and Seasonings

1 lime, cut into wedges

Granulated sugar

Fish sauce

Red chile powder (page 181)

⅓ to ½ cup finely chopped roasted peanuts

Immerse the noodles in room-temperature water to cover for 30 to 40 minutes, until soft enough to wind around your fingers without breaking. Drain and cut into 6-inch lengths with kitchen shears. Set aside.

In a small bowl, stir together the sugar, tamarind, and fish sauce until the sugar dissolves. Set aside.

Heat 3 tablespoons of the oil in a wok or a 14-inch skillet over medium-high heat. When the oil is hot, add the drained noodles and stir until the noodles are coated with the oil and have become more pliable but not yet cooked through, about 1 minute. Add the prepared sauce and stir-fry for 1 minute to coat the noodles with the sauce. Push the noodles to one side of the pan, add the remaining 2 tablespoons of oil to the empty side of the pan, and add the shallot, garlic, radish, tofu, and dried shrimp and stir-fry for 1 minute on their side of the pan while the noodles are cooking in the sauce on the other side. Add the fresh shrimp to the shallot side of the pan and

continued

stir-fry until the shrimp are half cooked, about 1 minute. Stir the noodles around once while still keeping them on their side of the pan.

Make a well in the center of the pan, add the eggs to the well, and scramble and shred them with the tip of the spatula until the egg bits are cooked through, about 1 minute. By this time all the moisture should have evaporated, the noodles should have become softened, and the shrimp should have been completely cooked. Do a strand check to see if the noodles are soft enough. If all of the moisture has evaporated and the noodles are still undercooked, add a little water as needed.

Once everything is ready, remove the pan from the heat. Fold in the chives and half of the bean sprouts and let the residual heat wilt them.

Plate the noodles and serve with the remaining bean sprouts and the table condiments and seasonings for adding as desired.

ก๋วยเตี๋ยวแกงใส่ไก่

CURRY NOODLES with CHICKEN

kuai-tiao kaeng sai kai

This is a quick version of my favorite Muslim-style curry noodles, a common dish in food shops specializing in Thai Muslim food. With boneless chicken, it can be done in less than a half hour. The ingredients list is long, but if you have made pad thai (page 123), you know that the two dishes have some ingredients in common. So if you have some dried rice noodles, preserved radish, extra-firm tofu, bean sprouts, and peanuts left over from making pad thai, you can use them to make these satisfying curry noodles. **SERVES 4**

1½ pounds boneless, skinless chicken thighs (great) or breasts (okay)

1 tablespoon vegetable oil

½ cup coconut cream (from the top of a can of coconut milk)

3 tablespoons homemade red curry paste (page 175), or 2 tablespoons store-bought

2 tablespoons kari ("yellow") curry paste, homemade (page 177) or store-bought

2 tablespoons packed grated palm sugar, or 1½ tablespoons packed light brown sugar

3 tablespoons fish sauce

1½ cups coconut milk

3 cups sodium-free chicken stock, homemade (page 178) or store-bought

6 ounces extra-firm tofu, cut into matchsticks 1 inch long and ¼ inch wide and thick

2 teaspoons curry powder

8 ounces mung bean sprouts (about 4 cups)

8 ounces dried rice sticks, 3 millimeters (about ⅛ inch) wide

¼ cup finely chopped preserved radish (optional)

¼ cup fried shallots (page 183)

¼ cup packed fresh cilantro leaves

⅓ cup finely chopped roasted peanuts

2 hard- or medium-boiled eggs (page 195), peeled and halved lengthwise

Table Seasonings

2 or 3 limes, cut into wedges

Fish sauce

Granulated sugar

Red chile powder

Cut the chicken against the grain and on the diagonal into thin, bite-size pieces. Cover and refrigerate until needed.

In a 1-gallon saucepan, combine the vegetable oil, coconut cream, and curry pastes, and stir over medium-high heat until fragrant, about 2 minutes. Add the chicken and stir for about 1 minute, until the chicken is coated with the curry paste. Add the sugar, fish sauce, coconut milk, and stock, stir well, and bring to a very gentle boil. When the chicken is cooked through, after 3 to 4 minutes, stir in the tofu and curry powder, mixing well to distribute the curry powder evenly. Turn down the heat to the lowest setting; keep the curry warm.

continued

Have ready 4 large individual serving bowls. Half fill another 1-gallon saucepan with water and bring to a boil. Add the bean sprouts, stir, and then immediately fish the bean sprouts out of the water with a wire-mesh skimmer, shaking off the excess water. Divide the bean sprouts evenly among the bowls. While the water is still boiling, add the dried noodles, stir to submerge, and cook until they have softened through, about 15 minutes. Taste a strand to make sure they are ready. Drain the cooked noodles through a large colander placed in the sink and rinse off all starchy liquid that clings to them with running hot tap water. Shake off the water. Divide the noodles evenly among the bowls.

Immediately ladle the curry over the noodles, dividing it evenly. Sprinkle each serving with an equal amount of the radish, fried shallots, cilantro, and peanuts. Top each serving with an egg half. Serve immediately with the limes, fish sauce, sugar, and red chile powder for adding as desired.

เสือร้องไห้กับแจ่วมะเขือเทศ

GRILLED STEAKS with ROASTED TOMATO DIPPING SAUCE (Crying Tiger)

suea rong hai kap jaeo ma-khuea thet

Crying tiger, tiger's tears, weeping tiger—where did all of these odd names on Thai restaurant menus come from? They make you wonder how a tiger got involved, why it is upset, if the tears are real or a bold pitch for public sympathy, and whether any tiger is even capable of psychogenic lacrimation.

Some say this dish owes its name to the fact that it once called for a cut of beef so tough that even a tiger could not chew it without weeping in pain. Others claim the opposite: the tiger, seeing how the human zeroed in on the most tender part of the cow for the dish, could not contain its envy-induced tears. And still others wave off both theories as implausible, insisting instead that the dipping sauce is so spicy that it makes even a tiger cry. Since my attempts to reach the tiger's publicist for comment were unsuccessful, I am not taking sides on the origin of the name.

The dipping sauce included here is the one that my mother made quite often. It calls for roasted tomatoes and is quite thick (you can thin it to a desired consistency with more fish sauce and lime juice). If you are pressed for time, you can skip this sauce and instead serve the steak with the simpler dried chile dipping sauce (page 190). Serve the steak and dipping sauce with glutinous rice (page 169) or long-grain rice (page 168) as part of a *samrap*, or offer it with beer as an appetizer. **SERVES 4 • PICTURED ON PAGE 32**

3 (8-ounce) rib-eye steaks

1 tablespoon thin soy sauce

1 tablespoon oyster sauce

1 tablespoon vegetable oil

½ teaspoon ground white pepper

4 ounces cherry tomatoes

3 large cloves garlic, unpeeled

1 large shallot, about 1 ounce, unpeeled

1 tablespoon fish sauce

1 tablespoon freshly squeezed lime juice

2 tablespoons red pepper flakes

½ teaspoon packed light or dark brown sugar

2 tablespoons coarsely chopped fresh cilantro leaves, plus ½ cup loosely packed whole leaves

2 tablespoons coarsely chopped fresh sawtooth coriander (optional)

½ English cucumber, or 2 pickling cucumbers, sliced crosswise ¼ inch thick

2 large Roma tomatoes, sliced crosswise ¼ inch thick

Position an oven rack in the middle of the oven and preheat the broiler.

Put the steaks in a wide, shallow bowl. Add the soy sauce, oyster sauce, oil, and white pepper and turn the steaks to coat them evenly with the ingredients. Cover and refrigerate for 1 hour.

ราดหน้าเนื้อ

RICE NOODLES with BEEF and CHINESE BROCCOLI GRAVY

rat na nuea

One of the most delicious street foods in Bangkok is rice noodles sautéed with dark sweet soy and topped with a savory, translucent gravy laced with tender meat and greens. This recipe was inspired by the version served at one of my favorite *rat na* joints in Bangkok's Wang Bura-pha neighborhood. I use the Chinese method of tenderizing meat with baking soda, so that the beef is extra tender and very smooth. You can use the same method for pork and chicken. **SERVES 2 GENEROUSLY**

Beef

8 ounces chuck or rib-eye steak

1 teaspoon baking soda

¼ teaspoon ground white pepper

1 tablespoon thin soy sauce

Gravy

12 ounces Chinese broccoli or regular broccoli florets

1 tablespoon oyster sauce

1½ teaspoons salted soybean paste (optional)

3 tablespoons tapioca starch (preferred) or cornstarch

3 cups sodium-free chicken stock, homemade (page 178) or store-bought

1 tablespoon vegetable oil

2 cloves garlic, minced

Noodles

1 pound fresh wide rice noodles, or 8 ounces dried wide rice noodles, prepared according to instructions on page 212

1 tablespoon vegetable oil

1 tablespoon thin soy sauce

2 teaspoons dark sweet soy sauce

Table Condiments and Seasonings

Ground white pepper, for dusting

Granulated sugar

Fish sauce

Red chile powder (page 181)

Vinegar with pickled chiles (page 192)

To prepare the beef, cut it against the grain and on a sharp diagonal (20-degree angle) into thin bite-size pieces. In a bowl, combine the beef, baking soda, pepper, and soy sauce and mix well. Cover and refrigerate while you ready the gravy ingredients and the noodles.

To prepare the ingredients for the gravy, if using Chinese broccoli, trim about 1 inch off the bottom of each stalk end. Cut the stalks on the diagonal (about a 45-degree angle) into ¼-inch-thick pieces, and cut the green leafy parts crosswise into 2-inch pieces. Keep the stalks and leafy parts separate. In a small bowl, whisk together the oyster sauce, soybean paste, tapioca starch, and stock until no lumps of tapioca starch remain; set aside along with the oil and garlic.

To prepare the noodles, if they are in sheet form, rather than precut, cut them length-wise into 1-inch-wide strips and separate the layers into singles. Place 2 individual serving plates (preferably with raised edges) near the stove.

Heat a wok or a 14-inch skillet over high heat until the pan is smoking. Add the oil and swirl it to coat the surface of the pan. Add the noodles, drizzle the thin and sweet soy sauces over them, and stir once to distribute the sauces and to spread the noodles evenly over the bottom of the pan. Stop stirring and let the noodles sit undisturbed over high heat until browned on the underside, about 1 minute. Flip the noodles over and brown the second side for 1 minute. Remove the pan from the heat and divide the noodles evenly between the 2 plates.

To cook the gravy, remove the beef from the refrigerator. Return the pan to high heat, add the reserved 1 tablespoon oil and the garlic, and fry for about 30 seconds, until fragrant. Add the beef and the broccoli stalks (the broccoli floret people do not add anything here) and stir until the meat is almost cooked through and very little pink remains, about 2 minutes. Whisk the sauce mixture again briefly (the tapioca starch may have sunk to the bottom) and pour it into the pan. Add the leafy parts of the broccoli or broccoli florets and stir until the gravy has thickened, about 1 to 2 minutes.

Ladle the gravy over the prepared noodles. Dust with the white pepper and serve with the sugar, fish sauce, chile powder, and vinegar with pickled chiles for adding as desired.

ก๋วยเตี๋ยวเนื้อสับ

RICE NOODLES with BEEF-TOMATO GRAVY

kuai-tiao nuea sap

I do not remember much about my sixth-grade year, but I do remember the day I was invited to my best friend's house for lunch and was introduced to rice noodles with beef-tomato gravy, a dish that inexplicably was regularly made by everyone's mother except mine.

I also recall how, in the middle of the meal, my friend's mother asked the other adults at the table if they thought the dish might be a Thai riff on pasta Bolognese. That question prompted a spirited discussion on a number of other issues, such as whether curry powder should be added, whether lettuce was a necessary garnish, and which restaurant originated the dish. Although no fists were slammed on the table and no lettuce was hurled across the room, I remember thinking to myself that these adults sure took their food seriously. I also remember that none of what they said mattered to me and my friend. We simply smiled at each other, kept our heads down, and enjoyed every single bite of our noodles. **SERVES 2 GENEROUSLY**

1¼ cups sodium-free chicken stock, homemade (page 178) or store-bought

2 tablespoons cornstarch or tapioca starch

3 tablespoons thin soy sauce

2 tablespoons oyster sauce

½ teaspoon granulated sugar

2 teaspoons curry powder

4 green lettuce leaves

1 pound fresh wide rice noodles, or 8 ounces dried wide rice noodles, prepared according to instructions on page 212

2 tablespoons vegetable oil

1½ tablespoons dark sweet soy sauce

2 large cloves garlic, minced

8 ounces lean ground beef

1 small yellow or white onion, about 4 ounces, cut into ½-inch dice

1 large Roma tomato, cut into ½-inch dice

1 tablespoon preserved cabbage (optional)

2 small stalks Chinese celery, cut into ½-inch pieces, or ¾ cup ¼-inch-diced leafy parts of regular celery

Ground white pepper, for dusting

In a small bowl, whisk together the stock, cornstarch, 2 tablespoons of the thin soy sauce, the oyster sauce, the sugar, and the curry powder until no lumps of cornstarch remain; set aside.

Divide the lettuce leaves between 2 individual serving plates and place the plates near the stove.

If the noodles are in sheet form, rather than precut, cut them lengthwise into 1-inch-wide strips and separate the layers into singles.

Heat a wok or a 14-inch skillet over high heat until the pan is smoking. Add 1 tablespoon of the oil and swirl it to coat the surface of the pan. Add the noodles, drizzle the remaining 1 tablespoon thin soy sauce and the sweet soy sauce over them, and stir once to distribute the sauces and to spread the noodles evenly over the bottom of the pan. Let the noodles sit undisturbed until brown on the underside, about 1 minute. Flip the noodles over and brown the second side for 1 more minute. Remove the pan from the heat and divide the noodles evenly between the 2 plates.

Return the pan to medium-high heat. Add the remaining 1 tablespoon oil and the garlic and fry for about 30 seconds, or until fragrant. Add the beef and cook and stir, breaking up the meat with the spatula, until no pink remains, about 2 to 3 minutes. Add the onion, tomato, and preserved cabbage and continue to cook until the onion is soft and translucent and the tomato has softened, about 2 to 3 minutes. Whisk the sauce mixture again briefly (the cornstarch may have sunk to the bottom) and pour it into the pan. Add the celery, increase the heat to high, and stir until the gravy has thickened, about 1 to 2 minutes.

Ladle the gravy over the prepared noodles. Dust with the pepper and serve immediately. The garnish of lettuce leaves will have been slightly wilted by the heat of the noodles and gravy. Some people do not eat them, but I do, and I recommend that you do, too.

ก๋วยเตี๋ยวผัดขี้เมาไก่

RICE NOODLES "DRUNKARD'S STYLE" with CHICKEN

kuai-tiao phat khi mao kai

To understand this dish, you need to know that it is a spin-off of *phat khi mao*, a spicy stir-fry that has nothing to do with noodles. In his book, *The Principles of Thai Cookery*, and in a 2013 interview with me, Mom Luang Sirichalerm "McDang" Svasti pointed out that this type of stir-fry was created to accommodate drinkers who wanted something hot and spicy to eat as they drank, hence the name. And that is how a spicy stir-fry with garlic, shallots, fresh chiles, and shrimp paste as its base and holy basil as its accent was born. Any protein can be prepared this way, as long as it is chunky enough to eat with a fork in one hand and a glass of whiskey on the rocks in the other.

At some point, someone came up with the idea of making stir-fried noodles in the style of this dish. But exactly how that noodle dish has morphed into no more than a spicier version of *phat si-io* (page 120) at many overseas Thai restaurants, I have no clue.

This recipe is based on the version that my mother regularly made. It inexplicably has a tomato in it, is soy heavy, and does not call for shrimp paste. Mom's version falls somewhere between the traditional *phat khi mao* and what has become the standard version of drunkard's noodles in Thai restaurants around the world.

Your favorite Thai restaurant's version of this dish may or may not include eggs. I have chosen not to add eggs, but if you prefer the dish with eggs, add them: after the chicken is cooked through, stir in 2 eggs, lightly beaten, before you add the noodles and then proceed as directed. If you cannot find holy basil, Thai sweet basil or regular sweet basil can be substituted. **SERVES 2**

2 fresh bird's eye chiles, or fewer or more to taste, stemmed

2 large cloves garlic

1 large shallot, about 1 ounce

1 pound fresh wide rice noodles, or 8 ounces dried wide rice noodles, prepared according to instructions on page 212

8 ounces boneless, skinless chicken breasts

2 tablespoons vegetable oil

1 yellow or white onion, cut into 1-inch-wide wedges

1 tablespoon fish sauce

2 tablespoons oyster sauce

2 tablespoons thin soy sauce

2 tablespoons sweet dark soy sauce

2 teaspoons packed grated palm sugar, or 1 teaspoon packed light or brown sugar

1 fresh large red or green Thai long chile, cut lengthwise on the diagonal into ¼-inch-wide strips

1 Roma tomato, quartered lengthwise, then quarters halved crosswise

1 cup loosely packed fresh holy basil leaves

In a mortar or a mini chopper, combine the bird's eye chiles, garlic, and shallot and grind to a fine paste. Set aside.

If the noodles are in sheet form, rather than precut, cut them lengthwise into 1-inch-wide strips and separate the layers into singles. Cut the chicken against the grain and on the diagonal into thin, bite-size pieces.

continued

Heat the oil in a wok or a 14-inch skillet set over medium-high heat. When the oil is hot, add the prepared paste and stir until fragrant and slightly thickened, about 1 minute. Turn up the heat to high, add the onion wedges and let them brown on the underside, undisturbed, for 2 minutes. Flip them and brown the second side for 2 minutes. Add the chicken and fish sauce and stir until the chicken is cooked through, about 2 to 3 minutes.

Add the noodles, oyster sauce, thin soy sauce, sweet soy sauce, sugar, long chile, and tomato and stir to mix. Cook, stirring occasionally, until the noodles soften and the sauce is absorbed, about 5 minutes.

Remove the pan from the heat, add the basil, and stir just until wilted. Serve immediately.

บะหมี่หอยลายผัดน้ำพริกเผา

EGG NOODLES with CLAMS, CHILE JAM, and BASIL STIR-FRY

bami hoi lai phat nam phrik phao

I make this one-plate meal a lot when I entertain at the last minute. I put a large platter of warm, springy egg noodles with an abundance of clams on top in the middle of the dinner table and my guests typically think that I spent hours in the kitchen before they arrived. Nothing could be further from the truth. The egg noodles are store-bought. The clams do not need to be sliced, chopped, marinated, tenderized, or anything. The complex, full-flavored sauce forms itself once the delicious juice of the clams and my hero, chile jam, meet. Indeed, this dish can be made from start to finish in less than a half hour. **SERVES 4**

3 tablespoons vegetable oil

4 pounds small clams, cleaned

2 large cloves garlic, minced

¼ cup chile jam, homemade (page 184) or store-bought

2 fresh Thai long chiles, slivered lengthwise

1 tablespoon fish sauce

1 cup packed fresh Thai sweet basil or regular sweet basil leaves

12 ounces fresh egg noodles

Fill a 4-quart saucepan three fourths full of water and bring to a boil over high heat.

While waiting for the water to boil, make the stir-fry. Pick through the clams and discard any that fail to close to the touch. Heat 2 tablespoons oil in a large wok or a 14-inch skillet over high heat. When the oil is hot, add the garlic and fry until lightly browned and fragrant, about 1 minute. Add the chile jam and stir for 30 seconds to loosen the jam. Add the clams, chiles, and fish sauce, cover, and let the clams cook for 5 minutes. (If you do not have a lid for the pan, use a large heatproof plate or bowl or tent with aluminum foil.)

Remove the pan from the heat, uncover, and pick out and discard any clams that failed to open. Taste for seasoning and add more fish sauce if needed. Add the basil and stir briefly just to wilt the leaves in the residual heat in the pan; keep warm. When the water boils, unravel the egg noodles, add them to the boiling water, and cook until the noodles are softened but still have a slight bite, about 2 to 3 minutes. Drain the noodles, shaking off the excess water, and then toss them with the remaining 1 tablespoon of the oil to keep them from sticking together. Divide the noodles evenly among 4 individual serving plates or put them all on a single large platter. Spoon the stir-fry over the noodles and serve immediately.

ข้าวคลุกกะปิ
SHRIMP PASTE RICE
khao khluk kapi

Ruam kan rao yu yaek mu rao tai is a popular Thai saying that translates to "Together we live, separate we die." Although the original idea behind it has nothing to do with food and everything to do with how being part of a group ensures survival and being isolated leads to ruin, the saying very much applies here.

In isolation, each member of this dish is deficient, wanting, fragmentary—a lone piece of a culinary jigsaw puzzle looking for its rightful spot in the big picture. None of them does well on its own. The rice is funky and salty. The pork is rich and cloying. The raw long beans are crunchy but tasteless. The green mango is so tart that it makes you squint. But when you put all of these components together, you get one harmonious bite after another of salty, sweet, sour, pungent, and spicy—in other words, you get a cohesive group.

So, even though the ingredients list is long, every item is needed for this dish to succeed. Some of them, such as the dried shrimp and the shrimp paste, will require a trip to an Asian market or online shopping, so plan ahead. This dish is definitely worth the extra effort. **SERVES 4**

½ cup meaty dried shrimp

½ cup boiling water

3 large shallots, 1 ounce each

2 large cloves garlic

½ teaspoon ground white pepper

1 cilantro root, or 1 tablespoon finely chopped cilantro stems

½ cup vegetable oil

2 eggs, lightly beaten

⅓ cup packed grated palm sugar, or ¼ cup packed light or dark brown sugar

2 tablespoons packed dark brown sugar

1 tablespoon fish sauce

¼ cup water or sodium-free chicken or vegetable stock, homemade (page 178) or store-bought

8 ounces boneless pork shoulder, cut into ½-inch pieces

2 tablespoons packed shrimp paste

4 cups cold cooked long-grain rice (page 168)

4 ounces long beans or green beans

4 fresh red or green Thai bird's eye chiles

8 ounces green tart mango or Granny Smith apple

¼ cup fresh cilantro leaves, for garnish

2 limes, halved lengthwise, cored, and seeded

Fish sauce, for serving

In a small heatproof bowl, combine the dried shrimp and boiling water and set aside.

Coarsely chop 1 shallot and put it a mortar or mini chopper along with the garlic, white pepper, and cilantro root. Grind to a fine paste and set aside.

Set a 14-inch skillet (preferably nonstick) over medium-low heat and add 1 tablespoon of the oil, coating the bottom of the pan. When the oil is hot, pour in the eggs and swirl the pan in a circular motion so the eggs form a thin sheet that covers the pan bottom. When the bottom of the egg sheet is set, after about 1 to 2 minutes, flip the sheet over

continued

with a heatproof rubber spatula and cook the second side for 20 seconds. Slide the egg sheet out of the skillet onto a chopping board and let cool. Roll up the sheet tightly like a scroll, then cut it crosswise into ¼-inch-thick slices. Unravel the egg strips and set aside.

Add ¼ cup of the oil to a wok (preferred) or skillet and place over medium heat. Line a small plate with paper towels and place it next to the stove. Drain the soaked shrimp and squeeze out every bit of moisture. Gently drop the shrimp into the hot oil and fry them, stirring constantly, until browned and crispy, about 1 to 2 minutes. Using a slotted spoon, transfer them to the towel-lined plate; set aside.

Discard the oil in the pan and wipe the pan with a paper towel. Add 1½ tablespoons of oil to the pan and place over medium-high heat. When the oil is hot, add the prepared paste and stir until fragrant, about 1 minute. Add the palm sugar, dark brown sugar, fish sauce, and water and stir until the sugars have dissolved. Add the pork and cook, stirring, for 10 to 12 minutes, until the pork is just cooked through and the sauce has evaporated, thickened, turned the color of dark maple syrup, and formed a glossy coating on the pork. Remove the pan from the heat and transfer the pork to a bowl.

Place the pan over medium heat. Grab a wet paper towel with a pair of tongs and wipe the sticky sauce off the surface of the pan. Add the remaining 1½ tablespoons oil and the shrimp paste to the pan and begin frying, breaking up the shrimp paste with the spatula as you go. Once the shrimp has disintegrated, add the rice to the pan and do your best to mix the two together as thoroughly as possible. When the rice is heated through, remove the pan from the heat and cover to keep it from drying out.

Now prepare the raw components of the dish. Slice the beans crosswise ¼ inch thick. Thinly slice the remaining 2 shallots lengthwise. Thinly slice the chiles crosswise. If using the mango, peel it and grate with a hand grater into thin strips about 3 inches long (see box on page 35). If using the apple, there is no need to peel it. Halve and core it, then place each half cut side down and cut into slices ¼ inch thick. Stack 3 or 4 slices and cut lengthwise into ¼-inch-wide matchsticks. Repeat until all of the apple slices are in matchsticks.

Divide the fried rice into 4 equal portions. Pack a portion tightly into an 8-ounce bowl, and unmold onto an individual serving plate. Repeat with the remaining 3 portions. Divide the beans, shallots, chiles, mango or apple, egg strips, and fried shrimp into 4 equal portions, and arrange a portion of each ingredient around each portion of rice. Sprinkle one-fourth of the cilantro over each portion of rice, place a lime half on each plate, and serve. Pass the fish sauce at the table. Instruct diners to mix all of the components together and to squeeze the lime into the dish, as if they are tossing a composed salad, before eating.

ข้าวต้มกุ้ง

RICE SOUP with SHRIMP

khao tom kung

Depending on how you look at it, the list of so-called Thai breakfast dishes is either infinitely long, nonexistent, or very short. The list is infinitely long because *anything* can be, and is routinely, eaten for breakfast. But because no dishes are exclusively designated as the first meal of the day, no list exists. In Bangkok, dishes such as rich, hearty stewed pork leg on rice (*khao kha mu*) and clear soup of pig's blood cake with all manner of offal (*tom lueat mu*), which you might be inclined to regard as dinner, are available morning, noon, and night. Fish green curry on rice or noodles first thing in the morning? Hungry office workers on their way to work regularly "break their fast" with that dish or a similar one. And when breakfast is eaten at home, it usually consists of whatever is left from the day before.

At the same time, there is a very short list of popular breakfast items, such as Chinese-style warm soy milk (*nam tao-hu*) and crullers (*pa-thongko*), mini coconut-rice pudding cakes (*kha-nom khrok*), Chinese-style rice congee (*jok*), and rice in clear broth (*khao tom*). Of course, these dishes are also available and consumed any time of day and night at food shops and street carts, which brings us back to the fact that no dish is exclusively a breakfast dish in Thailand.

But if pressed to nominate a single candidate as the iconic Thai breakfast dish, I would name this rice soup, which is served at street carts and on most hotel breakfast buffets, where it is the Thai option to scrambled eggs, sausages, fruit salad, and pancakes. **SERVES 4**

8 cups sodium-free chicken stock, homemade (page 178) or store-bought

1 pound large shrimp in the shell, peeled and deveined

2 tablespoons fish sauce

2 tablespoons thin soy sauce

3 cups cooked long-grain white rice (page 168), kept warm

2 tablespoons preserved cabbage (optional)

½ cup finely chopped Chinese or regular celery leaves

1 green onion, white and green parts, thinly sliced crosswise

2 tablespoons coarsely chopped fresh cilantro leaves

2 tablespoons fried garlic (page 185)

Ground white pepper

Table Seasonings (optional)

Fish sauce

Vinegar with pickled chiles (page 192)

Red chile powder (page 181)

In a 2-quart saucepan, bring the stock to a boil over high heat. Turn down the heat to medium-low so the liquid bubbles very gently. Add the shrimp, fish sauce, and soy sauce to the simmering stock, stir, and cook for about 2 minutes, until the shrimp are cooked. Remove from the heat.

Divide the warm rice among 4 individual serving bowls that can hold up to 4 cups comfortably. Divide the cabbage, celery leaves, green onion, and cilantro evenly among the bowls. Ladle the broth and the shrimp evenly over the rice and aromatics. Top each bowl with 1½ teaspoons fried garlic, dust with the pepper, and serve immediately. Pass the seasonings at the table for adding as desired.

CHICKEN, WATER MORNING GLORY, and SATAY SAUCE on RICE

khao phra ram long song

I do not know which of the many aliases this dish used when it first introduced itself to you: Rama, Bathing Rama, Swimming Rama, Phra Ram, and more. All of these are literal or partial translations of its Thai name pointing to Rama, the main character in the *Ramayana*, the Indian epic that has had great influence on Thai language, literature, and art. From what I can gather, the name comes from the fact that Rama is typically depicted as having a green complexion. And the act of blanching the green Chinese water morning glory, an essential step in this dish, apparently conjures up an image of the green deity incarnate bathing.

Chinese water morning glory is a tropical green vegetable with sword-shaped leaves and hollow stems. It is available at most Asian grocery stores, where it is often labled *ong choy*. If you cannot find Chinese water morning glory, broccoli can be substituted. **SERVES 4**

---

1 pound boneless, skinless chicken breasts

2 teaspoons salt

2 teaspoons baking soda

1 pound Chinese water morning glory, or 12 ounces broccoli florets

4 cups cooked long-grain white rice (page 168), kept warm

About 2 cups satay sauce (page 188), warmed

¼ cup chile jam (page 184; optional)

2 fresh Thai long chiles, thinly sliced crosswise (optional)

Cut the chicken against the grain and on the diagonal into thin, bite-size slices. Put the chicken in a bowl, sprinkle the salt and baking soda over the top, and mix well (this is best done with your hands). Cover and refrigerate while you ready the other ingredients.

Half fill an 8-quart pot with water and bring the water to a boil over high heat. While the water is heating, if using water morning glory, trim off and discard the bottom one-third of each stem, which is too tough to eat. Cut the remainder of each stalk into 2-inch lengths. If using broccoli, cut into bite-size pieces.

When the water is boiling hard, lower the morning glory into it, stir, and cook for 30 seconds. Then, using a wire-mesh skimmer or a slotted spoon, lift it out of the water, shaking off the excess water, and set aside on a plate. If using broccoli, blanch it the same way until tender but still slightly crisp, about 1 to 2 minutes. Turn down the heat so the water is barely bubbling. Add the chicken and stir gently until it turns white and is opaque throughout, about 1 minute. Using the skimmer or slotted spoon, lift out the chicken, shaking off the excess water, and transfer to a second plate.

Divide the rice evenly among 4 individual serving plates. Place the blanched greens on the rice, then layer the chicken over the greens. Spoon the satay sauce evenly over the chicken. Top each serving with a dollop of chile jam and a few chile slices and serve immediately.

โจ๊กหมูใส่ไข่

RICE CONGEE with PORK DUMPLINGS and EGGS

jok mu sai khai

When I sit down to enjoy a bowl of this silky, comforting congee (a rice porridge of sorts), whether at home or in the narrow alleyway that is home to my favorite congee shop in Bangkok, my brain inevitably plays the old tune "I Started a Joke."

Let me explain why. My childhood was spent around adults who blossomed and peaked during the disco era, who knew everything about the Bee Gees, Marvin Gaye, ABBA, and their bell-bottoms-clad, chest-hair-baring contemporaries. One of my aunts could do a perfect lip sync of Donna Summer. When his wife called him, one uncle always answered the phone in Barry White's voice. My maternal grandmother, who peaked long before disco came along, was once spotted in the kitchen doing the hustle while making fried rice.

So when I was a kid and an uncle told me that one of the Bee Gees had written a song about rice congee, I was interested right away. I went and listened, and sure enough, the word for rice congee, *jok* (pronounced "joke"), came up repeatedly. Not knowing much English, I thought it was cool that a band like the Bee Gees would be singing about my favorite breakfast. And it was not until years later that I realized my impish uncle was, well, joking.

The pork dumplings should have the texture of sausage meat, that is, tender yet with some resistance when you bite into them—think Asian fish balls but a bit more substantial. In other words, this preparation is called *mu deng*—literally "bouncy pork"—for a good reason. The eggs are served partially cooked, so if you are concerned about the safety of raw eggs and your diners include members of a high-risk group (the elderly, the very young, pregnant women, or anyone with an impaired immune system), use pasteurized eggs or leave the eggs out. If you are sensitive to the heat of ginger, rinse the julienned ginger in cold water three or four times until the water runs clear and squeeze it dry before using. **SERVES 4**

Pork Dumplings

2 large cloves garlic

2 cilantro roots, or 2 tablespoons finely chopped cilantro stems

½ teaspoon white peppercorns

1 pound ground pork

1 tablespoon oyster sauce

1 teaspoon thin soy sauce

1 tablespoon tapioca flour or cornstarch

Congee

2 cups cooked long-grain white rice (page 168)

6 cups sodium-free chicken stock, homemade (page 178) or store-bought

½ cup tapioca starch or glutinous rice flour

1 cup water

4 eggs

Ground white pepper, for dusting

2-inch piece fresh ginger, peeled and julienned

1 green onion, white and green parts, finely chopped

¼ cup loosely packed fresh cilantro leaves

Table Seasonings

Fish sauce

Red chile powder (page 181)

Vinegar with pickled chiles (page 192)

To make the dumplings mixture, in a food processor, combine all of the ingredients and process until smooth and sticky (the consistency of whipped cream cheese). Transfer to a bowl, cover, and refrigerate.

To make the congee, in a blender, combine the rice and stock and blend to a coarse puree (the consistency of cooked steel-cut oatmeal). Pour the puree into a 1-gallon saucepan, place over medium-high heat, and bring to a gentle boil, stirring occasionally to keep the bottom from scorching. Meanwhile, whisk together the tapioca flour and water until homogenous. Drizzle the flour mixture into the gently boiling rice mixture with one hand while stirring with the other hand. Let the congee boil gently, stirring occasionally to prevent scorching, for 2 to 3 minutes, until nicely thickened. Adjust the heat so the congee bubbles gently.

Remove the dumpling mixture from the refrigerator. Using 2 teaspoons, form the dumpling mixture into balls about ½ inch in diameter, dropping them, one at a time, into the gently bubbling congee. When all of the dumplings have firmed up and turned opaque, after about 2 to 3 minutes, the congee is ready.

To serve, ladle half of the hot congee into 4 large individual serving bowls, dividing it evenly. Crack 1 egg into each bowl. Ladle the remaining hot congee over the eggs to bury them. Dust each serving with the pepper and sprinkle with the ginger, green onion, and cilantro. Serve immediately, accompanied with the table seasonings to add as desired. Each diner breaks the now half-coddled egg and eats it along with the congee.

ข้าวไก่กระเทียม

CHICKEN and FRIED GARLIC on RICE

khao kai kra-thiam

There is not any one-plate meal that I have made more often than this one. So easy. So good. So comforting. So inexpensive. You can use any quick-cooking meat you want, including seafood such as shrimp or squid. **SERVES 4**

1½ pounds boneless, skinless chicken breasts or thighs

3 tablespoons vegetable oil

2 tablespoons thin soy sauce

2 tablespoons oyster sauce

¼ teaspoon granulated sugar

1 teaspoon ground white pepper

4 cups cooked long-grain white rice (page 168), kept warm

½ English cucumber, or 2 pickling cucumbers, peeled and sliced crosswise ¼ inch thick

1 Roma tomato, sliced crosswise ¼ inch thick

¼ cup fried garlic (page 185)

Fresh cilantro leaves, for garnish

Chile fish sauce (page 193), for serving

Cut the chicken against the grain and on the diagonal into thin, bite-size pieces.

Heat the oil in a wok or a 14-inch skillet over high heat. When the oil is hot, add the chicken and stir-fry until it begins to turn opaque but is not yet cooked through, about 1 minute. Add the soy sauce, oyster sauce, sugar, and pepper; turn down the heat to medium-high and continue to stir-fry until the chicken is cooked through and is coated with the glistening sauce, about 2 to 3 minutes. Remove the pan from the heat.

Divide the rice evenly among 4 individual serving plates and spoon the chicken over the rice. Arrange the cucumber and tomato slices on the side of each plate. Sprinkle the garlic over the chicken, garnish with the cilantro, and serve immediately. Pass the chile fish sauce at the table.

ข้าวผัดไก่
FRIED RICE with CHICKEN
khao phat kai

This is the street-food fried rice of my childhood, which does not seem to be made much anymore—at least not this way. If you look at the ingredients, you may not see what is special about this dish. But make a batch, squeeze a wedge of lime over it, and serve it with chile fish sauce (page 193) and you will understand why this recipe needs to be here. If you cannot find the Chinese broccoli, just omit it, as there is no substitute for it in this recipe. **SERVES 4**

8 ounces boneless, skinless chicken breasts

4 ounces Chinese broccoli

2 tablespoons vegetable oil

2 large cloves garlic, minced

1 yellow or white onion, about 6 ounces, cut into ½-inch-wide wedges

1 Roma tomato, about 6 ounces, cut into ½-inch-wide wedges

2 tablespoons vegetable oil

3½ cups cold cooked long-grain white rice (page 168)

2 tablespoons dark sweet soy sauce

2 tablespoons thin soy sauce

1 tablespoon fish sauce

2 eggs

Ground white pepper, for dusting

2 limes, cut into wedges

Chile fish sauce (page 193)

½ English cucumber, or 2 pickling cucumbers, peeled and thinly sliced crosswise

Cut the chicken against the grain and on the diagonal into thin, bite-size slices. Set aside.

Trim about 1 inch off the bottom of each stalk end of Chinese broccoli. Cut each stalk on the diagonal into slices about ½ inch thick and 2 inches long. Cut the green leafy parts crosswise into 2-inch pieces. Keep the stalks and leafy parts separate.

Heat the oil in a wok or a 14-inch skillet over high heat. When the oil is hot, add the garlic and fry for about 30 seconds, until fragrant. Add the onion wedges and let them brown on the underside, undisturbed, for 1 minute. Flip them and let brown on the second side for 1 minute. Add the chicken, tomatoes, and the stalk pieces of the Chinese broccoli and stir-fry for 3 to 4 minutes, until the chicken is cooked through.

Add the rice, sweet soy sauce, thin soy sauce, and fish sauce and stir-fry to distribute the sauces evenly and heat the rice. Make a well in the center of the rice mixture all the way to the bottom of the wok and crack the eggs into the well. Lightly scramble the eggs with the tip of the spatula, then let them cook undisturbed for about 1 minute, until they brown on one side. Add the leafy parts of the Chinese broccoli and stir-fry everything together until they are evenly distributed and the Chinese broccoli has wilted, about 1 minute. Remove the pan from the heat.

Transfer the rice to a serving platter or individual serving plates. Dust with the pepper and serve with the lime wedges, chile fish sauce, and cucumber.

ข้าวหน้าไก่

CHICKEN in BROWN SAUCE on RICE

khao na kai

During my first year in the United States, I made *khao na kai* four or five times a week. I did not have much cooking equipment, and I lived on a food budget that was, as I found out later, smaller than my landlord's for his golden retriever. This simple and inexpensive one-plate meal saw me through those days; occasionally, there was even enough to share with others. Some of my American classmates who ate my *khao na kai* during that time became close friends, and later they made trips to Bangkok with me to eat at all of my favorite *khao na kai* restaurants.

For this dish, you can use 1½ pounds boneless, skinless chicken breasts or thighs, though I have found that combining the two makes the best dish. Marinate the chicken before you leave home for work in the morning. When you get back, dinner is just ten minutes away. **SERVES 4**

12 ounces boneless, skinless chicken breasts, cut into ¾-inch dice

12 ounces boneless, skinless chicken thighs, cut into ¾-inch dice

¼ cup thin soy sauce

½ tablespoon dark sweet soy sauce

¼ cup oyster sauce

3 tablespoons cornstarch or tapioca starch

2 teaspoons toasted sesame oil

2 tablespoons vegetable oil

1 teaspoon ground white pepper

2 tablespoons Chinese rice wine (Shaoxing) or sherry (optional)

2 cups sodium-free chicken stock, homemade (page 178) or store-bought

4 cups cooked long-grain rice (page 168), kept warm

¾ cup loosely packed fresh cilantro leaves

2 fresh green Thai long chiles, thinly sliced crosswise

4 crispy fried eggs (page 194; optional)

In a bowl, combine the chicken, thin soy sauce, sweet soy sauce, oyster sauce, cornstarch, sesame oil, vegetable oil, pepper, and wine and mix well. Cover and refrigerate for 8 to 10 hours.

Pour the stock into a wok or a 14-inch skillet and place over high heat. When the stock starts to bubble around the edges, add the chicken and stir. Continue to cook, stirring constantly, until the chicken is cooked through and the sauce has thickened, about 3 to 5 minutes. Just before the chicken is ready, check on the thickness of the sauce. If it is too thick, add water as needed to thin to a good gravy consistency.

Divide the rice evenly among 4 individual serving plates. Ladle the chicken gravy evenly over the rice. Garnish with the cilantro and chiles and top each serving with a fried egg. Serve immediately.

ข้าวราดผัดกะเพราไก่ไข่ดาว

SPICY BASIL CHICKEN and FRIED EGGS on RICE

khao rat phat ka-phrao kai khai dao

In theory, you can separate out just the stir-fry component of this one-plate ensemble and include it as part of a family meal (*samrap*). In practice, though, Thais seem to prefer serving the spicy basil chicken on top of rice with a crispy fried egg. This version is the one I grew up eating. It is the simplest and, in my opinion, the best.

This dish requires not just any fresh basil, but holy basil (*ka-phrao*). If you can find this variety, with its fuzzy leaves and stems and peppery flavor, I encourage you to use it. But if it is nowhere to be found, Thai sweet basil or even regular sweet basil can be substituted, in which case, replace the *ka phrao* part in the title with *hora-pha*. **SERVES 4 • PICTURED ON PAGE 118**

8 large cloves garlic	2 tablespoons thin soy sauce
5 or 6 fresh bird's eye chiles	1 tablespoon dark sweet soy sauce
1 large shallot, about 1 ounce, quartered	1 tablespoon oyster sauce
¾ to 1 cup vegetable oil	1 cup packed fresh holy basil leaves
4 eggs	4 cups cooked long-grain rice (page 168), kept warm, for serving
1½ pounds ground chicken (beef, pork, or turkey will do as well)	Chile fish sauce (page 193; optional), for serving
2 tablespoons fish sauce	

In a mortar or a mini chopper, combine the garlic, chiles, and shallot and grind to a coarse paste. Alternatively, mince them on a cutting board with a large knife.

Heat ¾ cup of oil in a wok or a 14-inch skillet over medium-high heat. Fry the eggs, one at a time, as directed on page 194, replenishing the oil as necessary to achieve fried eggs with crispy bottoms and edges. Transfer the eggs to a plate and set aside.

Discard all but 2 tablespoons oil from the pan and return the pan to medium-high heat. When the oil is hot, add the prepared paste and stir for about 30 seconds, until fragrant. Add the chicken and break it up with the spatula into small pieces. Add the fish sauce, thin soy sauce, sweet soy sauce, and oyster sauce and cook, stirring constantly, until the chicken is cooked through, about 2 to 3 minutes. Check the amount of liquid in the skillet; there should be about ¾ cup of it. If it is too dry, add a little water or sodium-free stock.

Remove the pan from the heat, add the basil, and stir briefly to wilt it in the residual heat in the pan. Divide the rice evenly among 4 individual serving plates, and spoon the stir-fry over the rice. Put 1 fried egg on each plate and serve immediately, accompanied with the chile fish sauce.

No-Bake Almond
Cookies (Golden
Supreme), page 152

ของหวาน

SWEETS

khong wan

The Thai people do not have strict rules about when sweets should be consumed. Just as they do not eat their meals in individual courses, they do not insist that every meal be followed by dessert, or even that desserts must be eaten after meals. In fact, the most common postmeal offering is fresh fruit or other light fare, such as fruit in iced syrup. That means that sweets can be enjoyed after meals or as between-meal snacks—or really whenever you feel like a sweet bite.

ขนมโสมนัส

TOASTED-COCONUT MERINGUE COOKIES

khanom sommanat

Meringue cookies? Thai food? Yes, they are. In fact, you will find many items in the Thai repertoire of sweets that have been influenced by the West.

Sommanat is an archaic and poetic word for "joy" or "gladness." What a beautiful, charm-
ing name. When my maternal grandmother was alive, she used to pack a big jar with these
meringue kisses and send off the jar to friends who lived far away. She would always enclose a
note explaining that the jar contained much joy—the joy that the friends brought into her life
even in their absence and what she hoped their lives would always be filled with. Grandma was
a romantic like that. **MAKES ABOUT 5 DOZEN SMALL COOKIES**

1½ cups unsweetened dried coconut flakes

2 egg whites

1 tablespoon packed light or dark brown sugar

⅓ cup granulated sugar

¼ teaspoon salt

¼ teaspoon cream of tartar, or ½ teaspoon
freshly squeezed lime or lemon juice

Put the coconut in a 14-inch skillet set over medium heat. Stir the coconut constantly
until it is thoroughly golden brown and has developed a "nutty" smell. This should take
about 10 minutes. Do not take your eyes off the pan even for a moment, as the coconut
can burn easily and quickly. Use gentle heat, take your time, and stir constantly to
prevent uneven browning. If you burn some of the coconut, throw out the entire batch
and start over. That burnt smell will end up ruining the cookies. When the coconut
is done, immediately transfer it to a plate (if it remains in the pan, it will continue to
darken) and place the plate in the freezer while you work on the meringue.

Position 1 oven rack in the middle of the oven and a second rack in the lower third
and preheat the oven to 300°F. Line 2 large baking sheets with parchment paper or
silicone mats.

Before you begin beating the egg whites, make sure that they are not contaminated by
even a speck of yolk; that the beaters of your electric mixer, the bowl, and the rubber
spatula you will be using are completely free of grease; and that the coconut does not
come in contact with the whites. The presence of any fat will prevent the whites from
forming stiff peaks. Put the whites in the bowl and beat with the mixer on medium
speed just until the whites are frothy. Add the brown sugar and half of the granulated
sugar, increase the speed of the mixer to high, and beat for 1 minute longer. Scrape
the bowl with the rubber spatula, making sure you get to the very bottom, where the
mixture often escapes the beaters (especially if you use a stand mixer). Any under-
beaten bits will cause the cookies to become misshapen in the oven. Add the remaining granulated sugar, the salt, and the cream of tartar, and continue to beat on high,
stopping to check the consistency every minute, until the mixture forms stiff peaks.

It is important that you beat the egg white mixture until the peaks do not droop when you lift the beaters straight up. This ensures that the cookies will hold their shape in the oven, rather than melting into puddles.

Remove the toasted coconut from the freezer. By this time, it should be at, or a bit lower than, room temperature. Using the rubber spatula, fold the coconut into the meringue by running the spatula around the side and along the bottom of the bowl and folding the mixture over onto itself until the coconut is thoroughly and evenly incorporated. Work gently so as not to deflate the egg whites.

Drop the meringue mixture by the rounded teaspoon onto the prepared baking sheets (this can be done more easily with 2 teaspoons, one for scooping the batter and the other for scraping it from the first spoon onto the baking sheets), spacing the cookies about 1 inch apart. Bake the cookies, switching the baking sheets between the racks and rotating each sheet front to back halfway through the baking, until they are firm and completely dry, about 40 minutes. Turn off the oven and leave the cookies in the oven to cool off and continue to dry for at least 3 to 4 hours or up to overnight.

The cooled cookies will keep in an airtight container at room temperature for up to 1 week.

ขนมทองเอก

NO-BAKE ALMOND COOKIES (Golden Supreme)

khanom thong ek

Because its name is propitious and its color and gold leaf decoration are evocative of prosperity, *khanom thong ek* (literally "golden supreme") is usually served on auspicious occasions, such as the New Year's celebration. The most common version of these rich, no-bake cookies calls for flour instead of almond meal. The dough is pressed into a small mold with a flower design, unmolded, and then, before serving, it is perfumed with the smoke of *tian op*, a Thai scented candle that is used only for scenting foods.

I prefer this version, which uses blanched almond meal instead of flour, thereby fastening the tie between this old Thai dessert and its European roots more tightly.

To form these cookies the traditional way, you will need plastic or wooden tray molds or a pan of flower-shaped individual molds measuring 2 inches across and about ½ inch deep. Failing those two options, I have provided an alternative method in the note at the end of the recipe. Thais like to present these special cookies with a tiny piece of edible gold leaf on top of each one, but you can skip that flourish if you like. **MAKES 16 PIECES • PICTURED ON PAGE 148**

¾ cup coconut milk

1 cup granulated sugar

6 egg yolks

1½ cups blanched almond meal, plus more for dusting the molds

¼ teaspoon salt

1 teaspoon jasmine, coconut, or vanilla extract

About ¼ cup cornstarch, for dusting

Edible gold leaf, for decorating (optional)

In a heavy 14-inch skillet, whisk together the coconut milk, sugar, egg yolks, almond meal, salt, and jasmine extract until smooth. Set the skillet over medium-high heat and stir constantly with a heatproof rubber spatula until a soft, sticky dough forms, about 20 minutes. The dough is ready when its surface is somewhat glossy and it leaves a thin, cloudy film on the bottom of the skillet (this will not happen if you use a nonstick skillet!).

Transfer the dough to a bowl and cover with plastic wrap, pressing the plastic wrap directly onto the surface of the dough. Chill the dough until it cools to room temperature.

Line a work surface with a clean kitchen towel. Lightly dust the molds (see headnote) with cornstarch. Take a piece of the dough, form it into a 2-inch ball, and press it into a prepared mold. Unmold the cookie by tapping the mold onto a towel-lined work surface. Repeat the process until no dough remains. Top each cookie with a tiny piece of gold leaf.

The cookies will keep in an airtight container at room temperature for up to 3 days, in the refrigerator for up to 2 weeks, or in the freezer for up to 2 months.

Note: If you do not have the appropriate molds for shaping these cookies, line the bottom and the sides of an 8-inch square baking pan with waxed paper, dust the paper with some cornstarch, press the dough into the lined pan, and then cut it into 16 squares with the tip of a knife moistened with warm water.

แป้งจี่กล้วย

CHEWY BANANA-COCONUT GRIDDLE CAKES

paeng ji kluai

This is what my maternal grandmother, who never let anything go to waste, would make whenever we had overripe Burro bananas (*kluai nam wa*)—shorter and flatter but just as tasty as the common Cavendish variety—and grated coconut meat (after the milk had been extracted from it) on hand. When she made the pancakes silver-dollar size, we usually ate them as a sweet snack. But sometimes Grandma would make them larger, 3 to 4 inches in diameter, and serve them on a plate with honey (infused with fresh jasmine flowers) drizzled on top. Then we would eat them as dessert with hot jasmine tea. **MAKES ABOUT 20 CAKES**

1 cup mashed overripe banana (from 3 medium bananas)

1 cup unsweetened dried coconut flakes

½ cup glutinous rice flour

2 tablespoons granulated sugar

2 tablespoons packed light brown sugar

⅛ teaspoon salt

Vegetable or coconut oil, for cooking

In a bowl, whisk together the banana, coconut, flour, granulated and brown sugars, and salt until a thick, sticky batter forms. Let the batter rest, uncovered and at room temperature, for 15 minutes to soften up the coconut.

Lightly grease a pancake griddle or a nonstick skillet with oil and set over medium heat. When the pan is hot, drop the batter by the tablespoonful onto the surface, spacing the spoonfuls at least 1 inch apart. With a moistened heatproof rubber spatula, press down on each mound of batter to form a round 2 inches in diameter. When the cakes turn medium brown on the underside, after about 1 to 2 minutes, flip them over and cook on the second side until the cakes are browned on both sides and firm in the center, about 2 minutes longer. Transfer the cakes to a plate and cover them loosely with a clean kitchen towel. Repeat until all of the batter has been used, greasing the pan as needed to prevent sticking.

Let the cakes cool to slightly warmer than room temperature before serving.

COCONUT ICE CREAM with JACKFRUIT

ai-sa-khrim kati sai khanun

This recipe came out of the dogged attempt by one of my aunts to re-create at home the coconut ice cream sold at our family's favorite ice cream shop. I do not think it tastes like what she was trying to replicate. It tastes better. The members of our clan made this recipe for many years after my mother and her siblings pooled their money to buy an old-fashioned hand-crank wooden barrel ice cream maker. After years of faithful service, that wonderful ice cream maker breathed its last breath sometime during the Clinton administration. But the recipe—which appears here—is still very much alive.

The texture of this light, eggless ice cream is almost like gelato, that is, smooth, dense, and soft, rather than rich and creamy like a custard-based ice cream. It takes a bit longer to set, but the result is well worth the extra time. I have mixed in bits of jackfruit, a tropical fruit with sweet yellow flesh, for extra color and flavor, but this coconut ice cream is delicious without any add-ins. If you like, you might sprinkle a few roasted peanuts on top of each serving. My grandfather loved it topped with canned creamed corn, which was a de rigueur ice cream topping in Thailand in the 1970s. You can try that, too—or not. If you want a true Thai ice cream experience, serve the ice cream on a soft, split jumbo-size hot dog bun, which is how all of the ice cream carts in Bangkok serve their flavors. **MAKES ABOUT 1 QUART**

3 cups coconut milk (absolutely not the reduced-fat type)

2 teaspoons unflavored gelatin powder

2 tablespoons cornstarch

1 cup nonfat dry milk powder

¾ cup granulated sugar

⅛ teaspoon salt

¾ cup ¼-inch-diced fresh, frozen, or canned well-drained jackfruit (optional)

Have ready an ice bath. Pour the coconut milk into a 2-quart saucepan. Sprinkle the gelatin on top and let sit for 2 minutes. Whisk in the cornstarch and milk powder, making sure there are no lumps. Whisk in the sugar and salt. Put the pan over medium heat and whisk constantly just until all of the solids dissolve; there is no need to boil the mixture. Remove the pan from the heat and nest it in the ice bath. Let the mixture cool completely.

Transfer the cooled coconut mixture to an ice cream maker and churn according to the manufacturer's instructions. Fold in the jackfruit during the final stage of churning. Transfer the ice cream to an airtight container and place in the freezer for 5 to 8 hours, until set. The ice cream will keep for up to 1 week.

กล้วยบวชชี

BANANAS in SWEET COCONUT CREAM
(Bananas in Nunhood)

kluai buat chi

You cannot invoke the name of this dish, literally "bananas in nunhood," without feeling the sense of peace and simplicity associated with both the religious calling and this ultimate comfort dessert. Creamy, sweet, simple ingredients, simple procedure—nobody can glamorize it even if they try. And there is no reason to try.

According to the Theravada school of Buddhism in Thailand, when a woman enters the nunhood, she shaves her head and eyebrows, puts on a white robe, and lives in a temple. When you see the off-white Burro bananas, the cultivar most commonly used in this dessert (shorter and more rotund than the common Cavendish type and available at some large Asian markets), enrobed in white coconut cream, you understand how this dessert got its name. **SERVES 4**

8 semiripe Burro bananas, or 4 semiripe regular bananas

1 cup coconut milk

1 cup water

½ cup granulated sugar

¼ teaspoon salt

Peel the bananas, halve them lengthwise, and cut each half crosswise into 2-inch pieces.

In a saucepan, combine the bananas, coconut milk, water, ¼ cup of the sugar, and salt and bring to a boil over medium-high heat, stirring occasionally. Immediately lower the heat to a simmer and cook until the bananas have softened but still retain their shape, about 2 to 3 minutes. Remove the pan from the heat. Taste to see if it needs more sugar. If so, add as much of the remaining ¼ cup of sugar as needed and stir gently just until the sugar dissolves.

The bananas taste best when served slightly warm, but they are also great at room temperature or chilled.

สับปะรดลอยแก้ว
PINEAPPLE in SCENTED ICED SYRUP

sapparot loi kaeo

At a glance, this looks like something unimaginative that cooks might try to pass off as a bona fide dessert. After all, it is just fruit and ice cubes swimming in syrup.

First impressions are often wrong. This Thai chilled dessert is best described by the phrase *simple elegance*. It is something you sit down properly to enjoy either at home or at a nice restaurant. It is not usually available from a street cart or even from a stall at a food court.

Loi kaeo is essentially a fruit or a mélange of fruits cooked gently in simple syrup that has been infused with one or more aromatics such as fresh jasmine. If the fruit comes with seeds or pits, care is taken to remove them without disfiguring the fruit.

As a child, I was completely enthralled as I watched my paternal grandmother deftly and swiftly insert a slim-bladed carving knife into one end of a shelled rambutan, a favorite local fruit, to remove its pit and then fill the space with a piece of pineapple. Unfortunately, some of her genes were lost in transmission, for I cannot carve anything well. That is why I have chosen pineapple for this *loi kaeo* recipe: it has no pits. **SERVES 4**

¾ cup granulated sugar	½ large pineapple (from one 4-pound pineapple), peeled, cored, and cut into 1-inch cubes
¾ cup water	
½ teaspoon salt	2 cups crushed ice
4 star anise pods	

In a 2-quart saucepan, combine the sugar, water, salt, and star anise over medium heat and bring to a boil, stirring to dissolve the sugar. Add the pineapple cubes, return the mixture to a boil, then lower the heat so the syrup is bubbling gently. Cook the pineapple, uncovered and without stirring too much, until it has softened slightly, about 2 minutes. Remove the pan from the heat and let the pineapple cool completely, uncovered. Both the pineapple and the syrup will taste too sweet at this point. But when the ice is added later, the dessert will taste just right.

Discard the star anise and divide the cooled pineapple mixture evenly among 4 individual dessert bowls, each with a capacity of about 1 cup. Top each serving with ½ cup of the ice and serve immediately. The crushed ice is stirred into the dessert as it is eaten.

ทับทิมกรอบ

CRUNCHY-CHEWY WATER CHESTNUT DUMPLINGS in ICED COCONUT SYRUP

thapthim krop

On their own, these crunchy-on-the-inside, chewy-on-the-outside little water chestnut dumplings are not something to write home about, as they are kind of bland. But when you tint them pinkish, float them in a sweet, aromatic coconut syrup, and top them with crushed ice, you have a unique dessert that is reminiscent of pomegranate seeds and is both beautiful and refreshing.

Red food coloring is typically used to dye the water chestnuts, but I have chosen to go the natural route and use beet juice. It turns the water chestnut cubes a stunning dark purplish pink without imparting the earthy beet scent to this delicate dessert. **SERVES 4 TO 6**

Coconut Syrup

1 cup granulated sugar

½ cup water

⅛ teaspoon salt

1½ cups coconut milk

½ teaspoon jasmine, coconut, or vanilla extract

Water Chestnuts

1 (4-ounce) beet, peeled and cut into small chunks

½ cup water

2 (8-ounce) cans whole water chestnuts in water, drained, rinsed, patted dry, and cut into ¼-inch cubes

¾ cup tapioca flour

3 cups crushed ice

To make the syrup, in a small saucepan, combine the sugar, water, and salt over medium-high heat and heat, stirring, just until the sugar dissolves. Remove the pan from the heat. Measure out ¼ cup of the syrup and put it in a bowl; stir the coconut milk and the jasmine extract into the syrup remaining in the pan and set aside until serving.

To prepare the water chestnuts, in a blender, combine the beet and water and puree until smooth. Strain the beet puree through a fine-mesh sieve (or a colander lined with a disposable coffee filter) placed over the bowl containing the ¼ cup syrup, then stir to mix.

Add the water chestnuts to the beet juice mixture and toss them with the liquid, making sure the water chestnuts are thoroughly coated with the liquid. Let sit for 10 to 15 minutes. Drain in a colander, shaking off the excess liquid.

Put the tapioca flour in a shallow bowl. Add the drained water chestnuts to the tapioca flour and stir with a spoon to coat all sides of every piece of water chestnut with the flour. Spread the coated water chestnuts in a single layer on a large plate. If any of the pieces stick together, separate them. Let the water chestnuts sit undisturbed for 10 minutes.

Meanwhile, fill a 2-quart saucepan half full with water and bring to a boil over high heat. Fill a large bowl with cold tap water and place the bowl next to the stove.

By the time the water boils, the coating on the water chestnut pieces should have changed from powdery and white to thick and pastel medium purple. Make sure this has taken place before you add the pieces to the boiling water or the coating will dissolve in the water.

Drop half of the water chestnuts into the boiling water and stir gently to keep them from sticking together. In less than 1 minute, the water chestnuts should float to the surface. When that happens, using a wire-mesh skimmer or a slotted spoon, transfer them to the bowl of cold water. Repeat the process with the other half of the water chestnuts.

Drain the water chestnut dumplings in the colander, then divide them evenly among 4 to 6 individual dessert bowls. Pour the coconut syrup over the dumplings and top each bowl with an equal amount of the ice. Serve immediately.

ข้าวเหนียวมะม่วง

MANGO and SWEET COCONUT STICKY RICE

khao niao mamuang

I must start this iconic recipe with some not-so-encouraging news: without the same resources that sweet coconut sticky rice (*khao niao mun*) vendors use in Thailand, it is going to take some effort to match the quality of what they sell. In Thailand, sweet sticky rice is most commonly prepared with high-quality glutinous rice from the north, where farmers are known for harvesting kernels with a beautiful glossiness and a long, slender shape (likened to snake's fangs) even when cooked until soft. Plus, the coconut cream used to steep the rice is freshly extracted. Its fat not only enriches, flavors, and perfumes the rice but also keeps the kernels shiny and slick. If you swipe your hand in one quick motion across the surface of a mound of well-prepared sweet coconut sticky rice, no thick, gooey white sauce should stick to your palm.

Alas, the pasty, gooey appearance is unavoidable when you use canned or boxed coconut milk. In my experience, even the best brands do not give you the result that would be considered high quality in Thailand—not even if you carefully scoop out only the fatty part that rises to the top of the can. The result is even worse if you mistakenly buy canned coconut milk that includes a thickener. In other words, if you want to serve *khao niao mun* that is as good as what you get in Thailand, you must extract your own coconut milk.

Let's move on to the more encouraging news: it is okay if your sticky rice is not glossy.

In an ideal world, both your sticky rice and your mango will be of high quality. But if you were magically given the choice of a good mango paired with a serving of pasty, pudding-like sticky rice or well-prepared sticky rice alongside a bland and fibrous mango, you should definitely choose the former. Respectable Thai restaurants all list mango and sticky rice as a seasonal menu item; in other words, they serve it only when mangoes are at the peak of their season. They know that the quality of the dish is largely determined by the quality of the fruit, and that mediocre sticky rice can be saved by an exceptional mango.

So, my advice to you is to make this dish only if you can get really great mangoes. If the glutinous rice is not as good as what a Thai street vendor uses and you cannot get your hands on a fresh coconut, that is okay. The dish will still be delicious. In the United States, I look for sunny yellow, oblong Ataúlfo (sometimes labeled Champagne) mangoes, and instead of buying perfectly ripe fruits, I go for ones that are roughly one to two days away from being fully ripe. Ripe mangoes are fragile and are easily bruised, so it is better to let the mangoes ripen on your kitchen counter than in a huge pile at the store. **SERVES 4**

1 cup Thai glutinous rice, soaked in water to cover for 2 hours

1½ cups coconut cream, preferably freshly extracted (see page 172)

¾ cup granulated sugar

½ teaspoon salt

2 teaspoons rice flour

4 fully ripe, sweet mangoes

Sesame seeds, for garnish (optional)

continued

Rinse the soaked rice until the water runs clear, then drain well and steam the rice using your method of choice (see page 169). Depending on the type of steamer you use, it will take from 20 to 30 minutes for the rice to be fully cooked; keep checking. When the rice is completely translucent without any opacity left inside the kernels, immediately turn off the heat and keep the rice hot in the steamer. If the rice is not nearly as soft as you think it should be when preparing it to eat with rice accompaniments, do not worry; we intentionally leave it a little bit "thirsty" so it will soak up the hot coconut syrup without becoming too soft and mushy.

In a 1-quart saucepan, combine 1 cup of the coconut cream, the sugar, and ¼ teaspoon of the salt over medium heat and bring to a boil, stirring to dissolve the sugar. Add the hot rice to the coconut syrup, mix well, and remove from the heat. Cover and let the rice steep and cool down for 40 minutes, stirring once after 20 minutes.

While the rice is steeping, put the remaining ½ cup coconut cream and the remaining ¼ teaspoon salt in a small saucepan and whisk in the rice flour. Place the pan over medium heat and whisk constantly for about 2 minutes, until the mixture comes to a gentle boil and thickens. Remove the pan from the heat and set aside to using as a topping.

Working with 1 mango at a time, use a sharp paring knife or a vegetable peeler to peel off the skin. Hold the mango horizontally with the stem pointing toward you, and hold the blade of a very sharp knife parallel with the wide surface of the pit and positioned just above the stem. Now, imagining the mango as a fish and its pit as the spine bone, "fillet" the mango using a seesawing motion, removing the flesh in a single slab. Cut the mango "fillet" crosswise into thick slices. Flip the mango over and remove the flesh from the opposite side of the pit the same way. Repeat with the remaining mangoes.

To serve, arrange 2 mango "fillets" on each of 4 individual serving plates. Divide the sticky rice evenly among the plates. Spoon the coconut cream topping on top of the rice and sprinkle with sesame seeds. Serve immediately.

สังขยาฟักทอง

PUMPKIN CUSTARD

sangkhaya fak thong

This is a much easier version of the famous Thai steamed pumpkin custard that calls for hollowing out a pumpkin, filling it with custard, steaming it whole, and then serving it in wedges. Just the fact that pumpkins come in various sizes, flesh thicknesses, and volume capacities tells you that it is impossible to hope for consistent results.

With this easy version, you get the same taste without nearly as much fuss and uncertainty. You do not even need a steamer. Baking the custard in a water bath helps you achieve the same result. When I host a Thanksgiving dinner, I always serve this alongside a traditional pumpkin pie. SERVES 4

¼ kabocha squash (from one 2½-pound squash), peeled, seeded, and cut into ¼-inch dice (about 1¼ cups)

4 eggs

1 cup coconut milk

½ cup packed grated palm sugar or light brown sugar

2 tablespoons packed dark brown sugar

⅛ teaspoon salt

Preheat the oven to 350°F

Put a kettle of water (at least 4 cups) on to boil. Divide the squash among four 1-cup ramekins. Arrange the ramekins, not touching, in a large roasting or baking pan. Cut four 6-inch squares of aluminum foil.

In a bowl, whisk together the eggs, coconut milk, palm and brown sugars, and salt just until smooth. Do not overbeat or the mixture will become frothy. Strain the custard mixture through a fine-mesh colander and ladle it into the prepared ramekins, dividing it evenly. Cover each ramekin tightly with a foil square. Pour the boiling water into the pan to come halfway up the sides of the ramekins.

Carefully transfer the pan to the oven and bake the custards until the middle jiggles slightly when you tap the ramekins, about 40 to 45 minutes. Carefully remove the ramekins from the pan, uncover them, and let the custards cool. Serve slightly warm, at room temperature, or chilled.

บัวลอยไข่หวาน

STICKY RICE PEARLS in SWEET COCONUT CREAM with POACHED EGGS

bua loi khai wan

This dessert is the epitome of simple elegance in both its appearance and its essence, much like Bananas in Nunhood (page 156). I love its white-on-white color scheme, its short ingredients list, and the fact that it is easy (and fun) to make. More than anything, though, I love the serene imagery that its name, *bua loi* (floating lotus), conjures: a pond of white lotus flowers.

In the spirit of gilding the lotus, however, I am presenting one of the classic variations on this Thai dessert, which features poached eggs. The idea of poached eggs as part of a dessert may seem strange to you, especially if you are unfamiliar with this type of savory-sweet combination that Thai people love. But I hope you will try this recipe at least once. Enjoy this comforting dessert warm: break the yolk so that it oozes into the sweet coconut cream, and then savor the cream along with the tiny rice dumplings. If you have a well-stocked Southeast Asian market nearby, look for long, narrow deep green tropical pandan leaves, which impart a sweet, floral fragrance. **SERVES 4**

1 cup glutinous rice flour
1¼ cups coconut milk
⅛ teaspoon salt

1 fresh pandan leaf, tied into a knot, or 1 teaspoon vanilla extract
About ½ cup sugar, for sweetening
4 eggs

Put the flour in a bowl. Stir in room-temperature water, 2 to 3 tablespoons at a time, until a moist and silky ball of dough forms. You will need slightly more than ½ cup water total. Divide the dough into 4 equal portions, place 1 portion on a work surface, and keep the remaining portions covered with a kitchen towel. Using your palms, roll one portion of the dough back and forth on the work surface, stretching it out length-wise into a rope about ½ inch in diameter. Using a butter knife, cut off a tiny piece of the dough and, with the tips of your fingers, shape it into a pea-size ball. Place the ball on a large platter and repeat to make additional balls, arranging them, not touching, on the platter. Repeat with the remaining 3 dough portions.

In a 2-quart saucepan, combine the coconut milk, salt, pandan leaf, and sugar over medium heat and heat just until it is steaming hot; it does not need to boil. Taste the coconut sauce to see if more sugar is needed. Keep in mind that you will be introduc-ing one more component to the mix, the poached eggs, which are not sweet. If the coconut sauce is not sweet enough, the dessert will taste bland. Once the coconut sauce tastes right to you, stir in the vanilla extract, if using. Turn down the heat to its lowest setting to keep the coconut sauce steaming while you cook the dumplings on a nearby burner.

Fill a 4-quart saucepan half full with water and bring to a boil over high heat. Turn down the heat so the water is bubbling gently, then drop in one-fourth of the dough balls. In less than 30 seconds, the balls will float to the top. Using a wire-mesh skimmer or slotted spoon, scoop them out of the pan, shake off the excess water, and drop them into the pan of steaming coconut sauce. Repeat with the remaining dough balls in 3 batches until all the dumplings are cooked.

When the last batch of dumplings is removed from the water, leave the water simmering for poaching the eggs. Crack 1 egg into a small bowl. Then, holding the bowl right above the water, gently let the egg slide into the water. Repeat with the remaining eggs. Turn off the heat immediately and let the eggs poach in the hot water for 3 minutes.

While waiting for the eggs to cook, remove and discard the pandan leaf, if used. Give the dumplings a stir and check to make sure that there is about twice the amount of liquid as the solids. If not, add more water. Taste the coconut sauce again to make sure it is sufficiently sweetened; add more sugar, if necessary, and heat it through.

Spoon the dumplings and coconut cream into 4 individual dessert bowls. One at a time, scoop the poached eggs out of the water, shake off the excess liquid, and top each bowl with an egg. Serve immediately.

Clockwise, from top left: Cucumber Relish (page 191), Vinegar with Pickled Chiles (page 192), Peanut–Sweet Chile Sauce (page 11)

สูตรพื้นฐาน
BASIC RECIPES and PREPARATIONS
sut phuenthan

This section presents some basic recipes and preparations for anyone—whether you are a novice Thai cook who has never made a pot of rice, or an enthusiastic do-it-yourself type who enjoys making basic Thai ingredients rather than buying them from the store. You will find everything from how to cook rice, prepare coconut milk, and grind red chile powder, to how to make your own Thai-style Sriracha sauce at home.

ข้าวสวย

LONG-GRAIN WHITE RICE

khao suai

Jasmine rice, imported from Thailand, is what I recommend. In fact, the amount of water recommended here assumes that you use imported jasmine rice, which is almost always new-crop rice with a higher moisture content than that of old-crop rice, and, therefore, tends to be too wet and sticky with the 1:1 rice-water ratio. However, most types of long-grain rice work with Thai food, so if you use anything other than imported new-crop Thai jasmine rice, you will need to experiment with the amount of water that works best in creating soft and fluffy rice. This cooking method is for those who do not have a rice cooker. **MAKES 4 CUPS**

2 cups long-grain white rice
3¼ cups water

Put the rice in a fine-mesh sieve and rinse under cold running water until the water is no longer cloudy. Transfer the rice to a heavy 2-quart saucepan with a tight-fitting lid. Add the water and place the pan, uncovered, over high heat. Bring the water to a boil, stirring 2 or 3 times. When the water boils, cover the pan, turn down the heat to the lowest setting, and cook the rice, undisturbed, until the water has been absorbed and the kernels are tender yet firm, about 15 minutes.

Remove the pan from the heat, uncover, and let the rice rest for a few minutes. Fluff with a fork and serve.

ข้าวเหนียวนึ่ง

STEAMED GLUTINOUS RICE

khao niao nueng

Glutinous, or sticky, rice, a staple of northern and northeastern Thailand and of Laos, is cooked *above* boiling water, not *in* water. Forget how you may have learned to cook glutinous rice for other cuisines. Thai sticky rice, unless you are making a sweet rice pudding, is cooked by steam.

I have provided two basic methods here: The first requires either a tiered steamer (or, if you are cooking less than 2 cups raw rice, a Chinese-style bamboo steamer) or a traditional cone-shaped bamboo basket and a tall, narrow pot. In the case of the second method, I have gone rogue. I use a splatter guard, also known as a splatter screen, to steam the rice. It is an extrafine-mesh screen that is typically placed over a pan on the stove top to contain grease splatters, and if you do not have one, it is a tool worth acquiring. Not only is the fine mesh perfect for regulating steam from below and eliminating hot spots, yielding evenly cooked rice, but it is also easy to clean, since the rice does not stick to the superfine screen. The rice grains all cook at the same rate and do not easily turn mushy.

What if you want to cook more than 2 cups rice and do not have a steamer? Well, again, you need to go rogue. Several of my blog readers have written to say that for larger amounts of glutinous rice—say, 3 cups or more—they have had success with a metal colander set over a pot with an opening just wide enough to allow the bottom of the colander to rest inside the top of the pot, much the same way the traditional cone-shaped basket does. This approach is covered in method three on page 170. **MAKES 4 CUPS**

2 cups Thai glutinous rice, soaked in cold water to cover for 5 to 6 hours or up to overnight, then drained

METHOD ONE

Fill the steamer bottom with water. For the best results, keep the water level about 3 to 4 inches below the steamer tier. Line the steamer tier with a double layer of cheesecloth or a single layer of muslin cloth (if using a cone-shaped basket, skip the cloth lining). Put the drained rice on the cloth, forming it into a mound about 1 inch high. Cover and steam over boiling water until the rice is soft, translucent, and glossy and sticks together, flipping the rice over once halfway through cooking. Flipping the rice ensures even cooking and prevents the bottom of the mound from becoming soggy. The rice should be ready in 25 to 30 minutes.

continued

METHOD TWO

Select a saucepan that is slightly smaller in diameter than the splatter guard. Fill the pan with water and bring it to a boil. For the best results, keep the water level 3 inches below the screen. Place the splatter guard on the pot.

When the water begins to boil, put the drained rice in the middle of the splatter guard and spread it into a mound about 1 to 2 inches in height. This ensures even, quick cooking. Cover the rice mound with a domed pot lid that is higher than the height of the mound. The cover does not have to match the size of the pot opening. It is fine as long as it does not touch the rice and rests securely on the screen.

Steam the rice over boiling water until it is soft, translucent, and glossy and sticks together, flipping it over once halfway through cooking. Flipping the rice ensures even cooking and prevents the bottom of the mound from becoming soggy. The rice should be ready in 25 to 30 minutes. When the rice is ready, remove the splatter guard from over the water and scrape the rice off the screen. It should slide right off.

METHOD THREE

Select a pot in which the colander will fit securely inside the opening. Fill the pot with water and bring it to a boil. For the best results, keep the water level about 2 to 3 inches below the bottom of the colander. Line the colander with a double layer of cheesecloth or a single layer of muslin cloth and rest the colander in the top of the pot.

When the water starts to boil, put the drained rice on the cloth, forming it into a mound about 1 to 2 inches high. Cover the rice mound with a domed pot lid that is higher than the height of the mound. As with method two, the cover does not have to match the size of the pot opening. It can sit on the colander as long as it does not touch the rice.

Steam the rice over boiling water until it is soft, translucent, and glossy and sticks together. As with the methods one and two, flip the rice over once halfway through cooking to ensure even cooking. The rice should be ready in 25 to 30 minutes. When the rice is ready, remove the colander from over the water and transfer it to a container in which you can keep it warm until serving time.

น้ำมะขามเปียก

HOMEMADE TAMARIND PULP

nam ma-kham piak

Prepared tamarind pulp, sometimes labeled "tamarind juice" or "tamarind juice concentrate," is available in most Asian markets and online. But because ready-made tamarind pulp is almost always too watery, I prepare my own tamarind pulp from seedless tamarind sold in 14-ounce blocks (see page 210). In some recipes, the excess liquid does not matter that much. Other recipes, such as stir-fried noodles, can be ruined by too much moisture, however. In those cases, it is difficult to impart a good sour flavor without adding too much liquid.

I have found that the water-to-tamarind ratio that works best for me is to 2 tablespoons warm water to 1 ounce seedless tamarind. **MAKES 2 CUPS**

1 (14-ounce) block seedless tamarind
1¾ cups warm water

In a bowl, immerse the tamarind in the water and let sit for 15 minutes. Then, with your hands, break up the tamarind until you have a mixture of smooth pulp along with the stringy veins and seed-covering membranes that are often included with the pulp.

To separate out the undesirable membranes and veins from the pulp by hand, grab a handful of the tamarind mixture and squeeze very hard. The pulp will seep out between your fingers, leaving the tough membranes and other bits in your fist, which you can then discard. Repeat the process until you have only smooth, membrane-free tamarind pulp, which is ready to be used in a recipe. This is my preferred method.

If you do not like the idea of squeezing the tamarind mixture by hand, you can strain it through a fine-mesh colander. The pulp will be quite thick. You will need to use a rubber spatula to press the pulp against the colander, forcing it through the holes, and to scrape off the thick pulp that clings to the underside of the colander. This may prove just as challenging as the hand-squeezing method, plus you may end up having to thin out the unstrained pulp mixture with water just to strain it. That means you will have more pulp to strain, and the end product may be just as thin as store-bought tamarind pulp.

Regardless of which method you choose, store the strained tamarind pulp in a non-reactive container, such as a glass jar, in the refrigerator, where it will keep for up to 1 week. For longer storage, freeze the strained pulp in ice-cube trays, pop the frozen cubes out of the trays into a resealable plastic bag, and keep them in the freezer indefinitely, thawing only as much as you need each time.

กะทิสด

COCONUT MILK from SCRATCH

ka-thi sot

Although most of the time I use prepared coconut milk that comes in a can, I sometimes make my own coconut milk from scratch. Admittedly, it is not a pleasurable activity. The process is messy and somewhat labor-intensive, and can be dangerous if done carelessly. However, when it comes to certain dishes, such as sweet coconut sticky rice (page 161), canned coconut milk only does an okay job whereas freshly extracted coconut milk performs consistently well.

To make coconut milk, you need a mature coconut, because only a fully ripened coconut can yield the rich, fatty milk you want. Mature coconuts have a hard, dark brown, hairy shell, which sets them apart from their younger counterparts, which sport their off-white inner husk in markets and, at least in the United States, come wrapped in plastic. Mature coconuts typically weigh 1½ to 2 pounds.

In Thailand, a specific tool is used to grate coconut for extraction, but it is hard to come by in the United States and is a bit tricky to use. So I am recommending this alternative blender method that uses kitchen tools you already have on hand.

The first and trickiest step is to crack the coconut. This is the part where things get messy and potentially dangerous (you may want to put on protective eyewear). **MAKES ABOUT 1½ CUPS COCONUT CREAM AND 2 CUPS COCONUT MILK**

1 mature coconut, 1½ to 2 pounds
3 cups water

First, locate the 3 "eyes" on one end of the coconut and puncture one of them with the tip of a knife or a screwdriver. You will discover that only one of the eyes is soft enough for you to puncture; the other two are not so easy. Drain out all of the coconut water. Unlike the water in an immature coconut, the water of a mature coconut does not taste very good. But if you do not want to waste it, you can drink it. Now, holding the coconut over the sink in your nondominant hand, rotate the coconut with that hand while striking the center—"the equator"—of the coconut with either a hammer or a large Chinese cleaver wielded by your dominant hand. Keep rotating and hitting on the equator until the coconut pops open.

Using a sturdy butter knife positioned where the meat touches the shell, pry the meat out of the shell. With a sharp paring knife or a vegetable peeler, peel off the brown skin from the coconut meat. Chop the coconut meat into roughly 1-inch pieces.

In a blender, combine the coconut meat and 1½ cups of the water and blend until smooth. Line a large colander with a double layer of cheesecloth or a single layer of muslin cloth and place the colander on a clear glass bowl or a 1-quart glass measuring cup. Gather the corners of the cheesecloth to form a bag and squeeze out every bit of the liquid from the cloth.

Return the pulverized coconut meat to the blender, add the remaining 1½ cups water, and blend until the liquid becomes opaque white. Strain the liquid into the same glass container. (If you have a large, high-speed blender, this can be done in one batch.)

Let the coconut milk sit undisturbed for 30 minutes. The coconut cream will rise to the top and the see-through glass container will allow you to see clearly the demarcation line between the coconut milk and the coconut cream.

Scoop out the cream to use in a curry starter or other applications as desired. The remaining liquid is coconut milk. Both the cream and the milk can be stored in airtight containers (preferably nonmetallic) in the refrigerator for up to 24 hours or in the freezer for up to 2 months.

น้ำพริกแกง

CURRY PASTE from SCRATCH

nam phrik kaeng

When preparing curry paste, begin by toasting the dry spices (with the exception of white peppercorns) in a skillet over the lowest heat possible before grinding them in a mortar or spice grinder. If grinding the curry paste in a mortar, once the dry spices (including the white peppercorns) are ground, add the toughest and most fibrous ingredients next, followed by the softer, wetter ingredients. Always pound each ingredient until smooth before adding the next one.

The following recipes list the ingredients in the order in which they are added to the mortar. If you are making the curry paste in a food processor, toast and grind the dry spices first, then grind all of the ingredients together in one go. Even though you process everything at once, it is still a good idea to prepare each ingredient as if you were going to grind it manually in the mortar. As powerful as a food processor is, I have noticed that certain items with tough fibers, such as lemongrass stalks, break down into a smooth paste more easily when you slice them crosswise.

Ideally, curry paste is made fresh and used immediately, but that is not always possible. I have found that the most economical and efficient way to prepare curry pastes from scratch is to make a large amount when the ingredients are fresh and then freeze the paste for when I need it.

The flavor of the herbs stays true and fresh longer if you make the curry pastes and freeze them rather than freeze the herbs individually and then thaw them to make the pastes. Freezing the finished pastes is also practical if you live in an area where the availability of some key ingredients, such as kaffir limes or galangal, is unreliable. I pack 1/4-cup portions of fresh paste into small freezer bags, press all of the air out, seal, and then freeze the paste for up to 6 months (but it is best within 2 to 3 months). Thaw for 5 to 10 minutes at room temperature before using. **MAKES 1 CUP**

น้ำพริกแกงเผ็ด

RED CURRY PASTE

nam phrik kaeng phet

1½ tablespoons coriander seeds, toasted in a dry skillet over low heat until fragrant (about 1 minute)

2 teaspoons cumin seeds, toasted in a dry skillet over low heat until fragrant (about 1 minute)

1 teaspoon white peppercorns

7 dried Thai long chiles, seeded, soaked in hot water until soft, and drained

10 dried bird's eye chiles, seeded, soaked in hot water until soft, and drained

2 teaspoons salt

2 tablespoons finely chopped galangal

2 tablespoons thinly sliced lemongrass (see page 206)

2 teaspoons finely chopped kaffir lime rind

2 teaspoons shrimp paste

2 tablespoons finely chopped cilantro roots or stems

10 cloves garlic

1/2 cup sliced shallots

continued

น้ำพริกแกงเขียวหวาน

GREEN CURRY PASTE
nam phrik kaeng khiao wan

1½ tablespoons coriander seeds, toasted in a dry skillet over low heat until fragrant (about 1 minute)

2 teaspoons cumin seeds, toasted in a dry skillet over low heat until fragrant (about 1 minute)

1 teaspoon white peppercorns

2 teaspoons salt

2 tablespoons finely chopped galangal

2 tablespoons finely sliced lemongrass (see page 206)

2 teaspoons finely chopped kaffir lime rind

2 teaspoons shrimp paste

10 fresh green Thai long chiles, seeded and roughly chopped

15 fresh green bird's eye chiles

2 tablespoons finely chopped cilantro roots or stems

10 cloves garlic

½ cup sliced shallots

น้ำพริกแกงมัสมั่น

MATSAMAN CURRY PASTE
nam phrik kaeng matsaman

1½ tablespoons coriander seeds, toasted in a dry skillet over low heat until fragrant (about 1 minute)

2 teaspoons cumin seeds, toasted in a dry skillet over low heat until fragrant (about 1 minute)

4 whole cloves, toasted in a dry skillet over low heat until fragrant (about 1 minute)

2 Thai or green cardamom pods

1 teaspoon white peppercorns

5 dried Thai long chiles, stemmed, soaked in hot water to cover until soft, and drained

6 dried bird's eye chiles, seeded, soaked in hot water to cover until soft, and drained

2 teaspoons salt

2 tablespoons finely chopped galangal

2 tablespoons finely sliced lemongrass (see page 206)

2 teaspoons finely chopped kaffir lime rind

2 teaspoons shrimp paste

2 tablespoons finely chopped cilantro roots or stems

10 cloves garlic

½ cup sliced shallots

For this paste only, fry the paste in ¾ cup vegetable oil over medium heat for 5 minutes, then let cool completely before using or freeze for later use.

น้ำพริกแกงกะหรี่

KARI (YELLOW) CURRY PASTE

nam phrik kaeng kari

1½ tablespoons coriander seeds, toasted in a dry skillet over low heat until fragrant (about 1 minute)

2 teaspoons cumin seeds, toasted in a dry skillet over low heat until fragrant (about 1 minute)

2 teaspoons fennel seeds, toasted in a dry skillet over low heat until fragrant (about 1 minute)

1 teaspoon white peppercorns

3 dried red Thai long chiles, seeded, soaked in hot water to cover until soft, and drained

5 dried bird's eye chiles, seeded, soaked in hot water to cover until soft, and drained

2 teaspoons salt

1 tablespoon finely chopped galangal

2 tablespoons finely sliced lemongrass (see page 206)

2 teaspoons finely chopped kaffir lime rind

2 teaspoons shrimp paste

4-inch piece fresh turmeric, peeled and chopped

2 tablespoons curry powder, homemade (page 180) or store-bought

2 tablespoons finely chopped cilantro roots or stems

10 cloves garlic

½ cup sliced shallots

น้ำพริกแกงส้ม

SOUR CURRY PASTE

nam phrik kaeng som

10 dried red Thai long chiles, seeded, soaked in hot water to cover until soft, and drained

2 shallots, 1 ounce each, peeled

6 large cloves garlic, peeled

1 tablespoon shrimp paste

Puree everything in a food processor until smooth.

น้ำซุป

STOCKS

nam sup

Stocks in modern Thai cooking typically require fewer ingredients, have a lighter and less complex flavor, and are used somewhat differently from stocks in Western cuisines. I use them in the same way that some cooks use monosodium glutamate crystals (MSG), that is, to add umami flavor to dishes that lack it, such as soups or curries made with boneless meat that are cooked relatively quickly as opposed to those made with bone-in meat that are cooked longer.

In order to control the level of salinity in the dishes to which the stock is added, I do not add salt to the stock. This means that it tastes quite bland on its own. But that is fine, as stock is always used as a flavor enhancer in my recipes, never as a stand-alone dish.

If you are pressed for time and must buy stock, see my guidelines for purchasing store-bought stocks in the introduction to the Soups section on page 36. **MAKES ABOUT 8 CUPS**

CHICKEN or PORK STOCK

4 pounds raw chicken carcasses or pork neck bones

16 cups water

4 Chinese celery stalks, or 2 cups chopped regular celery

1 yellow onion

¼ cup cracked white peppercorns

8 large cloves garlic

8 cilantro roots, smashed, or 1 cup roughly chopped cilantro stems

In a stockpot, combine all of the ingredients and bring to a boil over high heat, skimming off any foam that forms on the surface. Lower the heat to a simmer, cover, and cook for 3 hours.

If there is any fat on the surface, skim it off. Strain the stock through a fine-mesh sieve into a clean container. Use immediately, or let cool, cover, and refrigerate for up to 1 week or freeze for up to 6 months.

VEGETABLE STOCK

Substitute an equal amount of peeled daikon or turnip or a combination of peeled daikon and green cabbage for the chicken carcasses or pork neck bones and proceed as directed, except that you will not need to worry about skimming off any foam or fat.

สามเกลอ

BASIC AROMATIC PASTE

"sam kloe" ("three buddies")

In Thailand, this aromatic paste of garlic, white peppercorn, and cilantro roots isn't really considered a stand-alone, composite ingredient—unlike red curry paste, for example. However, this team of three buddies—hence the nickname—plays a prominent role in Thai cooking. It lies at the heart of many meat marinades; it also serves as a base for various dishes in much the same way as how *sofrito* or *refogado* is used in Spanish, Portuguese, and Latin American cuisines.

I often make a large batch and keep it in the freezer for convenience. If you have a mortar, you can start out with whole white peppercorns. However, if you make the paste in a food processor, grind the peppercorns first in a coffee grinder, dedicated to spice grinding, because the peppercorns often escape the food processor blades. Of course, for convenience, you can also use store-bought ground white pepper, which is not as fragrant but will do. **MAKES 1½ CUPS**

4 heads garlic, separated into cloves and peeled

2 tablespoons whole white peppercorns or ground white pepper (see note above)

10 cilantro roots, or 1 cup loosely packed chopped cilantro stems

Grind the ingredients in a mortar or food processor into a smooth paste. Store loosely in a resealable plastic bag and freeze for up to 1 month. Thaw for 5 to 10 minutes at room temperature before using.

ผงกะหรี่

CURRY POWDER

phong kari

Although curry powder is not the core ingredient in classic Thai curries, as some folks mistakenly assume, it has found its way into Thai cooking. I have used this recipe for many years. It mimics the taste of my favorite Thai brand of curry powder, which I have been unable to find in the United States. The quality of your curry powder depends on the quality of the spices that go into it, so use the best and the freshest spices you can find. **MAKES ABOUT 1 CUP**

⅓ cup less 2 teaspoons ground coriander

⅓ cup ground turmeric

2 tablespoons ground cumin

1 tablespoon ground cinnamon

2 teaspoons ground cloves

1 teaspoon ground cayenne pepper

In a small bowl, stir together all of the ingredients until well mixed. Transfer to an airtight container and store in a cool, dry place for up to 2 months or in the freezer (my favorite place to store spice blends) for up to 6 months. Toast curry powder in a dry skillet over very low heat before using in a recipe. The heat helps enliven its aroma, which becomes dull during storage.

พริกป่น

RED CHILE POWDER

phrik pon

Pulverized toasted dried red chiles—exactly what this is—is widely available. However, when you make it from scratch, you are rewarded with fresher and more fragrant chile powder. This also allows you to determine the level of heat that suits your taste. Red chile powder made from dried red bird's eye chiles, for example, is much hotter than red chile powder made from dried red long chiles. Therefore, if you want the kind of red chile powder that lends a beautiful reddish color to your food without giving it too much heat, make it with dried red long chiles or half dried red long chiles and half dried red bird's eye chiles. As you can see, I like my *phrik pon* very hot. **MAKES 1 CUP**

2 cups loosely packed dried bird's eye chiles

In a dry skillet, toast the chiles over low heat for about 3 minutes, until fragrant, brittle, and slightly darker (but not browned and blistered). Pour onto a plate and let cool completely. Transfer to a granite mortar, a food processor, a spice grinder, or a coffee grinder dedicated to spices and grind to the consistency of coarse cornmeal. Store in an airtight container in a cool, dry place for up to 6 months.

ข้าวคั่ว

TOASTED RICE POWDER

khao khua

Toasted rice powder is neither a condiment that you serve alongside a dish nor a flavor enhancer that you use to adjust the taste of a finished dish. It is instead an essential ingredient in a handful of Thai dishes, mostly from the northeast. One of the best known of these northeastern dishes is the minced chicken salad on page 74.

Opinions vary as to which type of rice is most appropriate for toasted rice powder: long-grain white rice or glutinous rice. Because I find the texture of the hard, dense long-grain rice less pleasant than the texture of the softer, lighter glutinous rice, I usually use the latter. But you can use either type. **MAKES 1 CUP**

1 cup Thai glutinous or long-grain white rice

Put the rice in a dry 12-inch skillet (cast-iron or triple-ply stainless steel is best) over medium-low heat. Shake the skillet and stir the rice every 30 seconds to make sure the rice is toasting evenly. Do not be tempted to increase the heat in the hope of speeding up the process, as you want every rice kernel to cook slowly and thoroughly all the way to the core. After 20 to 25 minutes, the rice should be medium to dark brown and have a nutty aroma. Remove the pan from the heat and immediately transfer the rice to a heatproof plate to cool. Be careful as you work, as the rice is very hot. Do not leave the rice to cool in the skillet, or it may burn in the residual heat. Let the rice cool *completely* before moving to the next step.

Grind the cooled rice in a mortar, a spice grinder, a coffee grinder dedicated to spices, or a food processor to a medium-fine powder, roughly the texture of uncooked grits or slightly finer. If you use a mortar, you will have more control over the final texture. Be sure to apply pressure through the pestle in a circular motion, rather than in an up-and-down pounding motion, or the kernels will fly free of the mortar. It is easiest if you grind the rice in batches of roughly 2 tablespoons, adding more toasted kernels to the ground rice in the mortar after each batch is sufficiently ground.

Store the rice powder in an airtight container at room temperature for up to 6 months. Its shelf life is longer than that—as long as a year, perhaps—but the aroma noticeably dissipates after 6 months.

หอมเจียวและน้ำมันหอมเจียว
FRIED SHALLOTS and FRIED SHALLOT OIL

hom jiao lae nam man hom jiao

Fried shallots are used as an accent ingredient in a few Thai dishes. You can make them in advance to cut down on cooking time. The key in achieving evenly browned and thoroughly fried shallots that also stay crispy throughout their storage life is to start out with everything—including the skillet—at room temperature. The oil can be used in any of the recipes in this book that call for both shallots and vegetable oil; it can also be used to fry eggs (page 194) to give them extra flavor. **MAKES ½ CUP FRIED SHALLOTS AND ¾ CUP SHALLOT OIL**

4 shallots, about 1 ounce each, thinly sliced
lengthwise
¾ cup vegetable oil

Set a small fine-mesh strainer on top of a heatproof bowl and place both close to the stove. In a cold 6- or 8-inch skillet, combine the shallots and the oil and heat over medium heat. Stir the shallots around with a spatula to separate them. Cook, stirring occasionally, until the oil becomes hot and starts sizzling, about 5 minutes. Turn down the heat to medium-low and continue to cook, stirring occasionally as the shallots around the edges of the pan tend to cook faster than those in the middle. After 5 minutes, the shallots should be the color of honey (if not, turn the heat down to low and continue to cook for 1 to 2 minutes longer). Immediately remove the skillet from the heat and pour the contents through the prepared strainer. Let both the crispy shallots and the oil cool completely before storing them in 2 separate airtight containers at room temperature. The crispy shallots keep for 3 weeks and the oil keeps for 2 months.

น้ำพริกเผา

CHILE JAM

nam phrik phao

If you have never had Thai chile jam before, I recommend that you start with commercial *nam phrik phao* from Thailand, which you can buy at most Asian markets and some well-stocked groceries like Whole Foods (look for the label "roasted red chile paste"). This helps you get used to its flavor and texture. **MAKES 4 CUPS**

5 dried Thai long chiles, seeded and seeds reserved

About 1½ cups vegetable oil

2 small heads garlic, separated into cloves, peeled, and sliced lengthwise paper-thin

3 large shallots, about 1 ounce each, sliced lengthwise paper-thin

¼ cup dried shrimp

1 tablespoon packed shrimp paste

1 cup packed grated palm sugar, or ¾ cup packed light or dark brown sugar

¼ cup tamarind pulp, homemade (page 171) or store-bought

¼ cup fish sauce

1 cup water

In a dry wok or skillet, toast the chiles over medium-low heat for 5 to 8 minutes, until their texture changes from rubbery to somewhat brittle. Transfer them to a plate.

Add ¾ cup of the oil to the same pan and set over medium heat. When the oil is hot, add the garlic and fry until light brown and crisp, about 10 to 12 minutes. Using a slotted spoon, transfer the garlic to the plate with the chiles. Fry the shallots the same way and add them to the same plate. Add the shrimp to the hot oil and fry until golden and crispy, about 5 to 7 minutes. Using the slotted spoon, transfer them to the same plate. Remove the pan from the heat.

Add everything on the plate and the shrimp paste to a food processor, then process the mixture until pulverized to a paste.

Add oil to the wok as needed to total about 1 cup. Stir in the prepared paste, the sugar, the tamarind, the fish sauce, and the water and place over medium heat. Fry, stirring occasionally, until the ingredients are well blended and the mixture has developed the consistency of a loose jam, about 15 minutes.

Remove the pan from the heat and let the mixture cool completely. Transfer the jam to a glass jar and cap tightly. There is no need to drain off the oil, as it adds extra flavor and color to the food to which it is added. Store the jam in the refrigerator for up to 1 month. To ensure against spoilage, be sure to use a clean spoon every time you scoop jam out of the jar. Chile jam can also be frozen for up to 6 months.

กระเทียมเจียวและน้ำมันกระเทียมเจียว
FRIED GARLIC and FRIED GARLIC OIL

kra-thiam jiao lae nam man kra-thiam jiao

Fried garlic is used as an accent ingredient in much the same way as crispy shallots, albeit much more widely. Like crispy shallots, you can make them in advance to ensure that you always have some on hand whenever a need arises. Start with all ingredients, including the skillet, at room temperature to achieve evenly browned and thoroughly fried garlic that stays crispy throughout its storage life. Fried garlic oil can be used in lieu of plain vegetable oil in stir-fried dishes. It can also be used to fry eggs (page 194) to give them extra flavor. **MAKES ABOUT ¾ CUP FRIED GARLIC AND ¾ CUP GARLIC OIL**

2 heads garlic, separated into cloves
and peeled

¾ cup vegetable oil

Pound the garlic in a mortar (preferred), food processor, or mini chopper coarsely. You do not want to grind them too finely or—worse—into a paste. However, you want all the garlic bits to be the same size—roughly the size of a raw rice kernel—so they cook at the same rate and brown evenly. Set a small fine-mesh strainer on top of a heatproof bowl and place both close to the stove. Combine the garlic and the vegetable oil, put them in a 6- to 8-inch skillet, and put the skillet over medium heat. Cook, stirring occasionally, until the oil is hot and sizzling, about 5 minutes. Turn down the heat to medium-low and continue to cook, stirring often, until the garlic pieces are light brown, about 2 to 3 minutes. Immediately remove the skillet from the heat and pour the contents through the prepared strainer. Allow the fried garlic and the oil to cool completely before storing them in 2 separate airtight containers. The fried garlic keeps for 3 weeks and the oil keeps for 2 months.

ซอสศรีราชา

SRIRACHA SAUCE

sot si racha

This recipe gives you a result that resembles the commercial Sriracha sauce commonly used in Thailand (see page 209). It is runnier, sweeter, and milder than the widely available American-made Sriracha sauce, nicknamed "rooster sauce" because of the rooster on its label. **MAKES 2 CUPS**

12 ounces fresh red Thai long chiles, stemmed

2 heads garlic, separated into cloves and peeled

¼ cup distilled white vinegar

¾ cup water

1 cup and 2 tablespoons granulated sugar

3 tablespoons salt

In a blender, combine the chiles, garlic, vinegar, and water and blend until smooth. Strain the mixture through a fine-mesh sieve placed over a half-gallon saucepan, forcing as much liquid through the sieve as possible. Add one-third of the pulp from the sieve to the liquid in the pan and discard the remaining pulp.

Whisk the sugar and salt into the mixture in the pan. Place over medium heat and bring to a boil, stirring occasionally. Reduce the heat to a simmer and cook uncovered, stirring occasionally, until the sauce is reduced to about 2 cups and has thickened slightly, about 12 to 15 minutes. If you like your sauce thicker, reduce it longer; the recipe will yield less volume, but the flavor of the sauce will be more intense.

Remove the pan from the heat and let the sauce cool completely. Transfer the sauce to a glass jar and cap tightly. It will keep in the refrigerator for up to 1 month. The sauce tastes best if allowed to mellow for 2 days before using. To ensure against spoilage, be sure to use a clean spoon every time you scoop sauce out of the jar. The sauce can also be frozen for up to 6 months; thaw in the refrigerator.

น้ำจิ้มไก่
SWEET CHILE SAUCE

nam jim kai

As noted earlier, the primary use for this sauce is to accompany grilled chicken; hence, the Thai name *nam jim kai*, literally "dipping sauce [for] chicken." It is sweet, sour, and so mild that even young children can enjoy it. It is versatile, too, used as a dipping sauce for various savory appetizers and snacks and other grilled or fried meats.

This sauce is not very hot to begin with, and the heat dissipates quickly upon storage. But if you like your sauce extremely mild, devein and seed the chiles before adding them to the blender. **MAKES 1 CUP**

3 large cloves garlic
2 fresh red Thai long chiles, stemmed
¼ cup distilled white vinegar
½ cup granulated sugar

1½ teaspoons salt
¾ cup plus 2 tablespoons water
1 tablespoon tapioca flour, potato starch, or cornstarch

In a blender, combine the garlic, chiles, vinegar, sugar, salt, and ¾ cup of the water and blend until the mixture resembles a smooth salsa. Transfer the mixture to a small saucepan, place over medium-high heat, and bring to a boil, stirring occasionally. Lower the heat to medium and simmer uncovered, stirring occasionally, until the garlic and chile bits have softened, about 3 minutes.

Meanwhile, in a small bowl, whisk together the tapioca flour and the remaining 2 tablespoons water until the flour dissolves. Whisk the flour mixture into the sauce and continue to simmer until the sauce thickens slightly, about 1 minute longer. Remove the pan from the heat and let the sauce cool completely.

Transfer the cooled sauce to a glass jar and cap tightly. Store in the refrigerator for up to 1 month.

น้ำจิ้มสะเต๊ะ

SATAY SAUCE

nam jim satay

Both of the following recipes make a great Thai-style satay sauce. One is the quick, easy, and somewhat unconventional recipe that my whole family has loved and used for decades. It calls for unsweetened, unsalted natural creamy peanut butter—essentially ground roasted peanuts, always with a layer of oil on top—and two nontraditional ingredients, granulated sugar and distilled white vinegar, and is ready in less than 10 minutes. The second recipe is more time-consuming, though not by much, and uses ground peanuts. Choose the one that works best for you. I like them both, though the less-easy version is more similar to what you get on the streets of Bangkok.

Regardless of which method you use, the sauce can be packed into an airtight container and refrigerated for up to 2 to 3 weeks or frozen for 3 to 4 months. Thaw, if frozen, and reheat to slightly warmer than room temperature before using. Also, because the sauce tends to thicken during storage, you will need to thin it with water to the desired consistency. **MAKES 3½ TO 4 CUPS**

THE EASY VERSION

1½ cups coconut milk

¼ cup homemade red curry paste (page 175), or 2 tablespoons store-bought

¾ cup unsalted, unsweetened natural creamy peanut butter

1½ teaspoons salt

½ cup water

2 tablespoons distilled white or cider vinegar

½ to ¾ cup granulated sugar or packed brown sugar

In a 2-quart saucepan, combine the coconut milk, curry paste, peanut butter, salt, water, vinegar, and ½ cup of the sugar and bring to a gentle boil over medium heat, whisking constantly. Turn down the heat to low and let the mixture simmer, whisking occasionally to keep the bottom from scorching, for about 3 minutes, until the sauce is homogenous and smooth. Taste and whisk in more sugar if you prefer a sweeter sauce, making sure the added sugar dissolves. Remove the pan from the heat and let the sauce cool to room temperature or slightly warmer than room temperature before serving.

THE LESS-EASY VERSION

¼ cup homemade red curry paste (page 175), or 2 tablespoons store-bought

1 tablespoon coconut, peanut, or vegetable oil

1½ cups coconut milk

¾ cup packed grated palm sugar

1½ teaspoons salt

1 tablespoon tamarind pulp, homemade (page 171) or store-bought

½ cup water

2 cups roasted peanuts, ground to a smooth paste in a mortar or food processor

In a 2-quart saucepan, combine the curry paste, oil, and ½ cup of the coconut milk and fry over medium-high heat until the curry paste is fragrant and the coconut fat separates, about 2 minutes. Add the remaining 1 cup coconut milk, sugar, salt, tamarind, water, and peanuts and cook, stirring constantly, until the mixture is homogenous and a thin layer of oil forms on its surface, about 2 to 3 minutes. Remove the pan from the heat and let the sauce cool to room temperature or slightly warmer than room temperature before serving.

แจ่ว

DRIED CHILE DIPPING SAUCE

jaeo

This simplified version of *jaeo*, a relish popular in northeastern Thailand, is often used in the central plains as a dipping sauce for grilled meats, typically grilled chicken and beef steak. **MAKES 1 CUP**

1 large shallot, about 1 ounce, thinly sliced lengthwise

¼ cup finely chopped fresh sawtooth coriander or cilantro

½ teaspoon minced galangal (optional)

⅓ cup fish sauce

3 tablespoons freshly squeezed lime juice

2 teaspoons packed grated palm sugar or light or dark brown sugar

1 tablespoon toasted rice powder (page 182)

1 tablespoon red chile powder (page 181), or to taste

In a bowl, mix together all of the ingredients. Adjust the taste with more fish sauce, lime juice, or sugar if needed. The sauce should be predominantly sour and salty. The amount of red chile powder is your call. Use immediately, or transfer to a glass jar, cap tightly, and store in the refrigerator for up to 3 days.

อาจาด

CUCUMBER RELISH

ajat

This fresh relish is also called quick pickled cucumber. It is usually served with South Asian–or Middle Eastern–influenced Thai curries, which are made with warm dried spices and are not as hot or herbal as some indigenous Thai curries. I recommend that you serve this condiment along with *kaeng kari kai* (page 99) the way it is often done in Thailand. *Ajat* is also an indispensable part of a satay (page 19) set; the tartness, the crunch, and the heat all bring a nice balance to the grilled meat and the rich peanut dipping sauce. **MAKE ABOUT 1 CUP • PICTURED ON PAGE 166**

½ cup granulated sugar

½ cup distilled white vinegar

2 tablespoons water

¼ teaspoon salt

½ cup thinly sliced English or pickling cucumber

1 large shallot, about 1 ounce, thinly sliced lengthwise

1 fresh Thai long chile, cut crosswise into ¼-inch slices

8 to 10 fresh cilantro leaves

In a small saucepan, combine the sugar, vinegar, water, and salt and bring the mixture to a gentle boil over medium heat, stirring, just until the sugar dissolves. Remove the pan from the heat and let the syrup cool completely.

Stir the cucumber, shallot, chile, and cilantro into the cooled syrup seconds before you serve the relish, as the cucumber will get mushy and dilute the syrup with the moisture that it releases.

น้ำส้มพริกดอง

VINEGAR with PICKLED CHILES

nam som phrik dong

This is one of the most common members of the seasoning caddy found on every table of every noodle stall in Bangkok. I highly recommend that you serve this condiment along with *rat na* (page 128) and *phat si-io* (page 120), the two Chinese-influenced one-plate noodle dishes in this book, which benefit the most from the sharp vinegar and a little bit of heat from the chiles. Do not go fancy with the vinegar here. The simple distilled white vinegar used by street vendors is the best. If you find its taste too harsh, cider vinegar or *unseasoned* rice vinegar can be substituted. **MAKES 2 CUPS • PICTURED ON PAGE 166**

2 cups white distilled vinegar

3 fresh Thai long chiles, sliced crosswise
¼ inch thick

Put the vinegar and chiles in a glass jar, cap tightly, and refrigerate for up to 2 months. For the best flavor, wait for 2 days before using.

น้ำปลาพริก

CHILE FISH SAUCE

nam pla phrik

You cannot sit down at a rice-curry shop—Thai-style fast-food eatery—without finding a bowl of this simple condiment on the table. Think of it as the Thai equivalent of salt and pepper shakers. **MAKES 2¼ CUPS**

2 cups fish sauce

15 fresh bird's eye chiles, sliced crosswise ⅛ inch thick

5 cloves garlic, cut crosswise into paper-thin slices (optional)

In a bowl, stir together the fish sauce, chiles, and garlic. The sauce can be used immediately, but I think it tastes best if the chiles are allowed to soften and mellow for 2 to 3 hours. Store the condiment in a tightly capped glass jar in the refrigerator for up to a month, though the chiles will have lost their heat by 2 weeks.

ไข่ดาว

CRISPY FRIED EGGS

khai dao

If you have spent any amount of time in Thailand or around Thai people, it cannot escape your observation that we love our fried eggs. We serve them on the side of some rice-based one-plate meals, such as fried rice, and even as a stand-alone main dish as part of a *samrap*. Cooked in quite a bit of oil and over medium-high heat, Thai-style fried eggs are crispy on the bottoms and around the edges, just the way we like them. **MAKES 1**

½ cup vegetable oil
1 egg

Heat the oil in a small (6-inch) skillet or a wok over medium-high heat. When the oil is hot, crack the egg into it. The egg will start bubbling up right away. With a spatula, splash some of the oil around the edges and over the top of the egg to partially cook the part that does not touch the oil directly.

If you like the yolk runny, remove the egg from the oil as soon as it is crispy on the bottom and around the edges. If you like the yolk softly cooked, continue to splash more oil around the edges and over the top of the egg and remove it just as the yolk starts to firm up. If you like your fried egg cooked through and crispy on the top as well as on the bottom, once the bottom turns crispy and brown, flip the egg over and crisp up the other side.

ไข่ต้มยางมะตูม
MEDIUM-BOILED EGGS

khai tom yang matum

This method produces medium-boiled eggs with tender yet firm whites and soft, sticky yolks—the kind you most often find at rice-curry shops in Bangkok—which can be consumed as they are or used in any recipe in this book that calls for hard-boiled eggs. You can apply this method to any number of eggs, but let us start with 8 large eggs, so you can use them to make the recipe for Son-in-Law Eggs (page 47) without having to do any math. **MAKES 8**

8 eggs

To prevent cracked eggs, make sure that the eggs are at room temperature before you begin. If they have been refrigerated, leave them out to warm up on the counter until they are no longer cold. Meanwhile, half fill a 1-gallon saucepan with water and bring it to a boil over high heat. When the water boils, gently lower the eggs into it with a ladle, one at a time. Once the last egg goes in, immediately set the timer at 7 minutes. Lower the heat to medium-high so that the water is boiling gently. Stir the eggs around with a spoon a few times to center the yolks.

After 7 minutes, immediately drain off the water and cover the eggs with cold tap water. The cold water will become warm right away because of the hot eggs, so you need to repeat the process 4 or 5 more times until the eggs are at room temperature, which is when they can be consumed, used in a recipe, or refrigerated in the shell for up to 3 days.

If you want the eggs hard-boiled instead of medium-boiled, simply add 2 minutes to the cooking time.

Thai bird's eye chiles (*phrik khi nu*) and Thai long chiles (*phrik chi fa*)

Ingredients Glossary

The ingredients used in Thai cooking are so numerous that to list and discuss even one-fourth of them here would take dozens of pages. Instead, I have limited the entries, divided by category, to noteworthy ingredients used in the recipes in this book.

CHILES AND PEPPERCORNS

Dried red chiles (พริกแห้ง · phrik haeng).
Ripe, red chiles are dried and used in Thai cooking, and despite what some folks think, these dried chiles are not inferior to fresh chiles. Both fresh and dried chiles have specific functions in Thai cooking and are interchangeable only sometimes. For example, in a pinch, you can use fresh chiles in place of dried chiles in some salads or dipping sauces. But red curry, *phanaeng* curry, sour curry, and most orange-colored curries can only be made with dried chiles.

It is often easier to find dried bird's eye chiles than it is dried Thai long chiles, which is why I frequently buy functionally similar dried chiles at Latino groceries, where I look for árbol, guajillo, or New Mexico (aka Hatch) chiles, any of which can be substituted, alone or in combination, for dried Thai long chiles. For example, I get great results when I combine árbol chiles and guajillo chiles in my curry pastes. If you cannot find dried bird's eyes, pequin or árbol chiles—both of which are available at Latino groceries—can be substituted. Dried chiles keep for several months in a container with good ventilation, such as a loosely woven bamboo basket, in a cool, dry, bug-free place.

Fresh chiles (พริกสด · phrik sot). I call for two types of fresh chiles in this book: bird's eye chiles (*phrik khi nu*) and Thai long chiles (*phrik chi fa*). Bird's eye chiles are small, ranging from ¾ inch to just a little over 1 inch long, but they are packed with heat, registering 50,000 to 100,000 heat units on the Scoville scale. This is why Thais use this type of chile to describe someone who is small but powerful. Bird's eye chiles are often labeled "Thai chiles" at Asian supermarkets in the United States. Look for fresh, firm, vibrant, shiny pods with bright green stems, signs that they are fresh. If they are hard to come by where you live, when you see them, be greedy and buy a bunch, then freeze them. They freeze beautifully, stay fresh in the freezer for 2 to 3 months, and thaw at room temperature quickly—actually in seconds, if you run them under tap water. For the most part, bird's eye chiles are used for their heat and fragrance as opposed to the pulp (of which they do not have much); when you absolutely cannot find them, any fresh hot chile peppers can be used instead. Simply use your taste and heat tolerance as a guide since chiles differ greatly in their levels of heat.

Long chiles, which—true to their name—are longer than bird's eye chiles and measure about 3 to 4 inches in length, have more pulp and are less hot than their smaller and more compact cousin.

They work best in preparations in which you want the green or red color of the pulp but not excessive heat, such as green curry paste. If long chiles are called for as an ingredient in a condiment or a curry paste and you cannot find them, fresno, serrano, or jalapeño chiles can be substituted in a 1:1 ratio. If you are slivering the chiles to use as an accent in a stir-fry or curry, bell peppers can be used in their place, just as most overseas Thai restaurants do. Like bird's eyes, long chiles can be frozen for 2 to 3 months. Because they are more pulpy, however, they tend to get soft and mushy once they are thawed.

Peppercorns (พริกไทย · phrik thai). Even though white peppercorns are used almost exclusively in Thai cooking, you can use either white or black peppercorns in the recipes in this book, including the basic aromatic paste (page 179).

COCONUT

Dried coconut flakes (มะพร้าวแห้ง · ma-phrao haeng). Do not confuse unsweetened dried coconut flakes with the sweetened flaked coconut in the baking aisle at the supermarket. Look for unsweetened dried coconut flakes in Southeast Asian and South Asian grocery stores and in health food stores.

Fresh coconut cream and milk (หัวกะทิ · hua ka-thi, น้ำกะทิ · nam ka-thi). Neither coconut cream nor coconut milk is what you hear sloshing inside a coconut. That clear liquid is coconut water. Instead, they are the liquid extracted from the finely grated meat of a mature coconut. The first pressing produces the fattiest and most concentrated yield. If left to stand for a half hour, the liquid will separate, with the fatty layer of coconut cream—what Thais call the "head"—settling on top and the thinner liquid, the coconut milk, on the bottom. The grated meat is usually pressed a

second time to produce more coconut milk. Subsequent pressings will yield only a thin liquid—called the "tail"—that is too weak to use as a stand-alone ingredient but is often used to thin out a coconut-based soup, curry, or dessert. Sometimes when a curry calls for a tough cut of meat that requires long cooking, the tail is used to cook the meat and the thicker cream and milk are added to the curry at a later stage.

For instructions on how to extract fresh coconut cream and milk, see page 172.

Ready-made coconut milk (กะทิสำเร็จรูป · ka-thi samret rup). An essential Thai pantry staple, prepared coconut milk is typically available in cans that contain either 13½ ounces or 14 ounces. But now markets in the United States are also carrying coconut milk in aseptic boxes.

When choosing canned or boxed coconut milk, make sure that it is unsweetened and does not contain any emulsifiers, thickeners, or other additives. From my experience, if you stick to these two rules when you shop, you will not end up with a bad can or box of coconut milk for Thai cooking. Many brands fit this description, so I suggest you try different ones to find the brand that tastes the best to you. My favorite coconut milk brands are Mae Ploy, Chaokoh, and Aroy-D. Mae Ploy and Aroy-D also market particularly good canned coconut cream that is richer than their coconut milk. It is more expensive than coconut milk, but you also get more mileage out of it.

Light coconut milk, sometimes labeled "lite" coconut milk, is not an ideal choice but is permissible. The downside of light coconut milk is that it tastes flat and almost always includes additives and thickeners. The upside is that it is lower in fat and has fewer calories, which some people find a good trade-off. Also, do not purchase drinkable coconut milk in a carton, which is designed as a dairy alternative and is inappropriate for use in

Thai cooking. For more information on how to use canned coconut milk in curry making, see page 36.

FLOURS

Use Thai brands whenever possible. I highly recommend Erawan brand from Thailand, which is widely available and inexpensive.

Glutinous rice flour (แป้งข้าวเหนียว · paeng khao niao). Glutinous rice flour or sticky rice flour in the context of Thai cooking is finely milled white flour made from white glutinous rice. It is used almost exclusively in Thai cooking to make desserts and sweet snacks.

Whenever it is used in a Thai recipe, it will be made clear that "sticky rice flour" or "glutinous rice flour" is required; if the recipe simply says "rice flour," use long-grain rice flour and do not use glutinous rice flour.

Rice flour (แป้งข้าวเจ้า · paeng khao jao). Rice flour in the context of Thai cooking is finely milled white flour made from white long-grain rice. It is used primarily to make traditional Thai steamed desserts; it is also used to thicken the coconut cream topping for some desserts or savory dishes.

Whenever a Thai recipe calls for "rice flour," use nothing else but flour that is made from finely milled white long-grain rice. There is no substitute—not even sweet rice flour or glutinous rice flour.

Tapioca flour (แป้งมันสำปะหลัง · paeng man sampalang). Tapioca flour is a fine white flour extracted from mature cassava roots. In Thai cooking, it is used in a variety of ways much like cornstarch.

FRUITS AND VEGETABLES

Chinese broccoli (ผักคะน้า · phak khana). This Chinese green-leaf vegetable with stalks similar to but slimmer and more tender than those of regular broccoli is used extensively in Thai cooking. Both the deep green leaves and the stalks are cut crosswise into bite-size pieces and used in stir-fries. The tender stalks are also served raw as a crudité. In the United States, Chinese broccoli can be found at most Asian grocery stores and some mainstream supermarkets; it is often labeled *kai lan* or *gai lan*.

Green mangoes (มะม่วงดิบ · mamuang dip). Green mangoes are used in Thai cooking to lend tartness to many savory dishes, such as Fried Fish and Green Mango Salad (page 67). Look for the mangoes in a Southeast Asian or South Asian grocery store. The most common type of mango sold in mainstream supermarkets, the Tommy Atkins, can look green and feel firm but is too bland for Thai cooking. When selecting green mangoes, look for ones that are rock hard and free of bruises and blemishes. If the mango yields even just a little when grasped, do not buy it.

See page 35 for tips on choosing the best tool for grating green mangoes for Thai cooking.

Green papayas (มะละกอดิบ · malako dip). Although papaya is technically a fruit, when it is still green, Thais treat it as a vegetable. Green papaya is used in many savory Thai dishes, from stir-fries to soups and curries. It is most commonly used, however, for making green papaya salad (page 79). Look for green papayas in Southeast Asian grocery stores. Some markets even sell grated green papaya by the pound, which is convenient if you are making a salad. Otherwise, look for bruise- and blemish-free whole fruits with bright green skin and stem. Just as with green mangoes, green papayas must be rock hard for use in Thai cooking. In a pinch, unripe smaller papayas sold in mainstream supermarkets or other mainstream stores can be used.

The easiest way to grate a green papaya is with a hand grater (page 35). To keep grated papaya fresh for up to a week, store it loosely packed in an airtight container lined with a double layer of paper towel, cover it with second double layer of paper towel, close the lid, and refrigerate.

Long beans (ถั่วฝักยาว · thua fak yao). Long beans, slender, deep green beans that can reach 2 feet in length, are also known as yard beans, yard-long beans, and sometimes snake beans. They are a common ingredient in stir-fries, curries, and salads and are also eaten raw as a side vegetable to spicy salads and relishes. Most Asian grocery stores and some supermarkets carry them. If unavailable, use green beans in their place.

Thai eggplants (มะเขือเปราะ · ma-khuea pro). These round eggplants, which sport green and off-white skin, are one of the most versatile and, therefore, most commonly used eggplants in Thai cooking. They are eaten raw, with the skin and seeds intact, as a vegetable to accompany different relishes, such as Shrimp-Coconut Relish with Vegetable Crudités (page 109), and are used in curries and spicy stir-fries. Bakers in Thailand even seed and candy them, tint them red or green, and use them instead of the more expensive imported candied cherries.

When you choose eggplants, go for the ones that are light colored, glossy, smooth, and firm, with nary a wrinkle. This tells you that the eggplants are fresh. But that is only half of the story. To be sure that the eggplants are both fresh *and* young, pay attention to their anatomy. The stem must look as if it is the claw of a small bird grabbing onto the eggplant. If the claw is no more than one-third of the height of the eggplant, that is good.

Unlike larger eggplants, except for removing the stem, you do not need to do anything to prepare these small round eggplants for eating as a side vegetable or for incorporating into a dish. There is no need to salt them, either. The only thing you must watch out for is oxidation. Once these eggplants are cut open, they turn brown almost instantly, especially if they are on the mature side. So either cut them open right before you are about to throw them into the curry, or keep the cut eggplants submerged in acidulated water (water with vinegar or lime or lemon juice mixed in) until ready to use.

Wood ear mushrooms (เห็ดหูหนู · het hu nu). It is interesting how wood ear mushrooms have become so closely tied to certain Thai dishes that to leave them out or use another type of mushroom is regarded as permissible but not recommended. For example, Chicken-Ginger Stir-Fry (page 38) is not as good without wood ear mushrooms.

In terms of flavor, wood ear mushrooms do not have much to brag about. It is the crunchy texture that people like about this ear-shaped black fungus. If you can find fresh wood ears, use them. If you cannot, dried wood ear mushrooms, which can be found at any Chinese or Southeast Asian grocery store, can be reconstituted in hot water—they take about 20 minutes—and used the same way (1 ounce dried mushrooms rehydrated is equal to 8 ounces fresh mushrooms). Whether you are working with fresh or dried mushrooms, be sure to rinse them well before use. Dried ones are notoriously sandy and must be rinsed well after they are reconstituted, or the sandy residue that adheres to them will ruin your dish. You may also need to cut away and discard any hard, knobby bits.

Thai eggplants (ma-khuea pro)

Mint and Thai sweet basil

HERBS, SPICES, AND AROMATICS

Basil One of the signs of deep familiarity with Thai food is an understanding of the roles of the three prominent types of basil used in Thai cooking: Thai sweet basil, holy basil, and lemon basil. Each is closely tied to the dishes with which it is traditionally used, and the three do not typically cross over into one another's territory. Even though these three herbs are different subtypes of basil, Thai cooks tend to treat them almost as if they are not botanically related. In other words, adding holy basil to central-style sour curry that traditionally does not call for basil or using lemon basil rather than Thai sweet basil in a red or green curry would be like rolling a pair of dice on a Scrabble board.

Holy basil (ใบกะเพรา · bai ka-phrao) has jagged-edged green leaves and soft, fuzzy hair on its stems and leaves. It is the definitive ingredient in the famous Thai basil stir-fry (page 147), and is also used in some spicy curries, such as jungle curry (page 102). When holy basil absolutely cannot be found, Thai sweet basil or Mediterranean sweet basil can be used instead.

Lemon basil (ใบแมงลัก · bai maeng-lak) is not used in central Thai cuisine nearly as extensively as Thai sweet basil or holy basil is. You will see it used more often in northern and northeastern cuisines. However, the few dishes in which lemon basil is traditionally used are perceived as weak or lacking when the herb is omitted and are considered negatively altered if another type of basil is used in its place. *Kaeng liang*, the classic spicy mixed-vegetable soup (page 89), is an example of such dishes.

Thai sweet basil (ใบโหระพา · bai hora-pha), sometimes referred to as Queen of Siam, is perhaps the most well known and frequently used Asian basil around the world. It has smaller and more slender leaves than the sweet basil used in Mediter-

ranean cuisines, and it sports purple stems and dark purple flowers. Thai sweet basil is added to some curries and to stir-fries toward the end of cooking to ensure that its distinct flavor and scent are not destroyed by extended heat. If you absolutely cannot find Thai sweet basil, substitute Mediterranean sweet basil, which is available at most grocery stores.

Cardamom pods (ลูกกระวาน · luk krawan). The cardamom pods used in Thai cooking are different from the green cardamom pods readily found in most supermarkets. The Thai pods, sometimes labeled "Siamese cardamom," are smaller, rounder, light beige, and have a more floral and milder flavor than green cardamom pods. If you cannot find Thai cardamom, green cardamom can be used in its place.

Chinese celery (ขึ้นฉ่าย · khuenchai). Chinese celery is smaller, more slender, and leafier than the common American celery. It is used mostly in Chinese-influenced Thai dishes, more as an aromatic than as a vegetable. If you cannot find Chinese celery, substitute the tender, leafy heart of regular celery.

Chinese chives (กุยช่าย · kuichai). Chinese chives, also known as garlic chives or nira grass, have a mild garlic flavor that distinguishes them from the common chives found in most markets in the United States. The leaves are flat, instead of tubular, and tender. Even the tougher parts are eaten raw as a side vegetable. In Thailand, Chinese chives are considered an indispensable ingredient of pad thai (page 123). At overseas Thai restaurants, they are often replaced with the cheaper and easier-to-find green onions.

Cilantro roots (รากผักชี · rak phak chi). The roots of cilantro plants are routinely used as an aromatic in Thai cooking, most notably as part of the aromatic paste (page 179) that is used both as a base for various dishes and in marinades. Because the roots are often pounded into a paste prior to being incorporated into a dish, you may not notice their presence. They are essential to authentic Thai cooking, however, and serious Thai cooks in the United States are constantly frustrated by the fact that most fresh cilantro in this country is sold without the roots attached. Cilantro stems can be used in lieu of cilantro roots, but they are not as fragrant. Coriander seeds—actually, cilantro seeds—taste markedly different from cilantro roots and must never be used as a substitute.

That is why I decided to take matters into my own hands: I grow cilantro in the summer to ensure a supply of roots year-round. If you do not have a garden, ask a vendor at your local farmers' market to sell you whole cilantro plants, roots and all. To store the cilantro roots, rinse them under running cold water until they are clean, blot them dry with a kitchen towel, and wrap them in two layers of dry paper towel. Place the wrapped roots in a resealable plastic freezer bag and freeze them to use throughout the year. Admittedly, cilantro roots start to lose their potency after 2 to 3 months in the freezer. However, in my opinion, milder cilantro roots are still better than no cilantro roots. If you live in an area where you can grow cilantro plants more than once a year, by all means, grow them as often as you can.

If growing your own cilantro is not an option and if you absolutely cannot find cilantro with the roots intact at your grocery store, use cilantro stems.

Coriander seeds (ลูกผักชี · luk phak chi). These tiny seeds of the cilantro plant, which is the same as the coriander plant, are used mostly in curry pastes and are generally toasted briefly before use to release their fragrance. They are also used as part of the marinade paste for meats.

Even though coriander seeds are often sold ground in the United States, it is always best to use the whole seeds and grind them yourself. Also,

although coriander seeds and cilantro leaves and roots are all from the same plant, they taste different from one another and can never be used interchangeably.

Cumin seeds (ยี่หร่า · yira). Shaped like rice kernels, these seeds are routinely used—albeit sparingly—in curry pastes, and their use does not seem to extend much beyond that in Thai cooking. They are often briefly toasted before use to heighten their fragrance. For the best flavor, always start with whole cumin seeds and grind them yourself.

Curry powder (ผงกะหรี่ · phong kari). Although curry powder is not the core ingredient in classic Thai curries as the name might suggest, this mix of spices, which varies in composition depending on the cook or the manufacturer, has found its way into Thai cooking. Some Chinese-inspired dishes, for example, are incomplete without this fragrant spice blend.

Although it is not a Thai product, I use Waugh's brand curry powder in my Thai cooking. But you can use any brand of Thai curry powder that you can find at your local Asian grocery store. A product marketed as Madras-style curry powder will work as well. You can also make your own curry powder by following my recipe on page 180.

Fingerroot (กระชาย · krachai). This rhizome has so many names it makes your head spin: lesser ginger, wild ginger, Chinese keys, fingerroot, as well as its Thai name, *krachai*.

Rarely will you find fresh *krachai* at markets outside Asia, but they are sometimes available at well-stocked Asian supermarkets in a large city. Choose ones that are firm, taut, and glossy. But most likely, this rhizome comes to you in vacuum-packed and frozen packages. Sometimes, you will also see it brined whole or slivered in a glass jar. All of these work very well in a curry paste where its texture is not as important as its scent and flavor. But when *krachai* is used to accent a curry or stir-fry, it is eaten as part of the dish, and the frozen variety does not work as well as the brined one as it tends to get soft and mushy upon being thawed.

There is no substitute for *krachai*. If you absolutely cannot find it in any form, the best thing to do is to leave it out.

Galangal (ข่า · kha). Not to be confused with ginger, galangal, also known as blue ginger, is a rhizome that is routinely used in Thai cooking as a curry paste ingredient and to infuse various soups. Unlike ginger, galangal does not have papery skin that needs to be removed before use. You can rinse the rhizome, blot it dry, and then cut it as directed in individual recipes.

When buying galangal, select rhizomes that are glossy, taut, and medium beige rather than reddish brown (a sign that the galangal has gone from strong and somewhat fibrous to bitter and woody). Wrap them whole in two or three layers of paper towel, slip the wrapped rhizomes into an airtight container, and refrigerate for up to 2 weeks. To freeze galangal, I recommend thinly slicing it, wrapping the slices in a paper towel, and then putting the wrapped slices in a resealable plastic freezer bag. Galangal will keep its potency for 2 months in the freezer, though it will turn slightly brown. Frozen galangal is fine for infusing soups, such as *tom yam* (page 86) and *tom kha kai* (page 84). For curry pastes, I recommend that you use fresh galangal and then freeze the prepared paste (see page 175).

Pass up dried galangal. It is bereft of its essential oil, even when it is reconstituted. Nor should you use ginger in place of galangal in any Thai recipe. They are not interchangeable, nor do Thai cooks think of them as a substitute for each other.

Ginger (ขิง · khing). Fresh ginger is used mostly in Chinese-influenced dishes, primarily stir-fries and steamed dishes. Young ginger, which is mild and tender, is eaten as a crudité with certain types of relish or sausage or julienned and added to salads. It is also perfect for pickling.

Most of the ginger you see in the United States is mature ginger, with brown, papery skin. It is stronger and more fragrant than young ginger and is thus used differently. The only thing to watch out for is that it can sometimes be quite hot, which can be an issue if the ginger is consumed raw (as in *miang kham* on page 25). You can take the edge off its excessive heat by rinsing the sliced or diced ginger in cold water three or four times until the water runs clear.

Choose ginger with thin, taut skin with no wrinkles, signs that it is fresh and not too fibrous. Whole ginger can be wrapped in two or three layers of paper towel, slipped into an airtight container, and stored in the refrigerator for up to 2 weeks. I do not freeze ginger, as it alters its texture, turning it soft, spongy, and mushy when thawed.

Kaffir limes, kaffir lime leaves (ลูกมะกรูด · luk ma-krut, ใบมะกรูด · bai ma-krut). The rind and leaves of kaffir lime are among the core ingredients in Thai food. Without them, your Thai cooking will definitely take a hit. If you think that is discouraging, here is more: no substitutes exist for either one. Wait, the bad news keeps going: these bumpy limes are among the hardest-to-find Thai ingredients outside Southeast Asia. And I am not done yet: dried kaffir lime leaves, which are sometimes sold at Asian grocery stores and are available online, are depleted of their essential oil—the very reason we use these leaves in the first place—and, therefore, utterly useless. Please put that tranquilizer dart away. I am just the messenger—and I have some good news. More and more Asian grocery stores in the United States have started to stock kaffir lime leaves, both fresh and frozen. That is one problem solved. It is the kaffir lime fruits that are still hard to find. But these days, you can order whole fresh kaffir limes from some online grocers. Ideally, you will only use fresh kaffir limes. However, since it is more economical to order several limes at once, I usually order a dozen of them every six months. I wash them thoroughly, peel off the rind (avoiding the bitter white parts) in large strips, wrap the strips into two or three layers of paper towel, put the wrapped strips in a resealable plastic freezer bag, and freeze them for up to 6 months, and then it is time to order again. For curry pastes, I usually recommend that you use fresh ingredients and then freeze the prepared paste (page 175); kaffir lime rind, however, is an exception because only a small amount is used in a batch of curry paste and most online grocers only sell kaffir limes by the dozen.

I store kaffir lime leaves the same way. They freeze beautifully without losing much of their fragrant essential oil; they also thaw quickly, in less than a minute at room temperature.

Kaffir lime rinds are usually thinly sliced before being pounded into a curry paste. The lime leaves are deveined and then either hand-torn into small pieces or bruised and used to infuse a soup or curry or cut into fine strips and added to a stir-fry or curry. When the leaves are torn, they are usually too tough to eat; when they are cut into fine strips, they are soft enough to eat.

The rinds and the leaves are all you need. Kaffir lime juice is normally not used in Thai cooking. It is used medicinally, however, mostly to fight dandruff.

Lemongrass (ตะไคร้ · ta-khrai). This long, slender stalky plant may look intimidating to anyone who has never cooked with it. When shopping for lemongrass, look for stalks that are firm when you press down on the bulbous part toward the root end, which should not yield at all. If you are able to find whole, untrimmed lemongrass in your area, choose them over the trimmed variety that comes in a plastic box, as untrimmed lemongrass stalks keep much longer. Once you bring them home, immediately put them in a vase filled with water and keep them at room temperature. Along the way, the lemongrass will grow new blades, which you snip off with kitchen shears to keep them nice and tidy; the lemongrass will also grow roots, which do not affect their quality and only means that you also have the option of planting them if you wish. Be sure to change the water and wipe off the slime that develops on the wet exteriors of the lemongrass bulbs every 2 to 3 days. Kept in this manner, the lemongrass stay fresh, with all the essential oil intact and the texture unaltered by refrigeration or freezing, for up to a month.

To prepare whole lemongrass for curry pastes, salads, relishes, and other dishes, trim off and discard the leafy parts of the lemongrass stalk, remove the tough outer leaves of the bulb portion until the smooth, pale green core is exposed, and trim off the root end. Working from the root end, cut the bulb crosswise into paper-thin slices, stopping once you reach the point where the purple rings disappear.

If you can only find pretrimmed lemongrass at the store, storing them in a vase will only cause them to rot. Instead, simply wrap them in a couple layers of paper towel and keep in an airtight container or a resealable plastic bag in the refrigerator for up to 7 to 10 days or in the freezer for up to 1 month. Frozen lemongrass takes only a few minutes to thaw at room temperature. Frozen lemongrass is good for infusing soups, such as *tom yam* (page 86) or *tom kha kai* (page 84). When making a curry paste, I prefer to use only fresh lemongrass and then freeze the prepared paste. Never use dried lemongrass, which lacks its essential oil.

Shallots (หอมแดง · hom daeng). One of the most frequently used aromatics in Thai cooking, shallots are an indispensable ingredient in many curry pastes, are added raw to various salads, and are

Kaffir lime leaves (*bai ma-krut*)

fried until crispy and used to accent several dishes. Shallots used in Thai cooking are much smaller than the shallots sold in American markets, so I have provided a weight measure as well as the number of shallots in ingredients lists. If you dine frequently at Thai restaurants in North America, you will notice that red onions regularly appear in dishes. Shallots are relatively expensive, and by using red onions in their place, restaurateurs are able to keep their menu offerings at reasonable prices. Although red onions are not used in Thailand, this practice is understandable and, fortunately, is a clever solution that does not lead to disastrous results in some cases. Using red onions in salads and stir-fries is reasonable, but I draw the line at using them in curry pastes, as their flavor is much too weak.

Star anise (โป๊ยกั๊ก · poi-kak, จันทน์แปดกลีบ · jan paet klip). This rust-brown, eight-spoke seedpod is used in many Chinese-influenced Thai dishes, most of which are braised or stewed. The spice is often lightly toasted in a dry skillet to release its licorice-like flavor before it is added to the dish. Look for star anise pods in cellophane packets or in jars in Asian markets and some supermarkets.

Turmeric root, ground turmeric (ขมิ้น · khamin, ขมิ้นผง · khamin phong). Turmeric is used mostly in southern Thai cuisine, where it imparts a beautiful deep orange-yellow color and a peppery, mildly bitter flavor to dishes. With the recent proliferation of South Asian and Southeast Asian grocery stores in the United States, fresh turmeric, which is commonly called turmeric root but is actually a rhizome, has become easier to find.

When shopping for fresh turmeric, choose roots that have bright orange peeking through the brown skin and are so firm that you can snap them in half with ease. Whenever I chance upon fresh turmeric roots, I buy a big batch and freeze them whole, where they stay potent for months. Freezing alters their texture slightly, but because they are usually pounded into a paste or smashed to infuse a soup, the textural change is acceptable.

If you cannot find fresh turmeric roots, ground turmeric, which is made by grinding cooked and dehydrated turmeric roots into a fine powder, is an acceptable substitute in most applications. It is commonly used in Thai dishes that have been influenced by Middle Eastern or South Asian cuisines. To substitute ground turmeric for fresh turmeric, replace every 1-inch piece of fresh turmeric with 1 teaspoon ground turmeric.

Young green peppercorns (พริกไทยอ่อน · phrik thai on). Young green peppercorns are used in Thai cooking more as an accent than a paste ingredient. They are added to some curries and spicy stir-fries, usually in addition to chiles, to provide a different kind of spicy heat that warms your throat rather than burns your tongue. As opposed to mature peppercorns, young green peppercorns are tender and mild enough so as to be eaten whole. Since fresh green peppercorns are not widely available in the States, you may have to use brined young peppercorns, which have lost some of their flavor and vibrant green color but are still delicious. If neither is available, simply leave them out, as there is not a substitute.

SAUCES AND SEASONING INGREDIENTS

Dark sweet soy sauce (ซีอิ๊วดำหวาน · si-io dam wan). This Chinese dark—almost black, really—sweet soy sauce, similar to the Indonesian *kecap manis*, is used in some stir-fried noodle dishes, such as *phat si-io* (page 120), where it lends its inimitable flavor: a heady mix of sweet and salty with a hint of smoky caramel. It is not used nearly as extensively as regular soy sauce or even oyster sauce, but when certain recipes call for it, it needs to be there, as its absence is apparent to anyone familiar with those dishes.

For the best results, use a Thai brand of sweet dark soy sauce. Healthy Boy and Dragonfly are two good choices.

Fish sauce (น้ำปลา · nam pla). What would become of Thai food without this primary source of salinity? This reddish brown liquid extracted from anchovies fermented with salt is one of the basic ingredients in Thai cooking as both a seasoning and a condiment.

Look for a Thai brand for the best results, choosing any brand that does not contain artificial coloring or flavoring or preservatives. Tra Chang, Golden Boy, and Tiparos are among the labels I use regularly.

Limes (มะนาว · manao). Limes are one of the most commonly used souring agents in modern Thai cuisine. Their juice imparts a distinctive and potent sour taste that is sharper than that of tamarind. That means there is no substitute for limes in Thai cooking. Thai cooks never use lemons, for example, and although vinegar is a popular souring ingredient, it is not interchangeable with lime.

When choosing limes at the market, select those with taut, smooth skins. They will have more juice than their bumpier kin. To cut lime wedges the Thai way to serve as a table seasoning, cut the lime in half lengthwise, positioning the knife slightly off to one side of the stem to avoid the core. Then cut each half around the core into two more wedges. Without the core, your lime wedges will be easier to squeeze.

Oyster sauce (น้ำมันหอย · nam man hoi). Made of sugar, salt, and oyster extract, oyster sauce is usually thickened with either wheat starch or cornstarch into a thick, dark brown sauce. Packed with savory taste, or umami, this Chinese ingredient is popular in modern Thai cooking in stir-fries and sauces and as a marinade ingredient.

I prefer the taste of Thai brands of oyster sauce, such as Maekrua and Healthy Boy (the latter also manufactures the vegetarian alternative made with mushrooms). But if you cannot find a Thai brand, any brand of oyster sauce will work. Lee Kum Kee and Roland are often found in the Asian foods aisle of many mainstream supermarkets.

Preserved cabbage (ตั้งไฉ่ · tang chai). Also called pickled Chinese cabbage, this accent ingredient adds both flavor and aroma to some Chinese-influenced Thai dishes. It almost always comes in an orange-shaped earthenware or clear plastic crock and is available at most Asian grocery stores. Preserved cabbage comes coarsely chopped and ready to be added to a dish straight out of the crock. It is very salty and is, therefore, used only sparingly.

Salted soybean paste (เต้าเจี้ยวดำ · taojiao dam). A Chinese seasoning ingredient widely used in modern Thai cooking, salted soybean paste is made from cooked soybeans, which have been salted and stored in large jars. Wheat and a fungal starter are added to the salted soybeans to create fermentation. The result is a paste that lends a complexly salty flavor to a dish.

Sriracha sauce (ซอสศรีราชา · sot si racha). A favorite condiment of Thais, Sriracha (pronounced see-rah-chah as if the first r is not there) sauce is a sweet and tangy chile-garlic sauce that goes particularly well with a Thai-style omelet and rice (page 50). It can also be used as a stir-fry sauce or marinade.

Be sure that you do not get Thai Sriracha confused with Sriracha sauce made by the United States–based Huy Fong Foods, Inc., which is quite a bit thicker, more garlicky, and less sweet, and has a sharper, harsher flavor. Look for such Thai brands as Shark or Sriraja Panich. If you can find only

Huy Fong Food brand (easily recognizable by the rooster prominently pictured on its label), you can mix it in equal parts with sweet chile sauce (page 187) for using in the recipes in this book. I have also included a recipe for homemade Sriracha sauce on page 186.

Tamarind (มะขามเปียก · makham piak). One of the most prominent and traditional sources of acidity in Thai cooking, tamarind is a dried podlike brown legume that is processed into a sour concentrated paste or pulp. When you are shopping, do not confuse this with its relative, sweet tamarind, which is eaten as a snack.

I prefer to make my own tamarind pulp from seeded tamarind sold in brick form (see page 171). It is more economical and allows me to control the water content, which is important if you do not want to end up with too much liquid in a stir-fry.

Thin soy sauce (ซีอิ๊วขาว · si-io khao). Also known as white soy sauce, Thai or Chinese light soy sauce is appropriate for the recipes in this book. To keep the flavor of your dishes as Thai as possible, use a Thai brand, such as Healthy Boy. Korean- and Japanese-style soy sauces taste quite different from Thai soy sauces, and I recommend against their use in Thai dishes. If you cannot find a Thai brand, use a soy sauce made in the Chinese tradition, such as Lee Kum Kee brand.

NOODLES
Dried rice sticks (ก๋วยเตี๋ยวเส้นเล็ก · kuai-tiao sen lek). These long, thin, flat dried rice noodles are also called pad thai noodles, in reference to the well-known Thai noodle dish in which they are used. They are also used in curry noodles (page 125).

Be sure to buy noodles that are flat, not round. They come in different widths, ranging from 3 to 9 millimeters (about 1/8 to 1/3 inch). For pad thai

and other stir-fried noodles, stay as close to the 3-millimeter width as you can. Anything wider than 5 millimeters (1/4 inch) is not traditionally used; it also falls into the category of wide noodles which require boiling as opposed to simply soaking (page 212).

To prepare dried noodles for stir-frying, soak them in room-temperature water until they are pliable yet firm. For 3-millimeter-wide noodles, plan on soaking them for 30 to 40 minutes. (If you are in a hurry, you can soak them in warm tap water to accelerate the softening process. Do not soak or blanch them in boiling water, however, or they will become soggy and fall apart in the wok.) You know the noodles are ready when they are opaque white and soft enough for you to twirl them around your fingers without breaking the strands. Then drain the noodles well before adding them to the wok.

When you prepare dried rice noodles for a soup, there is no need to soak them. Simply boil them in a large amount of water like you do pasta, drain them well, rinse off the excess starch, drain again, and use immediately or lubricate them with vegetable oil to prevent them from sticking together until you are ready for them.

Egg noodles (เส้นบะหมี่ · sen bami). These yellow noodles, which are used in Egg Noodles with Clams, Chile Jam, and Basil Stir-Fry (page 135), are made with wheat flour and eggs much like Italian pasta. The dough is cut into long strands of different thickness and widths (egg noodles of any size or shape are fine to use in the recipes in this book). They are then wound into bundles and packed into plastic bags. You can find them in the refrigerated section of an Asian grocery store and in some well-stocked mainstream supermarkets. If you cannot find fresh egg noodles, use dried Chinese-style egg noodles, which are available in the Asian aisle of most supermarkets. Cook them according to the package instructions.

Fresh rice noodles (ก๋วยเตี๋ยวเส้นใหญ่ · kuai-tiao sen yai). These fresh rice noodles are used in Chinese cooking and in quite a few Chinese-influenced dishes in Thai cuisine, such as *phat si-io* (page 120) and *rat na* (page 128).

They often come in several oil-lubricated layers of thin sheets, stacked together, packed in a disposable tray, and covered with plastic wrap. You can find them in the refrigerated section of most well-stocked Asian grocery stores. To prepare them for cooking, you need to cut the whole stack into strips about 1 inch wide and then carefully separate the layers into thin, wide ribbons. Sometimes the noodles come precut and require only that you separate them gently so as not to break them.

Purchase fresh rice noodles in small batches and use them right away, as they lose their suppleness and flexibility quickly on refrigeration. They must never be frozen. If you are ever stuck with old, doughy, hard fresh rice noodles, cut them into strips and separate them into strands as instructed above, then blanch them for no more than 10 seconds in boiling water before cooking.

If you cannot find fresh rice noodles, buy the widest dried rice sticks (9 millimeters/about 1/3 inch wide) you can find. It is important to remember that you cannot simply soak these wide dried rice noodles until pliable in the same way you prepare thinner dried rice sticks for pad thai (page 210). You need to be boil them in a large amount of water, as you would dried Italian pasta, and then drain them, rinse off any excess starch, drain them again, and use them like fresh rice noodles. Once cooked, dried wide rice noodles double in volume. Therefore, if a recipe calls for 1 pound of fresh wide rice noodles, you need 8 ounces of dried wide rice noodles to yield 1 pound of cooked noodles, which can be used the same way as fresh wide rice noodles.

Glass noodles (วุ้นเส้น · wun sen). Also known as bean threads or cellophane noodles, glass noodles are made of mung bean starch, extruded into long, thin strands, dried, and sold in bundles of different sizes. Do not confuse these noodles with dried rice vermicelli (used in Vietnamese cuisine), which look similar to cellophane noodles but are opaque white instead of translucent.

When buying glass noodles, make sure that they are made of 100 percent mung bean starch with no fillers. Pure bean threads are soft and chewy when cooked and stay that way longer. In contrast, adulterated bean threads are especially brittle when dried (and prone to breakage) and become mushy easily when cooked.

Oddly enough, in Thailand glass noodles have traditionally been used as an ingredient in a dish that is eaten as a rice accompaniment, rather than in a dish that is served as a one-plate meal. Stir-Fried Glass Noodles with Chicken (page 52) and Glass Noodle Salad (page 76) are two good examples.

To prepare glass noodles for cooking, soak them in hot tap water just until they are pliable enough to cut into desired lengths with kitchen shears, usually 15 to 20 minutes.

OILS

Coconut oil (น้ำมันมะพร้าว · nam man ma-phrao). Coconut oil is not a traditional Thai cooking ingredient. But it has been turning up on supermarket shelves in recent years because of its purported health benefits, and I have taken advantage of its availability. I do not use it for frying or stir-frying, but I do use it in my curry making: when I buy a container of ready-made coconut milk and the cream I scoop off the top does not have enough fat to "crack" when cooking it with the curry paste, I add some coconut oil (see page 36).

Vegetable oil (น้ำมันพืช · nam man phuet).
The best vegetable oil to use in Thai dishes is one that does not have any flavor or scent. Just as Thais prefer the rice that they eat with their meal to be plain, Thai cooks usually like their cooking oil unflavored. The most commonly used vegetable oils are soybean, palm, corn, and rice bran, because they are both flavorless and affordable. Peanut oil—and this may surprise many people—is seldom used.

When it comes to deep-frying, most Thai cooks use palm oil due to its high smoke point, affordable price, resistance to rancidity, and ability to produce fried foods that stay crispy longer. However, any bland vegetable oil with a high smoke point you can find, such as canola, sunflower, or safflower, works well, too.

RICE

Glutinous rice (ข้าวเหนียว · khao niao). The term *sticky rice* is used to describe several different types of short-grain rice, many of which are neither Thai nor appropriate for Thai preparations. True Thai sticky rice is medium grain and grown in the north and northeastern regions of the country. When you are making Thai desserts, like Mango and Sweet Coconut Sticky Rice (page 161), you can get by using a different type of short-grain rice, including Japanese sweet rice. The result will be different from what the Thai people consider traditional, however.

If you want to get Thai glutinous rice, shop at an Asian grocery store specializing in Southeast Asian, rather than East Asian or South Asian, ingredients. Look for the Thai word "ข้าวเหนียว" on the label. In fact, I make my non-Thai friends take a photograph of the word and store it on their phones, and none of them has ever bought the wrong kind of rice. When no Thai language is present on the label, look instead for the words *glutinous rice* or *sweet rice* and an indication that the rice is imported from Thailand. Failing the latter, try to find the word *Thai* somewhere on the bag.

Long-grain white rice (ข้าวเจ้า · khao jao).
With the exception of certain northern and northeastern Thai dishes, such as Northeastern Minced Chicken Salad (page 74), which are traditionally served with glutinous rice, Thai food is best served as an accompaniment to long-grain white rice. Short-grain rice, which is routinely consumed in East Asia and in other parts of the world, does not lend itself well to Thai food or the Thai way of eating.

It is impossible to talk about Thai long-grain rice without mentioning jasmine rice, Thailand's best-known rice around the world. Jasmine is by no means the only type of long-grain fragrant rice available and routinely consumed in Thailand, but it is most likely the only type of long-grain rice from Thailand available in other countries.

This strain of fragrant rice (*khao hom*) was officially named *khao dok mali* (ขาวดอกมะลิ; literally "white [like] jasmine") because of its color, which is similar to that of jasmine blossoms. Many people mistakenly assume that it is named jasmine rice because of its aroma, which is in fact closer to that of pandanus, a tropical palmlike plant whose blades are used in Southeast Asia as an aromatic, such as in the coconut cream on page 164.

MISCELLANEOUS INGREDIENTS
Dried shrimp (กุ้งแห้ง · kung haeng). In the Thai tradition, dried shrimp are made by cooking shell-on shrimp in brine and then drying them in the sun until they have shrunk to about half their original size. The shrimp are then agitated to separate them from their shells as completely as possible. The shells are discarded and what are left are meaty shrimp with a chewy texture and a slightly briny flavor. Excessive saltiness is a sign of badly made dried shrimp.

Dried shrimp are used routinely in Thai cooking, so if you plan to cook Thai food with any regularity, you should have some on hand. They are sold at Asian grocery stores and come in two main types, the meaty type and the scrawny type. The meaty shrimp are all about the flesh and not about the shell. These are premium shrimp and are thus more expensive than the rest. They are used either whole or pounded in a mortar until they are reduced to cottony flakes. This is by far the most commonly used type of dried shrimp in Thai cooking.

The scrawny shrimp are made with tiny shrimp, which are all about the shells and not much meat. This means they are cheaper than the meaty type. If you pound these scrawny shrimp in a mortar, you will get pulverized dried shrimp shells, not flaky shrimp meat. Pad thai vendors like to use these crunchy shrimp, because they are less expensive and make for salty, crunchy bits in the noodles.

I prefer dried shrimp made according to the Thai tradition, which are available at most Southeast Asian grocery stores. But if you cannot find them, you can use dried shrimp sold at any Asian store for the recipes in this book. Even the larger dried shrimp sold in Latino markets can be used in a pinch.

When a Thai recipe calls for dried shrimp flakes or asks you to pulverize dried shrimp into flakes, the meaty type of dried shrimp should be used. The best way to pound these chewy shrimp is in a granite mortar. Soaking them in hot water until softened and squeezing them dry before you begin to pulverize them will help speed the process. You can also pulverize dried shrimp in a mini chopper or in a coffee grinder dedicated to culinary uses. Unless you are pulverizing a relatively large amount of dried shrimp, a food processor will not work because the shrimp tend to escape the blades.

Palm sugar (น้ำตาลปีก • nam tan puek). Palm sugar comes from the sweet sap of the sugar date palm. Sometimes it comes in a soft, pasty consistency reminiscent of Play-Doh and is sold in Thailand in a large rectangular can; sometimes it comes in solid form, shaped like the top half of a hamburger bun.

The soft, pasty palm sugar is the best. It has the light caramel flavor that is the reason why Thai cooks use palm sugar instead of granulated sugar. It is also easy to scoop out of its container, measure, and melt. No chopping or grating is needed. I could wax poetic all day about how great this type of soft palm sugar is, but, much to my sorrow, it is not available in the United States.

What you will most likely find in the States is crystallized palm sugar (often a sign that cheaper cane sugar has been added), which comes in round shapes of various sizes or in a clear plastic tub. It cannot be measured by volume without first being grated or finely chopped, it will not dissolve into any liquid without being heated, and its flavor lacks depth. It also does not caramelize readily into a beautiful dark amber, which is what gives a dish like pad thai its signature color. But I am so grateful to have any palm sugar available where I live that I cannot complain too much.

My advice is to steer clear of the palm sugar sold in a plastic tub. It is the worst and is the most likely to be impure. Most of the time, the sugar is hardened to the point that it is impossible to scoop it out of the container without bending a spoon and/or letting out a few choice words. If you are stuck with this type of sugar, the only way to set it free is not to melt it in the microwave—you will melt the plastic, too—but to break the container open with a large cleaver. It works, and although I thought it might be fun, it was not.

If possible, opt for the half burger bun or flying saucer type. This type comes in different sizes and some are smooth all over and others are smooth on the underside but are rough and coarse with a spiral design on top. Both types are solid, but the one with the rough surface and the spiral design on top tends to be softer, sandier, and much easier to grate or chop and melt. The smooth type tends to be harder to begin with and becomes even more so with storage. At its hardest stage, I cannot even grate or chop it with a sturdy cleaver and often have to resort to attacking it with a granite pestle. And the only way to measure it precisely is to soften it briefly in the microwave, which gives you a small window of opportunity to measure out what you need before the softened palm sugar turns solid again.

To augment the anemic taste and color of crystallized palm sugar, I sometimes add brown sugar, either light or dark, to the recipe to achieve a deeper flavor and darker color that are closer to that of the soft palm sugar in Thailand. In a pinch, you can substitute brown sugar without disastrous results.

Shrimp paste (กะปิ · kapi). This dark purple paste is pungent, and if you are not familiar with it, just a whiff of it up close could make you question the strength of your desire to cook Thai food. But if you have eaten red or green curry, you have had your share of shrimp paste, for it is an indispensable ingredient in curry paste.

Shrimp paste usually comes in a small plastic tub with a layer of preserving wax on top. Remove and discard the wax and use only the dark purple paste underneath. Once opened, store the paste in the refrigerator, where it will stay fresh and moist for about 6 months.

Spring roll wrappers (แป้งปอเปี๊ยะ · paeng po-pia). Sometimes referred to as spring roll skins or spring roll pastry, spring roll wrappers are paper-thin pancakes made with a dough of wheat flour, water, and salt. The soft, smooth, and highly elastic dough is rolled by hand onto a hot carbon-steel griddle and swiftly lifted out so that only a thin film of dough sticks to the griddle, cooks, and is removed within just a few seconds. These thin wrappers, sold in stacks, can be used to make both fresh and fried spring rolls.

In the States, spring roll wrappers usually come in 4- to 8-inch squares although occasionally round ones show up, too. They are found in the freezer of Asian grocery stores. I highly recommend Spring Home and Aroy-D brands. Make sure that the frozen spring roll wrappers are completely thawed before using; this can be done overnight in the refrigerator or in 3 to 4 hours at room temperature. Always cover the unrolled wrappers with a thick kitchen towel to keep them supple and elastic.

Spring roll wrappers should not be confused with eggroll wrappers, which are often made with eggs and resemble wonton wrappers, albeit larger. These wrappers are often used to make the eggrolls you see at many Chinese restaurants in the United States, but they are not used by Thai cooks. Having said that, you can use eggroll wrappers in any recipe in this book that calls for spring roll wrappers.

Note on the Romanization of Thai Words

The romanization of Thai words in this book is based largely on the latest version of the Royal Thai General System of Transcription (RTGS), which was published by the Royal Institute of Thailand in 1999 and serves as the standard for bilingual road signs and government publications. The system is not intended for pedagogical purposes but as a means to help a casual reader pronounce Thai words with reasonable accuracy without inundating him or her with marks of vowel quantity or superfluous diacritics.

A hyphen is also employed in places prone to syllable misdivision, such as when a syllable ending with a vowel precedes a syllable beginning with a digraph, or when a syllable ending with a vowel precedes a syllable beginning with a vowel.

Note that *ph* is pronounced like *p* in English and not like *f*. The letter *h* functions here as a mark of aspiration (represented by the superscript *h* in the International Phonetic Alphabet).

The spellings of the words *satay* and *pad thai* follow the convention of the various English lexica to which they have been added. The romanization of these words, however, is consistent with the RTGS.

The only departure from the RTGS rules in this book is the use of the English *ch* and *j* to represent the Thai ช and จ, respectively. The RTGS instead employs the English *ch* for both ช and จ.

For more information on the RTGS, please visit www.royin.go.th/en/home. I would like to thank Associate Professor Wirote Aroonmanakun of the Department of Linguistics, Chulalongkorn University, for his input on Thai orthography, on the romanization of Thai words in general, and on the advantages and limitations of the RTGS. It must be noted, however, that every decision regarding the romanization of Thai words in this book is my own.

Mail-Order Sources

If you don't have easy access to an Asian grocery store, I recommend the following sources for mail-ordering harder-to-find Thai ingredients.

templeofthai.com

This wonderful website offers everything you need in your Thai kitchen, ranging from affordable mortar and pestle sets to miscellaneous kitchen gadgets to everyday pantry ingredients and fresh Thai produce. They also carry some premium brands of curry paste, such as Nittaya, which are popular in Thailand but difficult to find in the United States.

importfood.com

This is another fine option for sourcing both sundry pantry items and fresh ingredients. High-quality rare produce—such as kaffir limes, kaffir lime leaves, and fresh wild betel leaves—are available nearly year round. They also have a fine selection of specialty cookware and tableware as well as Thai street-vendor tools, which are difficult to find even at well-stocked Thai grocery stores.

Green papayas (*malako dip*) and green mangoes (*mamuang dip*)

Acknowledgments

I would like to thank the following people:

Polsri Kachacheewa, one of the best Thai food writers I know. I have adored his works since I was a little child going through my mother's food magazines. I was overjoyed to have met him and discussed several food-related topics at length when I was writing this book. My hero, as I've found out, is also a kind gentleman who is even wittier and funnier in real life.

Nidda Hongwiwat, Thavitong Hongvivatana, and Sangdad Publishing for the work of unmatched excellence they have completed in the past several years, helping to educate the Thai people about their own cuisine. I am a grateful beneficiary of their research and writings.

Sisamon Kongpan, one of the most knowledgeable and prolific authors of Thai cookbooks. I am inspired by her industriousness and energy even in her advanced age, and I am grateful for her encouragement for me to study hard, to write a lot, and to write well.

Mom Luang Sirichalerm "Chef McDang" Svasti for always making himself available for any questions I might have about anything related to Thai cuisine. He has been instrumental in helping me get out of my own head and see anew the things I once thought I understood, and I am so grateful for that.

The chefs, writers, restaurateurs, street vendors, and home cooks in Bangkok who graciously allowed me to interview them and observe how they work. Their collective wisdom permeates this book.

Mollie Katzen, the woman whose work nudged me to venture outside Thai cooking and my once-limited repertoire of Western dishes. Her book, *Vegetable Heaven*, was the first English-language cookbook I bought with my own money, and, oh, how I've treasured it. Mollie's gentle spirit, excellent work, artistic skills, and beautiful penmanship have been a source of inspiration for me all these years.

Bob del Grosso, who is my go-to person for any question related to food science. I'm in awe of his knowledge, and I'm touched by how he has generously shared it with me.

Rikker Dockum, the language whiz in whom I trust.

My friends T and K for lending their support in various ways while I was in Bangkok writing and researching this book.

Vera, for her encouragement and support and for lending a helping hand whenever I was overwhelmed with the amount of work I had to do throughout the long process of writing this book.

While not exactly a person, this place has long been anthropomorphized in my mind: the underground Pridi Banomyong Library in Bangkok, where I spent most of my time writing this book. I would arrive in the morning, lay all my cares and worries at its door, and enter into its sacred cradle where I was completely calm and secure, where I sat and wrote and wrote and wrote.

Mike Sula for always being there whenever I need a writer's opinions and insights. I have learned much from him and his works, and I sure want to be able to write like he does when I grow up.

My recipe testers: Sophie Laplante, Emily Fiffer, Heather Sperling, Mindy Reznik, Mike Sula, Andrew Shiue, Noah Sanders, Title Sritecha, Josh Edelstein, Benja Apisekkul, Sven Becker, Mingk-wan Suwan-ake, Chris Hoekstra, Kit Martin, Mike Reeder, Shao Zhi Zhong, Aaron Barnes, Dylan Perkins, Beth Gardner, Emma Cham, Tippy Jeng, Savitri Penkhae, Vanessa Wong, Ryan James, Tracy Collins, Liam Thomas, and TJ Walker. There were many other volunteers whom I was not able to accommodate. My thanks go to them as well.

The talented team at Ten Speed Press: Emily Timberlake, my patient and ever-optimistic editor, supporter, and cheerleader. I am thankful for her steadfast belief in this book and for working tirelessly with me to bring it to fruition. I am also grateful to Betsy Stromberg for making this book beautiful as well as Sharon Silva who amazes me with her wisdom and keen eye for detail.

Lastly, I would like to express my gratitude to the readers of shesimmers.com. Your support, advice, and encouragement mean more to me than you will ever know.

Index

Measurement Conversion Charts

Volume

U.S.	IMPERIAL	METRIC
1 tablespoon	½ fl oz	15 ml
2 tablespoons	1 fl oz	30 ml
¼ cup	2 fl oz	60 ml
⅓ cup	3 fl oz	90 ml
½ cup	4 fl oz	120 ml
⅔ cup	5 fl oz (¼ pint)	150 ml
¾ cup	6 fl oz	180 ml
1 cup	8 fl oz (⅓ pint)	240 ml
1¼ cups	10 fl oz (½ pint)	300 ml
2 cups (1 pint)	16 fl oz (⅔ pint)	480 ml
2½ cups	20 fl oz (1 pint)	600 ml
1 quart	32 fl oz (1⅔ pints)	1 l

Length

INCH	METRIC
¼ inch	6 mm
½ inch	1.25 cm
¾ inch	2 cm
1 inch	2.5 cm
6 inches (½ foot)	15 cm
12 inches (1 foot)	30 cm

Temperature

FAHRENHEIT	CELSIUS/GAS MARK
250°F	120°C/gas mark ½
275°F	135°C/gas mark 1
300°F	150°C/gas mark 2
325°F	160°C/gas mark 3
350°F	180 or 175°C/gas mark 4
375°F	190°C/gas mark 5
400°F	200°C/gas mark 6
425°F	220°C/gas mark 7
450°F	230°C/gas mark 8
475°F	245°C/gas mark 9
500°F	260°C

Weight

U.S./IMPERIAL	METRIC
½ oz	15 g
1 oz	30 g
2 oz	60 g
¼ lb	115 g
⅓ lb	150 g
½ lb	225 g
¾ lb	350 g
1 lb	450 g

Published in the United States by Ten Speed Press, an imprint of the Crown Publishing
Group, a division of Random House LLC, a Penguin Random House Company,
New York.
www.crownpublishing.com
www.tenspeed.com

Ten Speed Press and the Ten Speed Press colophon are registered trademarks of
Random House LLC

Library of Congress Cataloging-in-Publication Data

Punyaratabandhu, Leela.
  Simple Thai food : classic recipes from the Thai home kitchen /
Leela Punyaratabandhu ; photography by Erin Kunkel. — First edition.
    pages cm
  Includes index.
1. Cooking, Thai. I. Title.
  TX724.5.T5P86 2014
  641.59593—dc23

                              2013040575

Hardcover ISBN: 978-1-60774-523-5
eBook ISBN: 978-1-60774-524-2

Printed in China

Design by Betsy Stromberg

10 9 8 7 6 5 4 3 2 1

First Edition